願主
保佑!

Chusan

the forgotten story
of Britain's first
Chinese island

LIAM D'ARCY-BROWN

BRANDRAM

First published in Great Britain in 2012
by Brandram, an imprint of Takeaway (Publishing)

1st edition 1.0

Takeaway (Publishing), 33 New Street, Kenilworth CV8 2EY

E-mail: books@takeawaypublishing.co.uk

British Library Cataloguing in Publication Data.
A catalogue record for this book is available from the British Library

ISBN 978-0-9563847-7-5

Cover by Shine Design

Contents

   v   *Maps*

   x   *List of Recurring Characters*

  13   Prologue

  17   Scarce a day free from insults

  31   The Great Emperor and the men with red hair

  43   The slightest spark

  51   A thundering fire

  63   A Pompeii of the living

  77   An idle dream

  93   Go to hell!

105   We live among the dead

111   A Chinese Singapore

119   The celestials wish to measure their strength

129   Soothing the sores and bruises

135   We read this with fast-falling tears

147   You have done us incalculable injury

163   So ends the Chinese war

175   How muchie loopee?

183   *Tabula rasa*

205   A sportsman's paradise

215   In the hospital their hearts are soft

237   Apples of Sodom

257   No news could have given us such joy

269   Famous for their construction of guns

279   Epilogue

297   *Sources & Bibliography*

306   *Acknowledgements*

307   *Author's Note*

307   *Note on Romanisation and Names*

309   *Endnotes*

329   *Index*

for Rachel and Liam, my mum and dad

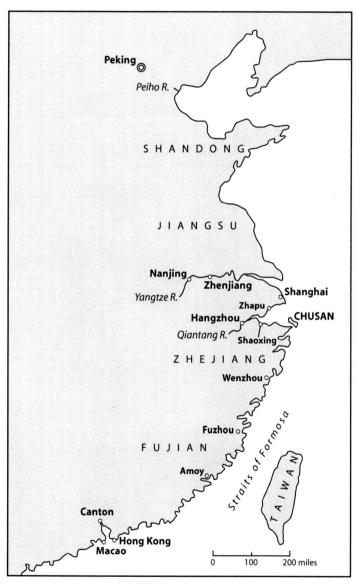

The China coast

Chusan and the southerly islands of the Chusan archipelago

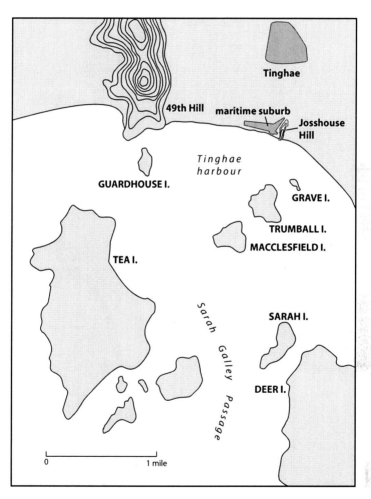

Tinghae

49th Hill maritime suburb

Josshouse
Hill

*Tinghae
harbour*

GUARDHOUSE I.

GRAVE I.

TRUMBALL I.

MACCLESFIELD I.

TEA I.

Sarah Galley Passage

SARAH I.

DEER I.

0   1 mile

Tinghae harbour and the harbour islands

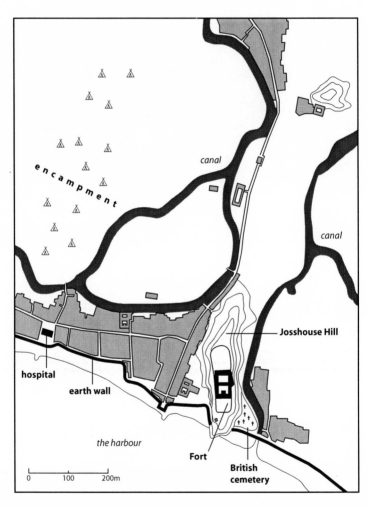

Tinghae's maritime suburb and Josshouse Hill

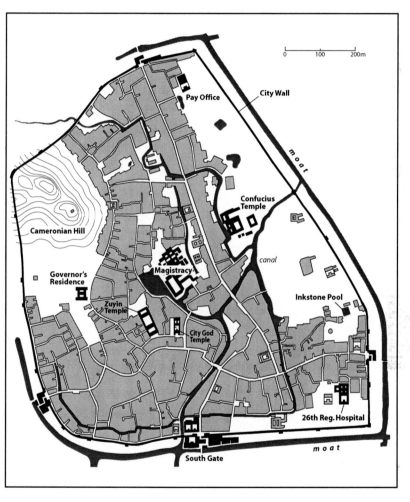

Pay Office

City Wall

moat

Confucius Temple

Cameronian Hill

canal

Governor's Residence

Magistracy

Zuyin Temple

Inkstone Pool

City God Temple

26th Reg. Hospital

South Gate

moat

0   100   200m

The city of Tinghae

List of Recurring Characters

Aldersey, Mary Ann Missionary and promoter of female education in Zhejiang.

Anstruther, Cpt Philip Officer of the Madras Artillery, kidnapped and imprisoned in Ningbo.

Bu Dingbang Comprador to the 1840 British expedition.

Burrell, George Commander of British land forces in China and governor of Chusan 1840-41.

Campbell, Lt-Col Colin Commanding officer of the 98th Regiment and governor of Chusan 1844-46.

Cree, Edward Assistant-surgeon of HMS *Rattlesnake*, diarist and watercolourist.

Daoguang Emperor of China 1820-50.

Davis, Sir John Governor of Hong Kong 1844-48.

Elliot, Cpt Charles Britain's chief superintendent in China before the first invasion of Chusan in 1840. Joint plenipotentiary alongside George Elliot until 1841.

Elliot, Adm George Joint plenipotentiary alongside Charles Elliot until 1841.

Fortune, Robert Plant-hunter sent to China in 1843 to collect botanical samples.

Gough, Sir Hugh Commander of British land forces in China from mid-1841 to the Treaty of Nanking in 1842.

Graham, Sir James British Home Secretary 1841-46.

Gützlaff, Karl Chinese-speaking German missionary who serves with the British expeditions in China.

Kangxi Emperor of China 1661-1722.

Lan Li Brigade general of the Tinghae garrison 1690-1701.

Liang Baochang Governor of Zhejiang province 1844-48.

Liu Yunke Governor of Zhejiang province 1840-43.

Lockhart, William Medical missionary in Tinghae 1840-43.

Martin, Robert Montgomery Journalist and polemicist who agitates for Chusan's retention as a colony.

Mu Sui Civil magistrate of Tinghae 1695-1715.

Noble, Anne Wife of the captain of the brig *Kite*, imprisoned in Ningbo after the *Kite* is wrecked.

Palmerston, Lord Britain's foreign secretary under prime minister Lord Melbourne.

Parker, Sir William Commander of British naval forces in China from mid-1841 to 1844.

Pottinger, Sir Henry British plenipotentiary in China after Charles Elliot's recall in 1841.

Qishan Governor-general of Zhili 1831-40. Governor-general of Liangguang 1840-41.

Qiying A Manchu of the Imperial clan and Chinese negotiator at Nanking, 1842. Governor-general of Liangguang 1844-48.

Shi Shipiao Brigade general of the Tinghae garrison 1701-8.

Schoedde, Sir James Commanding officer of the 55th Regiment and governor of Chusan 1842-44.

Urgungga Governor of Zhejiang province 1834-40.

Yijing Nephew of the emperor, given the title 'Awe-Inspiring General' and tasked with unseating the British in 1842.

Yilibu Governor-general of the Yangtze river provinces 1840-41. Special commissioner for the Zhejiang coast, 1841. Chinese negotiator at Nanking, 1842.

Yuqian Yilibu's successor as governor-general of the Yangtze river provinces and special commissioner for the Zhejiang coast, 1841.

Prologue

THE VILLAGERS who gathered on the road to Ningbo on the eighteenth day of September 1840 were treated to a thrilling spectacle: barefoot and filthy, and soaked to the skin in just the thin gown she had been wearing when the *Kite* had been wrecked, a pale-skinned woman was being paraded in chains across the flat farmland of Zhejiang province. Braving the rain through mile after mile of jeering crowds, soon Mrs Anne Noble found herself confined in a bamboo cage so tiny that her nose touched her knees, and so, without food or dignity, she was to spend the next two days. In the port of Ningbo she would pass five months in a dark cell, let out now and then to relate her tale to local mandarins; she was, they concluded despite her protestations, a sister of Queen Victoria. But Anne was just the wife of a sea-captain from North Shields, cast a prisoner upon the coast of China. In shock and grieving for her husband and infant son, both drowned only days before, she prayed and sang hymns to keep from losing her mind. She was just twenty-six years old, and pregnant.

Imprisoned nearby was a fellow Scot, though quite the opposite of Anne. Captain Philip Anstruther was a great hulk of a man, a roistering drinker with a full ginger beard, the epitome of the invading barbarians the Chinese had recently come to despise. As for many a son born to a military family in India, a public-school education in London had flowed seamlessly into a career in the Madras Artillery. He now enjoyed the questionable distinction of having been beaten and kidnapped by insurgents. Elsewhere in Ningbo there were others in the same precarious position — Hindu seamen, and soldiers and sailors from every corner of the British Isles, even a Chinese merchant who had fled his home near Hong Kong only to be abducted for collaborating with the enemy. Barely two months had passed since Anne, Philip and the rest had arrived on these shores, but in those few momentous weeks relations between the empires of Great Britain and China had changed for ever, and in ways that still reverberate down to the present day.

In Anne Noble's day a brig such as the *Kite*, up from Singapore with the wind in her sails, took three days to clear the Straits of Formosa and with them the tropics; then the Chinese province of Zhejiang would be sighted, and promontories so large they might hide an English shire. Stretched out now beyond the horizon, the 1,391 islands of the Chusan archipelago speckled the sea so densely that for 100 miles a lookout on a topgallant would never be out of sight of one or other peak. They skittered out into the Pacific as though some giant hand had scooped up the land and flung it far out over the water. In their midst sat the island of Chusan itself, a temperate paradise after the heat of the south. Its walled city, Tinghae, commanded a broad vale mid-way along the island's south coast, protected from the worst of the weather by the hills at its back.[1] Britons had known about its deep-water harbour for centuries, and they had eyed it with growing envy as their maritime power grew. Comfortably larger than the Isle of Wight, Chusan lay five miles off the Zhejiang mainland with its thriving markets in teas and silks, and was but a short sail from the mouth of the Yangtze and the vast interior of China that beckoned beyond. Its mountain spine receded into a cobalt haze, snow-dusted in winter, bringing to mind the Scottish glens. Merchants dreamed of building villas on its hillsides and wharves on its waterfront, missionaries of founding churches and schools, while colonial visionaries imagined plantations in its cool uplands and fertile valleys sown with wheat.

From the close of the seventeenth century, Chusan had been central to earnest attempts by the men of the British Isles to interact with the Manchu Qing dynasty which then ruled China. Commanding the trade-routes of the East China Sea, this strategically placed island sat squarely on what was fast becoming the new fault-line between East and West. With each new generation, men arrived under the Red Ensign bringing royal charters begging freedom to trade, with gifts for the emperor and letters of friendship from the Court of St James in London. Tinghae was the natural first landfall for diplomats sent by King George III in 1793. China's emperor, Qianlong, would thank King George for his humility but make it clear that the Celestial Empire had not the slightest need of his country's broadcloth and trinkets. Undeterred by China's insularity, the British were tenacious, and time and again during the coming century it seemed they might go so far as to wrest Chusan from China's hands forever. Under George's granddaughter Queen Victoria the island was thrice occupied by red-coated troops, but thrice handed back. Before ever the Union Jack flew over Hong Kong, it was raised on Chusan.

At a time when the Enlightenment's depictions of Cathay as a willow-pattern paradise were giving way to impressions of backwardness, tyranny and heathenism, the island of Chusan is where Britain and China took their first tentative steps at understanding one another. But while for a brief moment it was a household name in Britain, Chusan was swiftly eclipsed by Hong Kong's subsequent success. In today's People's Republic, though, the story of its pivotal role in the Opium Wars of the nineteenth century are familiar to every schoolchild. Like Dunkirk for the British, a resounding defeat at an obscure coastal town has become a focus for Chinese patriotism. And Chusan has become more, besides — a call to arms by an ever more nationalistic government. The People's Republic does not teach its schoolchildren that Britain, the archetypal colonial aggressor, handed back to an impotent dynasty an island known to be the superior of Hong Kong, and for the sake of national honour.

'We must religiously observe our engagements with China,' wrote the Home Secretary Sir James Graham with deep regret on the eve of the island's return to Chinese rule in 1846. 'But I fear that Hong Kong is a sorry possession and Chusan is a magnificent island admirably placed for our purposes.'[2]

Though the Chinese Communist Party would have it otherwise, the island of Chusan is an opportunity for Britain and China to deepen their friendship, not their enmity. This is its story.

Vale of Ting-Hai, Chusan (Thomas Allom, after Cpt. Stoddart)

1

Scarce a day free from insults

IT IS hard to imagine, in an age when staggering quantities of the world's consumer goods are manufactured in the People's Republic, that for centuries China suffered only the merest trickle of trade to pass through her gates. When European ships first arrived on her southern shores, China was still ruled by semi-divine emperors who perceived around them ever-widening circles of nations and tribes who grew less cultured and more barbarous the further they lived from the one, true civilization. There were many names for those unfortunate peoples, and it was fortuitous that the character chosen to describe Europeans depicted an archer holding a bow, for the Chinese were to learn that the men of the Great Western Ocean had a fondness for weaponry.

It was the Portuguese with their square-rigged carracks, a design of ship well suited to deep-sea voyages, who first rounded the Cape of Good Hope in the late 1400s and established themselves in trading enclaves along the rim of the Indian Ocean. Making their first landfall on Canton's Pearl River delta in 1513, by the mid-1500s they were trading as far north as the Yangtze.[1] Their buccaneering ways, though, proved unacceptable to the Chinese, who burned their ships and their warehouses and forced them to retreat to the tiny tidal island of Macao, where they settled down to live and trade. The Dutch, for their part, first reached China almost a century later in 1604. Rebuffed at Canton, they sailed to Taiwan, where for decades until their forceful eviction in 1662 they carried on a profitable business. But of the European nations who sought to trade with the Chinese in those early years, it was, surprisingly, the English who fared the worst; no sensible gambler of the sixteenth century would have staked money on them becoming the pre-eminent power on the China coast. In fact, England had grown to enjoy the luxuries of the East without any clear idea of their origins, her merchants unable to compete in the expensive and risky business of Oriental trade and obliged instead to rely on European rivals who closely guarded their knowledge of sea routes and safe harbours. And when the

English did finally gain the national self-confidence to challenge the Portuguese and the Dutch, things at first went badly: in 1596, the queen's favourite Sir Robert Dudley financed a flotilla of ships to sail to China bearing a letter from Elizabeth to the emperor; they were never heard of again. Alarmed by news of vessels laden with luxuries arriving in Amsterdam, London's merchants agreed that a government-backed company with a monopoly to trade to the East was essential if they were ever to punch at the same weight as their competitors. And so the first day of January, 1601, dawned upon a new contender for the riches of the Orient, the Governor & Company of Merchants of London Trading into the East Indies. This, the 'East India Company', would transform for ever the nature of China's relationship with the world.

Yet although they now enjoyed great privileges — they had a monopoly on English trade east of the Cape, and were permitted to carry valuable silver bullion out of the country to pay for it — the merchants of the East India Company still faced the most formidable of obstacles. A voyage to the far side of the globe and back could last years, and to be added to the privations en route, the threat of piracy, and the risk of armed conflict was the very real problem that English manufactures excited but little demand in the East. Still, by a process of trial and error in the matter of cargoes, by their meticulous management of provisioning and capital (and, it must be said, by the judicious use of gunpowder and shot when circumstances dictated), by the time of King Charles II's Restoration in 1660 the East India Company was a highly profitable venture. Within just a few years the English were carving out a niche for themselves in Thailand, Vietnam and Taiwan. Soon valuable ladings of tea, porcelain and, above all, silks were regularly being unloaded in London.

But mainland China herself remained elusive. In 1638 an English ship captained by one John Weddell had successfully made it up the Pearl River to Canton in the face of stiff opposition, fired upon from the shore with rockets and flaming arrows. In return, Weddell had burned junks and villages and carried off thirty head of swine, but his violent escapade had predictably failed to make a mark in the way he had hoped — peaceably and through commerce. Then in 1644 the Great Ming dynasty which for three centuries had ruled China was toppled by Manchu invaders from the northeast, and it was England's misfortune that two more vessels, the *King Ferdinand* and the *Richard & Martha*, reached Canton in 1658 during the ensuing ban on maritime trade and were obliged to leave without procuring a cargo. In 1664, the ship *Surat* visited Portuguese Macao but once again weighed anchor empty-handed. Finding it impossible to buy the cargoes it desired by trading directly with the Chinese, by the 1670s the East India Company had turned its attention to finding a backdoor route to their goods, sending ships to probe what cargoes might be loaded at entrepots from Indo-China in the south to Japan in the north. Slowly, persistence and a growing knowledge of the politics and geography of the region began to pay off. In 1684 the Manchus' Great Qing dynasty, by then fully in control of all the defeated Ming territories and desperate for tax revenue, lifted its trade embargo and opened a handful of coastal ports to foreign shipping. As the 1600s drew to a close, the East India Company's red-and-white striped flag had become a familiar sight from Canton in the south to Ningbo in the north.

Of all the Chinese ports which the Company frequented, however, Canton was by some measure the most important, due in no small part to its being the first mainland city which vessels reached after navigating the South China Sea. Home even then to more than one million souls, the city was itself no great centre of manufacture, but it had made its name as an emporium for goods transported across a vast hinterland. Foreign merchants quickly learned that the Cantonese, from the provincial inspector of customs down to the humblest lighterman, were raised to be preeminently skilled in business: each vessel to sound her way up the Pearl River was obliged to engage in endless rounds of hard-bargaining before filling her holds. An unpredictable labyrinth of cut-throat negotiations and cultural pitfalls, it was clear that the city's markets, profitable though they may be, would have to be bypassed if the East India Company were to expand its China trade and meet a growing demand back home for tea and silk. Perhaps, the Company's Court of Directors reasoned, if a man could be sent out with credentials enough to impress the mandarins further to the north, a market more lucrative than Canton might be established?

We will never know for certain precisely when it was that the name 'Chusan' was first spoken on English shores, nor even what English tongues made of it, for the word was at first set down in a bewildering variety of ways by people naturally unaccustomed to the Chinese language. Most likely, at some time during the early 1500s stories of a temperate island with good anchorages percolated back from the China seas amongst Portuguese cargoes of spice and silk. Yet by the time those cargoes reached London, Chusan would have been barely a whisper, its location merging imperceptibly into rumours of exotic lands.

The exact reasons why, as the China trade burgeoned in the late 1600s, the East India Company set its sights upon opening a 'factory' on Chusan rather than elsewhere in the province of Zhejiang are something of a mystery.[2] After all, the much larger river port of Ningbo, lying only forty miles to the west, had been visited by English vessels as early as 1683.[3] Yet Chusan's deep, sheltered harbour certainly made it desirable, as did its insular location, equidistant as it was from the provincial capital Hangzhou and the mouth of the Yangtze, and just a few days' sail from the outlying islands of Japan. We can at least be sure that hopes for a lucrative trade on Chusan must have been high: in the 1650s, atlases of the Chinese Empire had become available in Europe, compiled by missionaries such as the Jesuit Martino Martini. Chusan had appeared as a vast island (almost the twin of Taiwan, in fact, though Taiwan is seventy times larger), and it was said to be a potent kingdom with three score and ten cities upon it. More importantly, the province of Zhejiang was understood to be the ultimate source of much of the teas and silks which the Company was buying in Canton, hundreds of miles to the south. By tapping into markets closer to their origins, it was hoped that the overland transit duties paid to the imperial exchequer might be avoided, and ladings got more cheaply as a result. Besides, at those more northerly latitudes people might be more eager than their tropical compatriots to buy the warm, English woollens for which the Company sought a market.

And so it was in March of 1699 that the East India Company for the very first time, eager to test the market at untried northerly ports, handed to one Mr Allen Catchpoole a commission to act as King William III's consul-general to the Empire of China.[4] His trade mission was to be England's first official contact with the Chinese. A council was appointed, consisting of Catchpoole and four merchants — Henry Rouse, John Ridges, Robert Master, and a man named Solomon Loyd who had learned Chinese while trading with Taiwan — accompanied by five secretaries, five manservants, the Reverend James Pound, and a Scottish physician named James Cunningham. Late in the year 1700, almost a year after setting sail and having called at Borneo to buy a lading of pepper to sell to the Chinese, the ship *Eaton* was piloted into Chusan. Already at anchor in anticipation of Catchpoole's arrival were two Company vessels, the *Trumball* and the *Macclesfield*. Like all Company vessels, they held large quantities of silver coin — Spanish 'pieces of eight', Mexican dollars, Venetian duccatoons and French crowns — and woollen broadcloth from England. They saluted the *Eaton* with cannon, an act which enraged the Chinese who by tradition held that the firing of any levelled gun, even when unloaded, was an act of aggression. That simple misunderstanding would set the tone for the Company's entire venture on Chusan.

At first sight the city of Tinghae looked promising as a place of trade, but the English were frustrated to find that descriptions of the island had been somewhat exaggerated: the potent kingdom proved to have been the besieged refuge of a Ming prince whose entire population had been slaughtered when the conquering Manchus had overwhelmed him. Not a single building or mulberry tree, it was said, had been left standing. For a quarter of a century the Manchus had enforced their ban on shipping here, driving the entire coastal population inland to deny all succour to the last of the Ming loyalists. Earthen walls had been raised, and boundary stones set up, beyond which every last settlement was put to the torch and transgressors executed. For years, the seas around Chusan had been abandoned to pirates. At Catchpoole's arrival, barely a decade had passed since Tinghae had been rebuilt. The stonework of its city walls had only recently been completed, and the houses within them were as yet poor, the three or four thousand settlers there striking James Cunningham, physician to the factory, as little more than 'beggarlie'. And as for Chusan's supposed three score and ten cities, well, in truth there was but Tinghae and a scattering of hamlets.

Catchpoole and his council took up residence in a substantial building on the waterfront a short distance south of the city. Specially constructed for them in wood and whitewashed plaster, it consisted of fifteen handsome rooms in one, long row, a two-hundred-foot verandah running their length. Fitted out now to their satisfaction according to English tastes, we might surmise that they were soon indistinguishable from the home of any eighteenth-century gentleman back in London. Below these residential quarters were the warehouses, and across a yard from these stood a range of outhouses. An acre and a half of land, defined on its seaward side by stone embankments, provided a wharf for the Company's ships, while a creek behind the outhouses made landing cargoes easy.[5] From a surviving sketch in a ship's journal it looks neat and well-built.[6] The islanders took to calling it *Hongmaoguan*, the Red Hair Hall.

It would be fair to say that neither the Chinese nor the English were particularly clear in their own minds about how trade ought to be conducted. This was, after all, the first time that English ships had dropped anchor at Chusan, and the mandarins who resided there, though keen to profit from the Company's presence, had scant experience of Europeans. Clearly anxious to make his guests feel at ease, Chusan's military commander, General Lan Li, sent them presents (there were even a live deer and a large carp to celebrate King William's birthday),[7] despatched a guard to the factory to ensure that curious locals did not disturb their Sunday prayers, and invited them to a banquet served in what he mistakenly believed to be the English style. When this was brought in, it consisted of boiled and roast meats — pork, venison, bacon, whole pigs, geese and more. The servants knelt to disjoint the carcasses with their bare hands but with little decorum:

> Having cut the flesh into small pieces from the bones, the same was brought on a plate and thrown into a bowl upon the table, one sort of meat after another, but all put into the same bowl, which we took out with Chop-sticks and dipped into sauces lying on the table, eating the same without bread.[8]

The whole affair was sufficient, the English recalled, to turn a weak stomach.

The island's civil magistrate Mu Sui, thankfully, was more knowledgeable than his military counterpart in culinary matters, and when it was his turn to feast the English he even managed to procure knives and forks, plates, napkins, bread, 'and other things in very good order suitable to the English Eating.'[9] This first course having ended, the rest of the dinner was served in the Chinese fashion, accompanied all the while by a play, which the English considered very dull and noisy. Catchpoole in return feasted General Lan. As Chusan's more senior mandarin — he outranked magistrate Mu Sui — it was in Lan's gift to allow the English to live and work there, and it was essential to win him over. The Red Hair Hall had been built as his personal investment in the East India Company's success, and with his superiors expecting their palms to be greased it was important that Lan see a good return. Besides, as he explained to Catchpoole, he was personally responsible for the good behaviour of the English while they were in Chusan, and he could expect to lose his position — or worse — if he could not control them.

Once the mutual flattery had been concluded, trade talks began in earnest. Catchpoole was an experienced Company agent, and from time spent in the great Bengali trading centre of Cossimbazar he must have understood the importance of following local custom and cultivating powerful contacts.[10] Kneeling on the floor as Chinese protocol required, he was granted an official audience with General Lan. Despite Lan's honied words ('I am sorry,' he would say of the English, 'that I had not the happiness of a more early acquaintance with so worthy a people'),[11] Catchpoole began to realise that navigating a safe path through a maze of vested interests would be a treacherous matter. The English found themselves at the bottom of a pyramid of kickbacks and bribes, for an official posting for humble, county-level mandarins such as Lan would last just five or ten years before the emperor informed them that they were to be moved elsewhere, and they were fully expected to feather their nests for a comfortable retirement while they had the chance. Lan was duty bound to pay his superior officer, the military commander of Zhejiang, a cut of any money he squeezed from his official roles, and above this man was Zhejiang's provincial governor, and above him a governor-general…. Chusan's civil magistrate Mu Sui, too, had already been in the post for five years and must have been keen to grasp such a rare opportunity to provide for his future. And above Mu Sui, again, was the local prefect residing in Ningbo, and above him a powerful circuit intendant, each breathing down the other's neck for a cut of the East India Company's silver.

So if the Company had naïvely hoped that with increasing distance from Canton it might find more profitable markets, it was simply to be disappointed. For all an English consul was worth in Chinese eyes, Catchpoole might as well have been a Chinese fisherman turning up at Dover claiming the right to negotiate with King William himself. Any hopes he had harboured of encountering an enlightened and just bureaucracy in a famed Celestial Empire rapidly evaporated. For a start, General Lan would allow none but his own merchants to trade with the Company, all others being prohibited on pain of the most severe punishment.[12] One man, from whom the Company had privately agreed to buy 2,000 silk fans and thirty-six piculs of tea, was soon to face being beaten to death with bamboo rods if he dealt any longer with the English.[13] Lan, though, was not to be outmanoeuvred, and he flew into a foaming rage when told in direct terms that the English saw through these wiles.[14] 'Thus much for the general character of the Chinese functionaries here,' observed Catchpoole wryly.[15]

Catchpoole presented Lan with a list of the conditions under which the Company wished to trade.[16] Most were concerned with the details of commerce and duties and could be negotiated, but others proved to be quite out of the question: the English could not build houses for themselves, nor travel as they pleased; sailors who broke Chinese law were to be answerable to Chinese justice; Catchpoole was not at liberty to engage linguists of his own — men like Solomon Loyd — but had to rely on those provided by General Lan; there would be no overturning of the regulation requiring that English ships land their gunpowder and sails as signs of goodwill, nor would a cemetery be provided for all the Englishmen who would inevitably die while at anchor, and Lan would not stop the islanders selling sailors *samshoo*, the deceptively strong spirit for which Tinghae was famed.[17] Finally, it went without saying that Englishmen would not be permitted to meet the island's mandarins as equals — they would have to go on sitting before them upon a carpet to show their inferiority. In return for an official 'chop' — a stamped certificate allowing the Company to trade — the English agreed after some weeks of negotiation to pay General Lan a 2% tariff on everything they bought and sold, on top of a tax based on the dimensions of their ships.[18] This 'measurage' was noticeably lower on Chusan than it would have been at the going rate in Canton, but this was scant comfort when compared to Lan's insistence that two-thirds of all the bills owing to his merchants were to be paid in silver and just one-third in woollen broadcloth and trinkets, the very goods the English most wished to sell.

Catchpoole's hope that silver would be less in demand on Chusan than at Canton proved elusive for good reason: silver was the medium in which Zhejiang, just like Canton, paid its taxes to the emperor, while the Chinese simply did not wish to wear wool. Anyone who has spent time in China's tropics will understand why wool is not the most sought-after material there; yet even in Chusan, which in winter is bitterly cold despite lying at the same latitude as Cairo, the population proved far from eager to turn its back upon generations of tradition and cast off its homespun cottons. In any case, merchants familiar with the finest silks from Suzhou and Hangzhou were unimpressed with anything Kentish weavers had to offer. And as for the products of England's burgeoning workshops — mirrors, swords, guns and clocks, and objects of amber, coral and crystal — the Chinese had little need or interest.

Catchpoole was quickly learning that trading on Chusan would require a great deal of patience and silver, but as 1700 drew to a close the first of his ships did at least sail for England with a rich cargo. Despite Lan's cornering the market and his thirst for precious metal, consumers back home would soon be wearing silks and drinking tea from porcelain cups, all loaded in Tinghae harbour. Business seemed to be going rather smoothly, all things considered. So when one day General Lan summoned Catchpoole to tell him that their agreement was only a temporary measure, Catchpoole realised he had been misled; if the English wished to reside permanently in the Red Hair Hall, he was informed, they would need to send an embassy begging the emperor's personal favour and bringing his majesty £10,000 in gifts.[19] Any chop allowing the Company to trade on Chusan, it dawned upon Catchpoole, would have to be renegotiated with each new vessel, just as in Canton. This was precisely the stifling bureaucracy the Company had come to Chusan in the hope of escaping. Worse, General Lan's merchants were becoming capricious to the point of sheer dishonesty, seemingly changing the terms of each contract according to whim and demanding money to guarantee the timely delivery of their goods.[20] This was decidedly unlike home, where the commercial classes could appeal to an impartial court to decide their disputes. Unfamiliar with the intricacies of silk-weaving and tea production, and bemused both by Chinese obligations of gift-giving and by the relationship between Chusan's mandarins and their superiors on the mainland, Catchpoole saw only disingenuous hurdles placed in his path: 'There is no faith in these Chinamen,' he railed. 'We have chops, grants and articles, but they keep none of them but what they please.'[21]

Mr Robert Douglas, Catchpoole's chief 'supercargo' (the man ultimately responsible for buying and selling in Chusan on behalf of the Company), was equally damning:

The many troubles and vexations we have mett with from these subtile Chineese — whose principalls allow them to cheat, and their dayly practise therin have made them dextrus at it — I am not able to expresse at this time; and however easie others may have represented the trade of China, neither I nor my assistants have found it so, for every day produces new troubles.

As spring gave way to a hot summer, those troubles only seemed to worsen. General Lan Li was promoted to the command of distant Tianjin, and his successor General Shi Shipiao proved to be a man of rash temperament. When General Shi's appointed merchants proved unable to deliver great quantities of tea and silk that had already been paid for, the English threatened to cut their losses, weigh anchor, and leave. The prospect of watching the goose that laid the golden eggs paddling out of harbour seemed to invigorate General Shi, and he gave assurances of prompt delivery. But of course, in exchange for such guarantees, the Company would now be obliged to pay three quarters of its bills in silver and just one quarter in woollen broadcloth....[22] It was an even worse deal than before, but if Catchpoole wanted to build a profitable market on Chusan he had little choice but to agree. By the end of the year another ship full of luxury goods had sailed for home and contracts for more had been exchanged.

Yet it must have come as scant surprise to Catchpoole when, as completion on that lading neared, the same old demands resurfaced. Days of fraught talks in the cold of winter ended with the English squeezed of yet more cash, not to mention 24 lbs of silver as *cumshaw*, a gift for General Shi's elderly mother.[23] Civil magistrate Mu Sui, angered and insulted that the Company was sidelining him in its business dealings, harangued Catchpoole and his merchants over what a powerful man he was and demanded they console him with silver. The English refused, and amid a flurry of accusations and recriminations were ordered by an enraged Mu Sui to leave Chusan in the name of the Kangxi Emperor.[24] There was no counterargument to this ultimate method of expulsion, and little time to reship all the goods stored at the Red Hair Hall. Soon the wharf was a scene of confusion as personal possessions and merchandise were taken aboard. In the midst of the chaos a mob broke down the door to the Red Hair Hall and began to loot it. Escaping to the relative safety of their ships in the harbour, the English wrote to London that same day recommending that the Company refrain from ever again sending ships to Chusan: even a consul-general with a commission from King William himself had no status on this hateful island. They had lost some £20,000 in the venture, and could only lament the troubles that had dogged them ever since they had first set eyes on Chusan, 'having been scarce a day free from insults, impositions or hardships.'[25] Indignant at his treatment, Catchpoole sailed for Jakarta.

And there he resided at the pleasure of its Dutch rulers until, one summer's day in 1702, he decided to set a course once more for Chusan. A less tenacious man might have thought better of it, but Catchpoole's expulsion had benefited neither the East India Company nor General Shi nor Mu Sui, and Catchpoole was welcomed back with smiling reassurances of fair treatment. Within the month, another Company ship had sailed laden for home. But again, predictably by now though no less disappointingly for that, the situation deteriorated. The unexpected arrival of merchants acting for no less a personage than the future emperor of China provoked dismay: knowing full well that they could expect to be bled of any profit or severely punished for standing in their way, the local merchants simply vanished.[26]

'China is all trouble,' wrote Catchpoole in sheer frustration.[27] 'They will deliver no goods but what they please; no force can be used against them; and for the arguments of justice and reason, they laugh at us.'[28] Delays again grew, and prices rose. When the provincial inspector of customs, a mandarin of great authority on the Zhejiang coast, waded in, demanding a third of a ton of silver in unexpected taxes and duties, this was as much as Catchpoole could bear. He began to reship his stock with a view to leaving, only to be placed under house-arrest in a Red Hair Hall now flooded with Chinese soldiers. Liberty for His Britannic Majesty's Consul-General to China came only with what seemed little short of a ransom demand — 500 lbs of silver — while the price of freedom to go on trading was an agreement that nine-tenths of all future contracts be paid in silver coin.[29] These were devastating terms for a man who had dreamed of simply swapping English woollens for Chinese silks!

A final shipment of goods — silk, copper, tutenag and mercury — was loaded onto the Company's vessels. They were of good quality and would turn a profit in London. If nothing else, and rather late in the day, Catchpoole had learned that if the Company was willing to part with enough silver it could trade successfully on Chusan. But silver did not grow on trees, and the Company had wished for so much more: no permanent settlement had been established, and all they had to show for their troubles was a suite of rented rooms and warehouses from which they could be evicted at a whim, or which could just as easily become their prison. The game was not worth the candle. By December 1703, just three years after they had first arrived, the Company's ships had left for the South China Sea, taking with them English dreams of a settlement on Chusan.

Catchpoole had often recommended to the Company's Court of Directors in London that it annex instead the tiny island of Con Son, fifty miles off the Mekong delta, as a permanent base of operations in the China seas.[30] It was far less trouble than Chusan. The Court disagreed: Con Son's harbour was far from ideal, and it was not secure from surprise attack. They wrote to Catchpoole, then residing in the small English settlement on Con Son, ordering him to remove his stock to Borneo. He never read the letter: on March 3rd 1705, in the dead of night, the troops who occupied Con Son in the name of its Cochin-Chinese rulers burned the English factory and murdered Catchpoole and fifteen other Englishmen. Such were the terrible risks that Company men ran to make their fortune.

The South Gate of Tinghae as it was in 1793 (William Alexander)

2

The Great Emperor and the men with red hair

IN 1707 the kingdoms of England and Scotland united to become Great Britain. The fact that ships continued to drop anchor at Chusan under the new Union Jack for another half century is testament to the East India Company's faith that liberal trade could overcome the inertia of China's vast and mercenary bureaucracy. If the coming to the throne in 1736 of a new emperor, Qianlong, was remarked upon by British merchants, it certainly made no practical difference to them, for each one to visit Chusan faced the same intrigues and extortions, and each ultimately left disappointed and emotionally drained. Then, at last, fearing the loss of income that a successful Chusan venture might mean, the powerful guilds that had come to monopolize trade in Canton lobbied to close the island to foreigners once and for all. In 1757 Qianlong signed a decree raising the taxes on foreign trade upon the islands of the Chusan archipelago to double those in force in Canton, a simple move that made commerce all but impossible. In 1758 the *Onslow* sailed from Tinghae after negotiating a lading at great cost, her merchants having been warned that no more British vessels would be suffered to drop anchor.[1] The following year the *Chesterfield* was, true enough, turned away empty-handed.

Nobody could have argued that the British had not tried their damnedest to trade on Chusan. The plain truth — as over the course of half a century they had come to realize — was that self-sufficient China had no need of British manufactures, that her merchants and mandarins wanted nothing but silver dollars in exchange for their teas and silks. Accepting a little broadcloth besides, and some fancy gimcracks from the workshops of Birmingham and Manchester, was little more than humouring these persistent barbarians who set so much store by crude commerce. In the decades following the departure of the *Chesterfield* from Chusan, the emperor found no reason to question his edict confining foreigners to distant Canton, out of harm's way. These men from the distant land of *Yingjili* (the Chinese, following the rules of their own grammar, did not discriminate between 'England' and 'English' when they spoke of this new country) had tamely submitted to him.

The years went by, and generations of British merchants continued to buy silks, porcelains and other luxuries on the Canton market, but as time passed it was tea that became the mainstay of the China trade. As Britons from the middling and working classes developed a taste for it, by 1760 the East India Company was importing 3,000,000 lbs of leaf each year, and fully three times as much come 1790. Across Britain, people were drinking tea from China cups decorated with Minton's fanciful willow pattern and imagining a Chinoiserie world where their *twankey* and *lapsang-soochong* were grown; in Brighton, the future King George IV built a seaside pavilion chock full of the most sumptuously gaudy imaginings of Chinese aesthetics.

Half a world away in steamy Canton, by contrast, the onerous restrictions under which the tea trade was suffered to carry on was looking more and more at odds with Britain's growing global prestige as each year passed.[2] On the Pearl River there, upon a site safely outside the city walls, two-thirds of a mile of waterfront had been set aside for the foreign factories (for not just Britons but also Americans, Dutchmen, Frenchmen, Spaniards and others lived here during the trading season). It was not that the factories were inherently unpleasant; far from it: sturdily built of brick and granite and fitted with colourful blinds and shady verandahs, they were furnished much like a Pall Mall gentleman's club, with billiard rooms, libraries, dining rooms and private quarters, and they were certainly far better suited to Western ideas of comfort than even the very richest residences of Canton's mandarins. But when hundreds of men lived confined to these few acres for months on end their attractions faded. The Cantonese man in the street was openly contemptuous of foreigners, physically violent even. Wives and daughters were forbidden there. The local merchant guilds kept a tight rein on the Westerners, whose only avenue of appeal was through those very same guilds about whose abuses they wished to complain. The Chinese were forbidden from teaching their language to outsiders on pain of death, making the commercial stranglehold of the guilds all the more asphyxiating. And for Britain — the world's foremost industrial nation — to be running an enormous trade deficit with agrarian China was not just an insult to national pride but a huge drain on the exchequer. If only, the British lamented, they could produce something for which the Chinese truly had a yen....

It is not clear precisely how 'yen', originally a Chinese word, came to mean an intense craving in the English language, for there are two similar-sounding characters which fit the bill, one meaning 'addiction', the other 'smoke' — *opium* smoke. It turned out to be that hitherto minor Indian export which finally set Britain and China on a collision course over the island of Chusan. The trickle of Bengali opium arriving in Canton at the start of the eighteenth century became first a torrent then a flood, the demand so strong as to elicit silver from Chinese merchants without negotiation, *cumshaw* or politicking. Opium quite simply turned the China trade on its head. It was the Chinese now who were desperate to get hold of British goods, and trading with them had become easy.[3]

Opium was produced legally in India (the refined sap of *Papaver somniferum* was in fact a widely used medicine in Britain), but its sale inside China had been banned by imperial edict since 1729 for the simple reason that it sapped the mind and body of vitality and destroyed the lives of upright young men from good families. The emperor's reasoning might have been wrapped up in the Confucian ethics of the day, but, after all, this is fundamentally the same reason why heroin (an opium derivative) is today a controlled drug across the globe. The British government for its part did not question China's right to ban the import of any item of trade (or such at least was Britain's avowed position), but felt that if China wished to do so then enforcement should be the responsibility of Peking rather than of London.[4] The French, went one analogy of the day, could ban the import of British products through Calais, but Whitehall would not be obliged to enforce that ban on Britons who wished to break French law. The British would try time and again to persuade Peking to legalise opium, for at least this would allow the emperor to profit from its sale, but the emperor would not sacrifice his moral principles or accept advice from foreigners. The fact that China's long-standing opium ban was a dead letter most of the time played into the hands of those who thought the Chinese hypocritical: the trade in the drug was, after all, connived at and even monopolised by the relatively lowly mandarins in coastal ports — men like generals Lan and Shi on Chusan — who for the British merchants were their only experience of Chinese officialdom.

The East India Company, at least, pretended not to deal in opium bound for China, for fear of jeopardizing the agreements under which it traded in Canton. Instead the drug was sold in India to private merchants who entrusted its sale to agency houses on the China coast. Those agencies placed the opium into receiving ships, who sold it to Chinese smugglers who undertook the illegal act of landing and selling it on, while tier upon tier of bribable mandarins turned a blind eye and took their cut on the deal. The silver which had paid for the opium then found its way to the East India Company's offices in Canton to be exchanged for IOUs that could be cashed with clean hands in London. It was, in modern parlance, little short of money-laundering, though quite legal. The very same silver, meanwhile, was used by the Company in Canton to buy the tea which, when imported into Britain, provided the Treasury with valuable tax revenue. In essence, as the eighteenth century drew on, the British public was imperceptibly becoming addicted to tea, the Chinese to opium, and the Treasury to the money that the trade was generating. Yet despite the remarkable about-turn in the trade deficit which opium would make possible, the same old complaints still festered in Canton as they once had on Chusan: the arbitrary taxes and *cumshaw* remained, as did the unwholesome conditions in cramped residences beyond whose bounds Britons feared to tread (they had become, it was commented, little better than a commercial leper colony). Something had to be done.

And so a suitable man was chosen to lead Europe's first full-scale diplomatic mission to Peking, to seek better terms for

British merchants and to win over the Chinese with a demonstration of Britain's achievements in science and industry.[5]
George Macartney, Viscount of Dervock, was an Irish peer, an
ex-governor of Madras, and a proponent of the understandable
view that Britain was the most powerful nation on Earth. Lord
Macartney left Portsmouth in September of 1792 aboard the
64-gun man-of-war *Lion*, with the East Indiaman *Hindostan* and
others following close behind. His embassy, comprising doctors,
scientists, painters, musicians and scholars, was the largest ever
to have left Europe bound for the imperial court. Its holds were
crammed with gifts from King George III, chosen with care to
demonstrate that Britain was fit to be treated as an equal. There
were terrestrial and celestial globes, orreries, a planetarium,
the most advanced clocks, barometers and telescopes, the most
perfect glass lenses yet ground, Wedgwood porcelains, musical
instruments, sprung carriages, a hot-air balloon, air guns, rifles,
cannons, a perfect scale model of the navy's pride and joy the
110-gun *Royal Sovereign*, the finest cloths and carpets... the
inventory simply went on and on.

The Qianlong Emperor, the same man who in 1757 had agreed
to smother the Chusan trade with punitively high duties, was still
on the throne at the age of eighty-two (though he was piously to
abdicate in 1795 in favour of his son rather than enjoy a longer
reign than his grandfather Kangxi). Besides hoping — naïvely, in
retrospect — to impress this conservative old Manchu with the
fruits of Europe's Enlightenment, Lord Macartney carried a list of
practical aims. Of these, the most important was the opening of
Chusan's principal town Tinghae, amongst other ports, to British
trade. Then there was an end to the humiliating conditions in
Canton to be discussed, and the permanent cession of an island
in Eastern China to negotiate — it was assumed this would be
Chusan, already known to occupy an unrivalled position — where
Britons might live and work freely under extraterritorial British
law. It was almost a century now since Allen Catchpoole had laid
similar requests before a mandarin in Tinghae. Generals Lan and
Shi, like Catchpoole, were long dead, but Lord Macartney was
soon to learn how little things had changed.

On June 23rd 1793, having visited Macao, the *Lion* and the *Hindostan* passed within sight of an island known locally as Hong Kong without giving it a second thought, pressing on north-eastward to drop anchor in Chusan's waters. Soon they could scarcely manoeuvre for the press of sampans and junks crowding about their hulls. The *Lion* alone was hemmed in by some three hundred, while hundreds more were visible all the way to a thunderous horizon.[6] Supplies were eagerly offered — bullocks, goats, fowl and fish — and presently the decks were so crowded with curious fishermen that the crew was obliged to turn them off to make room for new arrivals.[7] They watched as men gaped at the height of the masts and measured heel-to-toe the length and breadth of the ships, the like of which had not been seen in those parts since the departure of the last East Indiaman a generation before.[8] Wandering quite at will, some of these smiling fishermen chanced upon the *Lion*'s great cabin and the portrait of the Qianlong Emperor that Lord Macartney had hung there. Falling to their knees, they prostrated themselves and kissed the floor.[9]

'On rising,' Lord Macartney's deputy Sir George Staunton would later recall, 'they appeared to have a sort of gratitude towards the foreigner who had the attention to place the portrait of their sovereign in his apartment.' Presently Sir George, a personal friend of Macartney from the days when his lordship had been governor of Grenada and, later, Madras, headed for Tinghae to enquire after pilots for the trip northward. The navigation to the mouth of the Peiho River (for this was the closest one could reach to Peking by sea) had only been attempted once before by a British captain, and even this was now some thirty years gone. Lord Macartney himself remained aboard the *Lion*, proudly determined that his first encounter with Chinese bureaucracy would come in Peking. He desired, it seems, to make as grand an entrance as could be stage-managed.

As the day's tide turned, Staunton's ship the *Clarence* moored off a tiny islet her charts called Tree-a-top (though it had lost its sole defining feature to a log-pile). A landing party rowed across to the neighbouring island of Lowang, and there the embassy of the Court of St James set foot on Chinese soil.[10]

Sir George walked unchallenged for some time until, descending a valley, he and his party met with an astonished-looking young peasant. In loose blue trousers and with a conical straw hat tied with twine beneath his chin, he was a fitting archetype. As this unlikely welcoming committee led them toward his village, the Englishmen were beckoned to enter an isolated farmhouse amidst a grove of bamboo and fan palms. Farmer and son stood and stared in wide-eyed amazement, as if the men before them had fallen from the sky, though their visitors were most struck not by their hosts themselves but by their apparent poverty. Sir George recalled the scene:

> The house was built of wood, the uprights of the natural form of the timber. No ceiling concealed the inside of the roof, which was put together strongly, and covered with the straw of rice. The floor was of earth beaten hard, and the partitions between the rooms consisted of mats hanging from the beams.

A pair of spinning wheels sat abandoned by womenfolk who had been whisked away at the men's approach. How different things would have been had a party of Chinese landed on the Scilly Isles and stumbled into a sturdily built cottage. The embassy was yet a thousand miles from Peking, and already China was proving to be like a different world.

The *Clarence* was escorted into Tinghae's inner harbour on the early morning tide the next day, firing a blank salute that only served to irritate the islanders and mooring half a mile from the former Red Hair Hall. A brightly painted junk presently came alongside bearing an elderly man, a merchant who in his youth had dealt with the East India Company. Despite the passing of over several decades he still spoke a little English and recalled with affection Fitzhugh and Bevan, two of the Company's agents. Sir George Staunton's delegation was welcomed ashore the next day and in Tinghae was treated to plays and entertainments just as Allen Catchpoole had once been. Of Tinghae itself Sir George was especially attentive, aware that Lord Macartney planned to ask the emperor for the right to settle in the archipelago. He would later write an account of the day, a depiction that would find a receptive audience in a British public eager to have its love of Chinoiserie flattered:

> Of the towns of Europe, Ting-hai bore the resemblance most of Venice, but on a smaller scale. It was, in some degree, surrounded, as well as intersected, by canals. The bridges thrown over them were steep, and ascended by steps, like the Rialto. The streets, most of which were no more than alleys or narrow passages just a dozen feet wide, were paved with square flat stones; but the houses, unlike the Venetian buildings, were low, and mostly of one story. The attention, as to ornament, in these buildings was confined chiefly to the roofs, which, besides having the tiles that cover the rafters luted and plastered over, to prevent accidents from their falling in stormy weather, were contrived in such a form as to imitate the inward bend of the ridges and sides of canvas tents, or of the coverings of skins of animals or other flexible materials, effected by their weight; a form preferred, perhaps, after the introduction of more solid materials, in allusion to the modes of shelter to which the human race had, probably, recourse before the erection of regular dwelling houses.

But if Sir George's guesswork as to the origins of the Chinese flying eave was wide of the mark, his description of Tinghae as a bustling commercial centre rings true. The town that sultry July 5th smelt of the incense that wafted from shops and temples into its busy streets. He was impressed by the rich displays of silks and cottons, of furniture, brightly painted coffins and animals fated for the pot — eels, fish, poultry, and even dogs. He noted the curious hairstyle all men adopted, their heads shaved leaving just a long pigtail (it was a legal requirement, and a sign of submission, for Chinese men to wear their hair in this style characteristic of their Manchu rulers) and the attractive way the women coiled their plaits into a topknot.[11] Their tiny bound feet, though, he considered a bad affair.

Staunton's curiosity was in turn more than matched by that of the townsfolk: though opium clippers were to be seen in Chusan's outer anchorages, no foreigner had set foot in Tinghae in recent memory, and the sight of aristocratic Britons swathed in dress-coats, stockings and breeches, buckled shoes and pomaded wigs had an electrifying effect. People crowded around the shore party, ignoring the efforts of Chinese soldiers to hold them back. The atmosphere was muggy, the visitors bound in layers of tight clothing and stifled by onlookers. Before nightfall, a sky which all day had glowered with the threat of rain suddenly turned black, and there arose a terrific thunderstorm.[12] Suffering from the heat, the party slipped into the City God's Temple to catch their breath, emerging in sedans to be carried back to the harbour. The crowd, which had waited outside for them to reappear, followed them all the way back to the old Red Hair Hall, inquisitive heads pushed every now and again through the drapes. That muggy summer's day, it was later remembered, the only words to be heard on the townsfolk's lips were *dahuangdi* and *hongmao*: 'the great emperor' and 'the men with red hair'.[13]

When it came to finding sailors who had been all the way north to the Peiho River, a number of miserable wretches were sniffed out but none were capable of piloting a ship. It was an most unexpected turn of events, since Chusan was known to be a centre of seafaring.[14] Eventually, two former merchants were found who in their youth had made the voyage many times. Despite their protestations that it would be ruinous to their businesses and their settled lives, they were commanded in the name of the emperor to prepare to leave. By dark, the *Clarence* was once more anchored off Lowang, and the next day she sighted the rest of the squadron. But the merchants turned out to be worse than useless as pilots, understandably frightened by the strange surroundings of a European warship and incapable of navigating out of sight of the shore.[15]

'It was in vain to make them endeavour to comprehend the difference in the draft of water between their ships and ours,' complained John Barrow, the overseer of the embassy's scientific instruments, 'although they were shown by a piece of rope the depth required. Indeed, their skill in navigation was held very cheap by the lowest seaman on board.' Still, taking on proper pilots in Shandong, the embassy safely reached the mouth of the Peiho. There its ships, drawing too great a depth of water to proceed, turned back for Chusan, while Lord Macartney's vast store of gifts for the emperor was meticulously trans-shipped into shallow-draughted junks.

On the slow and winding river passage to the capital, the question of ceremonial was raised. (Lord Macartney by now suspected that the Chinese understood his embassy in starkly different terms to himself, for lining the banks were banners announcing that he was bringing with him not gifts for the emperor but *gongwu*, the term reserved for items of tribute from a vassal nation. He objected, but his objections were ignored: he was, after all, a mere envoy from such a vassal nation and could be excused his ignorance of Qing practice). Macartney was informed that he would, of course, be performing the full kowtow before Qianlong — three genuflections and nine prostrations, touching the forehead each time on the floor — to demonstrate King George III's acceptance of his vassal status. But Macartney could not — *would* not — kowtow to anybody. The argument soured the atmosphere.

The emperor's birthday celebrations — the occasion on which Macartney was to meet him — were to be held in the imperial retreat at Chengde, a hundred miles beyond Peking. When the British finally arrived in the town, the only men to witness their entry were idle street people of the lowest order. The Chinese seemed to be making a point. They were handed a letter which Macartney had been jealously guarding since London. It came from King George III himself, and outlined the reasons for his embassy. King George concluded by declaring Qianlong to be his good brother and friend. To a demigod who counted the sun, moon and stars within his extended family, this claim to his fraternity was outrageous, a terrible diplomatic *faux pas*. The row over the kowtow simmered on, and at length Qianlong agreed that a single bending of the knee, as the form of respect Macartney might show to his own monarch, would suffice. But what to Macartney appeared a victory over protocol only served to affirm the British in Chinese eyes as the most unreconstructed of barbarians.

The long-awaited meeting with Qianlong, when it came, was not the focus of festivities that Macartney had hoped it would be. He found himself just one of three ambassadors presented to the emperor that day, the others Kalmuks from Central Asia and representatives of a Burmese prince who went barefoot and chewed betel-nuts like savages. When Macartney's turn came he knelt before Qianlong, handed a few of King George's presents to the waiting courtiers, and was ushered away in the same way as the Kalmuks and the Burmese. In an official reply to his letter, King George was praised for his humility and obedience, and for his willingness to incline his heart toward civilisation. But his requests for more equitable trading conditions — and this after all was the very point of the embassy — were dismissed with all the condescension of a stern parent toward a greedy and deluded child. There was no possibility of Britons being allowed to live and trade on Chusan. Worse, and despite every intention to the contrary, King George III had added his name to China's long list of vassal rulers. When a generation later frustration finally flared into violence, the Chinese could rightly rank the British as 'perfidious rebels'.

The situation went from bad to worse when sickness broke out aboard the embassy's ships as they sailed back from the Peiho to drop anchor off Chusan. A patch of rice-paddy north of the old Red Hair Hall was granted to the squadron's five dozen invalids, and near a large building given over as a hospital for them there sprang up a village of white canvas tents.[16] Guards were posted to prevent any contact between the British and the islanders, though the contamination feared was as much cultural as it was corporal. The weather in early autumn was still hot, and it was a struggle to find any clean water. On Chusan itself, and on the smaller islands of Tinghae's harbour, watering parties found the village wells to be reservoirs for surface run-off rather than bore holes.[17] On some days they might visit thirty or more without gathering enough. Worse, as villagers began to equate the appearance of

British boats with the theft of their irrigation water they would drain their wells of what little they contained and toss filth in to spoil what was left.[18] That, at least, was what the British suspected after the indignities they had endured elsewhere in China. But time ashore, even on the mosquito-ridden paddy, cured most of the dysentery cases (many had contracted malaria in its place, but at least this was curable with cinchona bark). Those who died were buried on Chusan. On the last day of November the *Hindostan* weighed anchor to leave Tinghae harbour. But there, as she struck a submerged rock, she gave a dreadful heel and water came close to flooding her gundecks. After fully half a minute, just when it seemed her keel would split under her weight, she floated free.[19] The embassy had so nearly ended in disaster as well as humiliation.

And so, a costly trade mission having been utterly rebuffed, Britain's commercial grievances festered, yet China paid them no heed. The British were, after all, being correctly managed by long-established protocols of the Great Qing dynasty, and they had willingly shown themselves to be vassals. When in 1816 a second embassy arrived in Peking in filthy weather in the dead of night, its ambassador was whisked bedraggled and tired to the Forbidden City and forced to kowtow to the emperor. There seems to have been a refusal, a scuffle, and Lord Amherst was ordered to leave in disgrace. If China would not of its own volition grant Great Britain the respect and the trading rights she expected, then only force, it seemed, remained, and Great Britain was growing certain enough of her military superiority to resort to it.

3

The slightest spark

THE COMING to the throne in 1820 of a new emperor — Daoguang was a grandson of the Qianlong Emperor who had confined foreign trade to Canton — made no difference to the arduous nature of living and working in China for British merchants. If anything it got worse, but the frugally minded Daoguang, his shoulders bearing the weight of an empire which was under threat from internal uprisings and natural disasters, had little time for, and, besides, no real understanding of British grievances. By the time Daoguang ascended the throne, nearly five thousand chests of Indian opium were reaching China each year.[1] The British government continued to tiptoe the narrow path between supporting and condemning the opium trade, Britain's superintendent in Canton being reminded that he should neither encourage opium traders in their activity nor lose sight of the fact that he had no authority to interfere with them, for they were not beholden to act according to government diktat.[2] From a Chinese perspective, of course, such fence-sitting was utterly incomprehensible: these were merchants from the land of Yingjili — how could it *not* be within the power of their chieftains to restrain them?

But while the merchants at the coalface of the China trade were prepared — if far from happy — to allow things to continue as they always had for the sake of predictability and profits, others were growing increasingly impatient with China's refusal to engage in anything approaching meaningful negotiations on trade. Besides, for the Court of St James far away on the northern edge of the Great Western Ocean, China's haughty assertion that the monarch of Yingjili was a mere barbarian prince was growing more unacceptable with every year that passed. And for the Treasury, the worrying tendency of the Chinese to unilaterally suspend the Canton trade at a whim, and so cut off vast sums in tax revenue, was beginning to threaten Britain's fiscal base.

In 1835, an essay was forwarded to Britain's foreign secretary, Lord Palmerston, from a rather unexpected quarter. Its author was a German missionary named Karl Gützlaff. Gützlaff, a Lutheran evangelist who spoke several oriental languages, had over the course of the previous few years formed strong opinions on the political situation on the China coast. He was candid in his observations:

> The Mandarins are taught from their childhood to look with contempt upon Barbarians. Under this denomination all foreigners are included, however civilized they may be, if they are not transformed by the laws of the Celestial Empire, they remain Barbarians and ought to be treated as such.[3]

China, Gützlaff went on, 'looks… with the utmost contempt upon the British Empire, and upon its Sovereign as a Barbarian King who has to tender obedience and homage to the Celestial Empire.' All that two embassies to Peking had achieved was to confirm the Chinese in their belief that Great Britain was merely a tributary vassal wholly undeserving of diplomatic recognition. 'We can demand everything from the fears of the Chinese government,' Gützlaff wrote, 'but nothing from their goodwill.' If the British desired the right to free trade in China, they must provoke a reaction in Peking, something their ambassadors had signally failed to do so far by pussyfooting around Chinese sensibilities:

> This haughty government must be lowered in the dust by distress, and come to offer terms instead of being permitted to reject ours. Once we have got the trading conditions we require, the government should be made to compensate us for our military forces.

As a first step, Gützlaff recommended to Lord Palmerston that any future stoppage of the Canton trade be met with the least bloody response — a naval blockade. Just a handful of British men-of-war would need to be stationed along the coast, off the great cities of the Yangtze, at the mouth of the Peiho, and on the ancient Grand Canal that linked Hangzhou to Peking. Gützlaff's reasoning was simple: such a move would stem the supply of rice to the capital. The Chinese government could sacrifice the lives of myriads without a groan, for the country teems with people… but it cannot do without its large supplies of grain, for it has to satisfy a host of hungry Tartars who are quite dependent on the coast.'

Next, a jumping-off point was needed, a fulcrum for all subsequent military action, and this role Gützlaff alloted to Chusan. The British occupation of that island, he concluded, would defy response and cause a sensation in Peking. The Chinese, finding a dagger pointed at their heart, would be forced to negotiate, but the British should remain aloof until presented with an offer too good to refuse. The man chosen to lead this expedition must have full plenipotentiary power to act, Gützlaff insisted, and must be a man of the utmost firmness. He needed to be equipped with enough firepower to make his point unambiguously. He should establish his HQ on Chusan and not leave until his demands were met.

'The Chinese will attempt to cut off our supplies,' Gützlaff predicted, 'and unless we have treated the people well, they might do us severe harm on this score. A paltry effort will be made to dislodge us.' The events of the coming years would prove Gützlaff to be a man of considerable prescience.

'To try by conciliatory measures to bring matters to a happy conclusion has been proven delusive,' he impressed upon Palmerston, 'and our whole diplomatic intercourse has been very justly compared to pouring water into a sieve, and wondering at its remaining always empty.' Force was now unavoidable if the doors of the China market were to be opened. 'The combustible materials are there, and the slightest spark will produce a flame.'

Who, then, was this Karl Gützlaff, this intriguing German who felt entitled to refer to himself and the British as 'we', as if he were little short of being a personal aide to Britain's foreign secretary? How had he come to know so much about the Chusan archipelago, when for more than a lifetime foreigners had been banned from trading there?

Born in the Prussian province of Pomerania, Karl Gützlaff had grown up to be an eccentric Lutheran preacher, an incorrigible self-publicist and fund-raiser exuding missionary zeal, and a rough-and-tumble, baptise-'em-or-hang-'em worker for God with a sound knowledge of Chinese culture. Though some thought him a man of specious manner and commented on his intolerable assumption of omniscience, most agreed that he was kind-hearted, if a little prickly and thick-skinned.[4] With great drollery he would dole out insights from his fund of anecdotes on China, keeping those about him in constant laughter.[5] Gützlaff looked and sounded the part, too — short and well-built, with a good-humoured face, a heavy German accent, and clothes that looked to have been cut in some remote Pomeranian village where the fashions of the town had yet to reach.[6] Yet he was almost unique among the men setting forth their suggestions for Britain's China policy in the mid-1830s in having actually spent time ashore in the Chusan archipelago. He well understood that his knowledge of Chinese — he could read and write it, as well as speak more than one coastal dialect — made him a most useful asset to the British government at a time when there was no professional body of interpreters to speak of. He knew, too, that the firepower of the Royal Navy was the best hope he had of getting unrestricted access to the tens of thousands of heathen souls who lived on Chusan. Little wonder, then, that he was so eager to direct that firepower as best he could.

He had first travelled east in 1826 aged just twenty-three, living first in Jakarta, then amongst the overseas Chinese community in Bangkok, then in a mission station at Malacca on the Malay peninsula where he married an Englishwoman, a teacher at a girls' school. He returned with Maria to Bangkok, and there they lived until in 1831 she died in childbirth. Time spent in Siam mixing with the overseas Chinese had opened Gützlaff's eyes to the boundless possibilities for mission work in China itself, and four months after his wife's passing he boarded a cramped and unhealthy junk bound for Chusan, her captain and crew alternately (and sometimes simultaneously) too stoned on opium even to sail her. Gützlaff had arrived in the archipelago only to be refused permission to go ashore: the prohibition on foreigners landing there was as valid as when the last East Indiaman had been forced to leave in 1759, and the Chinese did not differentiate between merchants and missionaries. But something about the islands' potential as a field for mission left its mark, and within the year Gützlaff was back as interpreter to the trading barque *Lord Amherst* to test the waters once more. Refused permission to enter Tinghae's inner harbour to drum up interest in her woven cloth (she intentionally held no opium, the better to approach the island with clean hands), the *Lord Amherst* instead made do with an anchorage off nearby Kintang Island, and Gützlaff set foot on Chusanese soil for the first time.[7] The island impressed Gützlaff — it was fertile, and its people friendly. He set about distributing religious tracts and medicinal ointments, browbeating the Buddhist priests who lived in Kintang's temples on the spuriousness of their faith. Islanders rowed out to the *Lord Amherst* to be cured of their ailments and rowed back clutching a treatise on Christ to boot.

'The word of God,' Gützlaff predicted, 'will doubtless find some serious readers among the intelligent natives of Kintang, and when I revisit the island, there will be some individuals who know that Jesus Christ is coming into the world to save sinners. This joyful hope animates me under all discouragements.' There would indeed be both animation and discouragement, for when next Gützlaff visited the archipelago it was aboard an opium clipper in the January of 1833, a winter so bitter that some of the lascars crewing the *Sylph* died of hypothermia. Once more his request to the city's magistrate to enter Tinghae itself was turned down (that honour would have to wait until he had the British army at his side to make his request all the more forcefully) but again he made up for his disappointment with zealous distribution of tracts wherever he could contrive to land unnoticed by Chusan's mandarins. On Kintang, he claimed, the locals recognised him and came to receive the scriptures once more, bringing their sick to be treated with his famed sulphur and mercurial ointment. On the Buddhist holy island of Putuoshan, he declared, priests swam out from the shore to meet his boat as it landed, exclaiming 'Praise be to Buddha!' and carrying every volume off in triumph. At the fishing village of Sinkamoon on Chusan's east coast, crowds of locals begged not to be sent away empty-handed, even going so far as to steal his tracts. But Gützlaff was a shrewd operator and understood the Chinese mindset. Despite the grandiloquence of the reports he sent home to raise funds, he must have known that any apparent appetite for the Word of God owed more to curiosity and raw greed than to any thirst for Salvation. Still, to a prosperous readership eager to believe any reports of success, no matter how far they stretched the truth, Gützlaff could enthuse over the potential for spreading the Word among the people of Zhejiang.

'What a field for missionary exertion they do present!' he predicted. 'We humbly trust in the wise government of God, that the doors to these parts will be soon thrown open.' Gützlaff, of course, knew very well that the tide was in any case turning in favour of blowing those doors off their hinges with British cannon: it was after all he who had recommended as much to Lord Palmerston.

The 'slightest spark' which in 1835 Gützlaff had predicted came in 1839, on the day a Chinese high commissioner took the step of seizing and destroying 20,000 chests of contraband opium, estimated to be worth the better part of £2,000,000. The destruction was the culmination of decades of slights to British pride and constant battles over the rules under which trade in Canton was carried out. The Chinese once more suspended trade in the port, robbing HM Government's Treasury of tax revenues, but the British government made it clear that it would not be stepping in to compensate merchants for their confiscated opium: *that* was up to the Chinese who had destroyed it. Lord Palmerston informed the Admiralty of his considered response: a military force would be sent, large enough to cow China's emperor into accepting the reality of British power.[8]

'It is expected that this expedition shall,' he explained, 'on arriving in the China Sea, proceed to take possession of some island on the Chinese coast.' Some easily defended island had to be selected, 'which might be permanently retained, if circumstances should render its permanent retention expedient.' The island he had in mind was, unsurprisingly given the attention that had been drawn to it, Chusan. Once it had been captured, warships were to sail for the mouth of the Peiho, just as Macartney and Amherst had done before, but when there they were to force the emperor to accept Palmerston's terms at the barrel of a gun. The man chosen to hold his finger over the trigger was one Charles Elliot, the British plenipotentiary in China.

Charles Elliot was a sailor by profession, a captain, born to an aristocratic family, yet he had worked his up through the ranks after volunteering for the Royal Navy at the age of fourteen just as the Napoleonic Wars were drawing to a close. As a midshipman and lieutenant he had seen action in Algiers and experienced life on the seas of the East Indies, Africa, and the Caribbean. After a Colonial Office posting to British Guiana as protector of slaves, Elliot found himself in Canton acting as a deputy to Britain's chief superintendent of trade just as the related questions of opium and trading rights were threatening to explode into conflict. A man of considerable conscience — he had no more sympathy for opium merchants than he had for slave-owners — he does not strike one with hindsight as the best man to set about lowering the haughty Chinese into the dust by distress, as Gützlaff had suggested.[9] But he was, at least, on the government payroll and on the spot, and Palmerston was willing to put his faith in him.

Charles held the role of British plenipotentiary jointly with his cousin, Admiral Sir George Elliot, whom Lord Palmerston had selected as naval commander-in-chief of the China expedition. George, by now in his mid-fifties and not in the prime of health, was like Charles a professional sailor who had seen action in more than one battle in the Mediterranean by the age of just ten. Admiral Nelson, under whom he had served aboard HMS *Victory*, described him as one of the best officers in the navy. An MP for a time, he was serving as Britain's naval commander-in-chief at the Cape when called upon by Palmerston to head for the China station to join Charles and set about rebalancing Anglo-

Chinese relations by force. He would prove to be considerably out of his depth in the role, a fact he himself admitted.[10]

As to Palmerston's terms, besides taking possession of Chusan and securing the opening of other coastal ports to British trade, Captain Elliot was instructed to demand compensation for the destroyed opium, for the cost of mounting the military expedition, and for debts owed by the unscrupulous merchant guilds of Canton.[11]

'We are going, it seems,' crowed the *United Service Journal* (it was the *de facto* magazine of Britain's armed forces and unsurprisingly jingoistic), 'to chastise the Chinese, and awaken them from their opiate dreams.'[12] China's haughty mandarins, who from ignorance or arrogance thought the British 'barbarians', needed to be taught a lesson in the harsh realities of the modern world, it thought. 'Tonawanta', a correspondent to the *Journal*, concurred, writing in favour of 'a short, vicious war': 'They are naughty children,' he observed, 'and rather sick. We must force a little wholesome medicine down their throats to cure them for the time being.'[13]

4

A thundering fire

THE BRIG *Kite* carrying Mrs Anne Noble and her husband and infant son, all three of them unaware of the terrible fates awaiting them, and the merchantman *Rustomjee Cowasjee* bearing Captain Anstruther and the Madras Artillery were just two amongst a British flotilla that reached the Chusan archipelago at the start of July, 1840.[1] Aboard some four dozen ships were almost 3,800 army officers and men and close on 1,000 Indian camp followers, more than half of these employed privately by the officers and the rest shared between the expedition's six regiments.[2] With a Royal Navy sloop carrying a complement of anything up to 125 sailors and a third-rate ship of the line (there were three — HMS *Blenheim*, *Melville* and *Wellesley*) carrying up to 650, not to mention the crewmen and their families upon the transports and store-ships that had been specially commissioned, the expedition consisted of the greater part of 10,000 souls. The population of Tinghae alone was more than twice that number.

They had had a torrid time of it since leaving Singapore on May 30th, the weather by turns squally and wet, thunderous or bright, but always unbearably hot: 'Roasting in own fat. Thermometer ninety degrees,' one ship's surgeon noted laconically in his journal.[3] Men-of-war, troop transports and supply ships played follow-my-leader around the narrow promontory that British charts called Kittow Point — the Chinese had named it the 'towering headland' for it fell away almost sheer into the sea — and by that unmissable landmark they dropped anchor.

The men of these islands, as always when a foreign hull was sighted, had at first been eager to do business. They crowded about the flotilla, unafraid to approach those men who had landed on the outlying islands and to ask them with hand gestures whether they had any opium to sell.[4] As for years those waters had offered anchorages for great numbers of opium clippers it must have puzzled the Chinese to see so many foreign keels but no-one willing to sell them the drug.[5] One of their number was taken aboard HMS *Wellesley* so that something of the local navigation might be learned. The poor man, spirited from his small fishing junk onto a 74-gun leviathan of towering white sails, was under-standably terrified and next to useless.

Next morning at daylight the flotilla weighed anchor and closed in on Chusan.[6] It was foggy, and the ocean raced through the network of channels between countless islands that loomed out of the mist. The tides here could spin a warship around like a toy, and they seemed to savour their power. Vessels fell foul of each other, had their jib-booms carried away in the crush, and grate-fully dropped anchor as the wind died. Then as the tide ebbed it revealed the stakes and nets of the local fishing fleet, strung like cobwebs across the sea. The British had anchored amongst the catch, their chains dragging over the islanders' livelihood.[7] A few brave men came aboard to remonstrate, only to be pressed into piloting the ships ever closer in. In thick fog the next morning, the Indian Navy paddle-sloop *Atalanta* sounded the final narrow passage into Chusan's inner harbour.[8] Her arrival aroused the greatest of interest — with twin paddle-wheels powered by a 210-horsepower steam engine, nothing quite like her had ever been seen on this coast. The islanders crowded the foreshore to witness this smoking iron monster inexplicably moving at will without sails.

A rowing boat was despatched from the *Atalanta* to take a closer look at the waterfront, and soon the Royal Navy was moving unchallenged and incongruous amongst war junks at anchor.[9] The Chinese seamen peered down from the crowded decks, faces wreathed in smiles of curiosity, though they had been forewarned these past few days to provide a show of naval strength against the British. Along the beach, a sprawl of warehouses and shops was seen to extend over a dozen acres. A pack of boys detached itself from the crowds that had gathered there, running and beckoning playfully and seemingly calling out to the foreigners not to be afraid. From a temple upon a hill on the shore, a platoon of soldiers waved flags to intimidate their uninvited guests. When the men of the *Atalanta* turned to leave, the soldiers raised a victory cheer: the barbarians had been repulsed.

The afternoon wore on. Aboard HMS *Rattlesnake*, the officers plied a boatful of inquisitive fishermen with drink and snuff in return for some of their smoked tea.[10] Though they were proving friendly enough on a personal level, still the fishermen were evidently unwilling for word to get out that they had been fraternising: 'I was taking the likeness of one of the fellows,' wrote Edward Cree, the ship's surgeon, 'who immediately dropped his soup and ran out as fast as he could!'[11] The Chinese soldiers waiting in the harbour, the *Atalanta* was able to report back, appeared equally unlikely to offer much resistance.

The flotilla upped anchor once more early on the morning of July 4th. The scenery was striking, each turn in the channel bringing into view sheets of water seemingly land-locked by countless verdant islands.[12] It seemed a shame to carry war to such a peaceful country.[13] HMS *Wellesley* sounded a suitable anchorage for herself in the inner harbour, and an official delegation was rowed across to the principal war junk (she was not hard to find, for painted on her high, flat stern were great tigers' heads, traditional symbols of martial authority).[14] Soon the delegation, to which Karl Gützlaff had attached himself as interpreter, found itself amidst a crowd of Chinese sailors straining eagerly to inspect their strange visitors. Others waded into the sea to get a better look. Tea was served, and presently the commander of the Chusan garrison arrived. His name was Zhang Chaofa, and like Lan Li and Shi Shipiao a century and a half earlier he held the rank of *zongbing* — brigade general — in the Chinese army of the Green Standards. A military man, General Zhang somewhat outranked Chusan's civil magistrate Yao Huaixiang who accompanied him, and from setting foot on his personal junk he made it clear that, of the two, it was his opinion that counted. He was elderly, a red-button mandarin, and, handed a note in Chinese, he would not stoop so low as to read it. It had been written by Gützlaff in an inexpert hand, and besides, it was utterly beneath his dignity to accept petitions from a barbarian officer. Instead he passed it to his aide-de-camp to read out.[15] The men who stood before General Zhang, the note explained, had the honour to inform him that they had come by command of the Sovereign of Great Britain for the purpose of occupying Chusan and its dependencies. If the inhabitants showed no resistance, it was not their intention to injure them of their property:

> We therefore summon your Excellency to surrender the same peaceably, to avoid the shedding of blood. But, if you will not surrender, we shall be obliged to use warlike measures for obtaining possession. The official messenger who transmits this letter will only wait an hour for an answer. When this time is elapsed, and your Excellency refuses to surrender, and does not return an answer, we shall then immediately open a thundering fire upon the island fort.

Though he was clearly angry at the threat of such unwarranted violence, General Zhang at least agreed to repair to HMS *Wellesley* to discuss the matter further. But there, even when the destructive power of a naval broadside was spelled out to him, he remained unmoved: he was not at liberty to surrender the emperor's territory to barbarians who had arrived in defiance of every protocol![16] Told that the deadline for surrender was noon the next day, his last words were delivered with a nihilistic smile: if the British did not hear from him before sunrise, let the consequences be upon his own head. The British could scarcely comprehend this ill-favoured old man, who to judge from his features was clearly an opium addict: what use this obstinacy, when his destruction was guaranteed the instant the *Wellesley* opened fire?

All that day, warships threaded a path into the harbour, while around them boats full of locals came and went about their everyday business. The only sign of resistance came from the troops arrayed on the decks of the brightly coloured war junks, who beat tinny gongs and set banners flying. At length it grew dark. Throughout the night the shoreline hummed with activity. Streams of lamps could be seen ascending to the temple on the hill, and there could faintly be made out the silhouettes of boats piled dangerously high with cargo and crowded with women and children.[17] The Royal Navy let them go quietly on their way.

After disembarking HMS *Wellesley*, General Zhang had hurriedly assembled his officers in Tinghae to decide what to do.[18] They agreed that the barbarians of the Great Western Ocean lived mostly on board ship and in war relied on their broadsides, a tactic of use only on water since their cannon weighed three tons apiece and could not be used as field artillery. Zhang did not anticipate the British possessing field guns that could readily be deployed against his city. Less excusable, though, was an unchallenged assumption in Chinese thinking: none had ever faced the British in a land engagement, and it was believed that this sailing nation shrank from them for fear of defeat. Mandarins had observed their tight trousers and jackets and concluded that once they had fallen over in battle they could not get up again. The very same Chinese commissioner who had destroyed the confiscated British opium in Canton informed the emperor himself how easy it would be for an infantrymen dressed in voluminous silks to kill a British soldier once he was helpless on the ground.[19] So a land battle seemed General Zhang's only hope of victory, and his officers urged him to sacrifice his junks and withdraw into Tinghae, leaving a detachment to occupy a pavilion that blocked the only road to the city.[20] But Zhang would not contemplate such a cowardly response and issued incontrovertible orders that his men were to face the British on the waterfront.[21]

It was inevitably going to be a one-sided engagement, for General Zhang's men, though regular soldiers on paper, were not remotely the equals of a professional British regiment. The Green Standards (they took their name from the colour of their battle flags) were drawn from the native Han population rather than from the hereditary warriors of the Manchu Qing dynasty that had conquered China by force of arms two centuries earlier. More a provincial constabulary than a campaigning army, in coastal regions like Zhejiang one of their more important roles was the suppression of piracy, and their instinct was to treat the British as not much more than buccaneers. Underpaid and undermotivated, and with only the most cursory of military training, they were armed, if at all, with a positively medieval assemblage of bows and arrows, pikes and halberds, interspersed with a few gingals — wall-mounted matchlocks that fired iron balls or grapeshot — and even these had been obsolete in England for at least a century.

Dawn revealed the Green Standards' handiwork. On the wharves below the temple hill they had piled up rice sacks to form crude batteries mounting guns of little more than 6 lbs. The temple itself had been provided with a handful of weapons, as had a small stone tower at its foot, upon which was a big, red flag. Fishing nets had been stretched over the waists of two dozen war junks to stop the British from boarding, and their decks bristled with small cannon. Wicker shields painted with roaring tigers were hung over their sides, and boards strung between them bore ugly black faces intended to terrify the enemy. A mile inland, the walls of Tinghae were lined with soldiers waving flags. What to the Green Standards must have seemed a formidable array of weaponry appeared to Western eyes as just a tragicomic display of theatricals. It was as if, ruminated one observer, the illuminated manuscripts of the Hundred Years' War had come to life.[22] They might as well have been kittens raising their hackles against a pack of ravening dogs.

The cloud that morning was low upon the hills framing the harbour, the atmosphere melancholic, and rain threatened.[23] Crowds could be seen squatting in the fields, smoking pipes and watching events unfold with detached interest. At 8 a.m. the Royal Navy received the signal to prepare for action. Noon came and went with no word from General Zhang, but by then the tide was ebbing and it made little sense to man the boats. Finally, at half past two o'clock, a 52-lb British cannonball slammed squarely into the stone tower, bringing down its red flag and sending up a great cloud of dust. As the report echoed and died away, the Chinese batteries returned a feeble salvo. There were a few final moments of calm before the air was torn by the roar of cannon. Raising a blue flag as a signal to the fleet's gunners, the *Wellesley* shuddered as she let fly a broadside into General Zhang's junk, which was all but obliterated, while the rest of the flotilla poured solid iron and explosive shells onto the shore. (The attack came a decade too late for Zhang's men to stand an earthly chance against the Royal Navy: in 1830 HMS *Excellent* had been founded as a gunnery training ship in Portsmouth. Three years before the assault on Tinghae, a rigorous drilling in the science and practice of naval gunnery had been extended to the entire fleet. Where Chusan's generals had syphoned off funds meant for its defence, the Admiralty was spending some £300 training each gunnery officer.)[24] Shots passed clean through the junks as though through paper before ricocheting about the warehouses. The Chinese soldiers simply dropped their arms and ran as musket balls buzzed about their ears. After scarcely seven minutes the signal to cease firing was hoisted, three cheers were given from the boats, and as the smoke dissipated men could be seen scurrying away in all directions. The junks, dismasted and peppered with holes, settled silently into the mud. The buildings along the shorefront had been devastated. The tower was in ruins and the rice-sack batteries had been tossed about like litter. A few mutilated bodies could be seen lying around. As for the Royal Navy, other than some chipped paint and a broken halyard the sole casualty was an unlucky gunner whose legs had been crushed by a cannon's recoil.

As the regimental band played, the Royal Irish Regiment landed and ascended the temple hill (the only opposition was a man who threw a stone at them and ran off)[25] to find a handful of cowering monks terrified half to death by the bombardment.[26] The first man to reach the top was a sailor from one of the landing boats. He appeared on a wall with an idol he had torn from its pedestal, holding it by the arms in a mockery of a dance before dashing it to pieces upon the floor. Then, taking a Union Jack handed to him by an officer, he shinned up a convenient flagstaff and made the British colours fast while the men of the fleet cheered him on.[27] By ten minutes to three on Sunday, July 5th 1840 the British flag was fluttering over the courtyard of an obscure Buddhist temple, the very first Chinese territory to be forcibly occupied by a Western power. Whatever remained of Mr Allen Catchpoole's Red Hair Hall lay in ruins below, just like any hope that Great Britain and China might solve their commercial disagreements peacefully.

The men who went ashore on the afternoon of July 5th had been raised from regiments serving in India and were a hotchpotch of nations and races. Beside the Englishmen of Her Majesty's 49th Regiment of Foot (they were known to all and sundry as the Hertfordshires), there were the Scots of Her Majesty's 26th Regiment of Foot (the Cameronians) and the Irishmen of the 18th Royal Irish Regiment. With them came the Hindus, Sikhs and Muslims of the Bengal Volunteers and a regiment each of Artillery and Engineers from Madras. Moving unhindered now among the remains of the wharves, the extent of the carnage became clear. Twenty bodies were removed from the half-sunken war junks, a handful of dead were discovered amongst the shattered houses, and others had died in the fields beyond, trying to reach safety. Those too wounded to flee were taken aboard the *Wellesley* for surgery.[28] Only one survived, a soldier with a shattered leg that was amputated despite his protestations. As for their weapons, it was discovered with some surprise that of the two dozen cannon which General Zhang had mustered on the foreshore the only decent piece had been cast in London in 1601, a relic perhaps of some forgotten attempt to trade with these islands.[29] It was primed and pointed squarely at HMS *Alligator*, but its crew had fled before firing it.[30] The contents of Zhang's arsenals (they better deserved to be called 'toy-shops upon a large scale')[31] were no more a match for the British army: hollow-cast iron guns packed with grapeshot, obsolete matchlocks that would have posed as much danger to the firer as to his foe, packets of quicklime, longbows, halberds, even pitchforks.... Carefully stored uniforms of padded cotton with metal studs harked back to the days when the sword was the principal threat.[32]

Climbing to the temple atop what was quickly renamed Josshouse Hill,* one could see the walled city of Tinghae itself, a mile away across the paddy fields. Upon the ramparts, lines of silk banners were still waving in defiance. Throughout the afternoon the Madras Artillery landed howitzers, mortars and cannons, unshipping each with difficulty onto the crowded wharf

---

* 'Joss-house' was a common name for an oriental temple.

before heaving them to the top of a low hill within just 400ft of the walls. By nightfall, under sporadic but pointless firing from the city (it served no purpose but to prove that the Chinese 'were utterly ignorant of gunnery'),[33] a battery had been set up ready to shell Tinghae come first light. At around midnight the Chinese guns fell silent. Exhausted from their exertions, the artillerymen snatched some rest. They spent that first night on Chinese soil surrounded by wet rice fields, feasted upon by mosquitoes that swarmed in their millions, kept awake by the noise of gongs from the city, the hammering of scaling ladders being prepared, and the croaking of frogs.[34] Those young men, for the most part illiterate Bengalis and Irish labourers, must have wondered to themselves what on earth they were doing there. Bivouacked around a large fire, their kit to hand and the guns ready to open up when called upon, they were unaware of the events unfolding half a mile away.[35]

In the century since the last East India Company merchants had traded upon Chusan, it had been forgotten that Tinghae's wharves existed mainly to store three commodities: one was timber, another dried fish, and the third a potent sorghum spirit called *samshoo*, produced in vast quantities for export. What precisely made *samshoo* so helplessly intoxicating was a moot point. Some said it was mixed with tobacco juice, others arsenic. That its name meant 'thrice distilled' is probably explanation enough. Thousands of soldiers had been landed by nightfall, and most were still awaiting muster. Sailors from the transports had been given permission to go ashore. In alleys choked with debris, pressed into tiny passageways to allow the artillery to roll by, some of the men forced the doors to the warehouses.[36] With the discovery of stores crammed room after room and floor to ceiling with large earthenware jars of *samshoo*, rank and file both British and Indian found to their delight that they had captured what amounted to a vast distillery.[37] The meagre ration of watered-down drink doled out daily aboard cramped ships had left them thirsting for the real thing. An eye-witness to the inevitable result, a young artillery officer named Charles Wyndham Baker, wrote to his sister disgusted at the troops' behaviour:

Its effect on them was of the most dreadful nature and very
different from that of the spirits we are used to in England. A
man no sooner took a small quantity than he was bereft of his
senses, and men were lying about in all directions in a most
dreadful state and committing the most dreadful atrocities,
which I am sorry to say are but too common in war.[38]

Under cover of darkness, orders to respect private property and
treat the Chinese with civility were ignored and discipline utterly
broke down; shops and homes were broken into, and women were
reported to have been raped. Officers tried to put a stop to the
drunkenness by smashing *samshoo* jars where they found them,
until the streets ran in torrents.[39] Wooden houses and timber-
yards were soon awash with volatile spirits,[40] while all around
lay ammunition tubs from the dismounted Chinese ordnance.[41]
At three in the morning the inevitable finally happened. Perhaps
an oil lamp or a candle was knocked over, or a lit pipe carelessly
dropped from insensible lips.[42] The blaze consumed a third of
the wharf district, bathing the temple on the hill and the ships
at anchor in an orange glow until sunrise. The next day the
Hertfordshires, too drunk to be of any use in attacking Tinghae,
re-embarked onto their troopships.[43] If the British had anticipated winning over the Chinese with a display of the civilising
arts, this was a most ignominious start.

Before dawn, with the wharves still burning, a party of sappers
crept across the fields to Tinghae intending to blow the south gate
open. Flags still fluttered dimly on the ramparts, but the gongs
and drums had been stilled: the garrison had abandoned the
city overnight. A party of officers requisitioned a ladder, scaled
the wall (ignoring one brave man who, though unarmed, tried
to prevent them) and hauled aside an impromptu barricade of
grain sacks.[44] Once a plank bridge had been erected over the city
moat (for the Chinese had demolished the bridge)[45] a more-or-
less sober company of soldiers filed silently through the gateway
to take possession of Tinghae in the name of Queen Victoria, and
at dawn hoisted a Union Jack. An entire Chinese city had fallen

to British forces for the first time. Captain Elliot seemed satisfied with his fiefdom and wrote to his superior, Lord Auckland, governor-general of India, with some pride:

> We are in possession of the Capital and Harbor of our New Kingdom. I have no hesitation in forwarding my opinion that the position is admirable in point of general situation, that the harbor cannot be safer when once in, and that the navigation is perfectly safe with due caution.[46]

As to the means of Dinghai's capture, though, he pronounced himself less comfortable:

> I think we might have achieved our conquest with much less destruction of property, and necessarily with a less serious shock to the confidence of the people in our considerateness and friendly disposition.

Elliot, no military tactician, admitted that he could not understand why his naval commander, Sir Gordon Bremer, had felt obliged to fire an unprovoked shot at the suburb, an act intended to force an impotent response, when there could have been no difficulty in taking Zhang's 'half dozen pop guns'. And did the army really need to land two thousand men to capture an undefended hill? In his inexpert view, violence had overshadowed political considerations when in fact his commanders might have taken the suburb without firing a shot, and certainly without destroying more than ten houses. Reading his letter, the thought must have crossed Auckland's mind that Lord Palmerston had chosen the wrong man for the job. 'But it is an ungrateful task to take exception,' Elliot continued in a more pragmatic tone,

> and it is but just to say that the catastrophe which befell the suburb may have indisposed the Mandarins to take a stand behind the walls of the city. In such a contingency its destruction would probably have followed, and that would have been a dismal calamity.

No more a calamity, though, than what was to follow.

A street in Tinghai, Chusan from *The Cree Journals*
(image © Webb & Bower; original watercolour © Henrietta Heawood)

Inside the Great Josshouse, Tinghai (the Zuyin Temple) from *The Cree Journals*
(image © Webb & Bower; original watercolour © Henrietta Heawood)

5

A Pompeii of the living

THE ARRIVAL of the British flotilla in the East China Sea had unleashed a flurry of dispatches between Zhejiang's mandarins and their superiors in Peking.[1] Tinghae might have been abandoned, but across the water on the mainland men of the Green Standards were already being gathered up and rushed toward the coast. Still, it was a full three days after the city's capture before the provincial governor of Zhejiang, a Manchu named Urgungga, knew enough of the situation to file a report: the foreigners who had been prowling around the coast had in fact opened fire on Chusan.[2] His report began in the formulaic language expected of all official contact with Peking:

> Your servant on bended knees memorialises on the matter of the English barbarians' passing a letter to the general of Tinghae, and on their flaunting of their refractory behaviour, which respectful memorial is sent with all dispatch by government courier, beseeching the imperial gaze!

Urgungga, wary of admitting the seriousness of the situation in his jurisdiction or perhaps hopeful still that things were not as bad as might be feared, exaggerated the extent of his forces' resistance. General Zhang's war junks, far from succumbing with scarcely a fight, were reported to have exchanged fire with the barbarians from sunrise until noon. The barbarians had then left their ships and bombarded the city throughout the night, finally smashing down the gate and swarming in. Chusan's civil magistrate and chief of police had both crept out of Tinghae under cover of darkness and drowned themselves rather than surrender. The elderly General Zhang himself had been seriously wounded, but with several of his officers had made it back to the mainland. Urgungga concluded his report in rousing fashion:

> These barbarian bandits, these vagabonds and rogues, arrived most precipitately, their hearts intent on evil, and we must deal out to them the most painful destruction so as to make manifest

the nation's prestige. The situation is changing day by day, and my heart burns with grief.

Twelve days later — for it took this long for a provincial memorial travelling by horse-back courier to reach the emperor's eyes — Daoguang himself added his vermilion script at its foot:

> The neglectfulness of Zhejiang's forces is clear to see without enquiring into it! Such trifling little ne'er-do-wells dare run amok, and the great civil and military officials array their troops only to go to pieces![3]

It was the use of such condescending terms that had so consistently maddened the British since the days of Allen Catchpoole. To the emperor, insulated from the reality of a changed world beyond China's borders, all non-Chinese races were barbarian, and barbarians were by definition inferior, just trifling little ne'er-do-wells. Blindfolded by its own semantics, how could Peking react to something it could not comprehend? Weeks of dispatches from Zhejiang detailing the British flotilla's every movement had not told the whole truth. The sparse nature of the Chinese characters *da yi chuan* — 'big barbarian ship' — to describe HMS *Wellesley* could not begin to explain the threat posed by just that single 74-gun man-of-war, honed to lethal perfection through centuries of European conflict. It had been boasted with no exaggeration that one or two British frigates could sink the entire Chinese navy,[4] and the Elliots commanded far more than just one or two frigates. Still, in Chinese eyes there was no excuse for such a humiliating rout. With over a thousand men at arms, a firm hold ought to have been kept on Tinghae. Why then had it fallen so rapidly? General Zhang was stripped of his rank while his fate was considered. Eventually sentenced to death for cowardice, he only escaped punishment by dying of his wounds before he could be beheaded.[5] His senior officers, meanwhile, were given one hundred lashes and banished to China's remote western deserts. It appeared the only ones to come out of the invasion with honour would be the two suicides: 'Their dying for their country is admirable,' Urgungga had gushed. 'Permit your servant to look into their circumstances so that their families might be offered relief!'

While the machinery of Qing government ground into action, the British began to explore their new conquest. The first curious individuals to inspect occupied Tinghae found just a few terrified beggars with nowhere to flee to, the elderly and the infirm who could not escape and who simply threw themselves at the feet of the invaders, and gangs of thieves who were busy ransacking the wealthier houses.[6] The soldiers who had feigned a defence from the walls had, it was guessed, cast off their effeminate silk uniforms and melted away. Half-starved dogs skulked about the streets. Shutters had been nailed down across shop fronts and windows, and doors had been secured as best the former occupants could manage. The last of the city's richer inhabitants were seen dropping chests of valuables over the wall and heaving them away.[7] Stories had circulated during the voyage to Chusan of how much the Han Chinese populace hated their Manchu rulers and longed for freedom, and the British had naïvely expected to be greeted as liberators. But instead of grateful crowds, the sound of prayers wafted from the temples as the few remaining citizens begged Guanyin the goddess of mercy for delivery.[8] Tinghae, as one eye-witness observed, had become overnight 'a Pompeii of the living — nothing wanting in the picture but inhabitants'.[9] Except for a few dozen, the city's entire population of more than 25,000 had fled in terror.[10] They had even left their food half-cooked in their kitchens, their china set out ready to eat, so hurried had been their departure when the *Wellesley* had opened fire.[11] And so, with Chusan's civil magistrate drowned and General Zhang under arrest on the mainland, it fell to the British to establish the rule of law in their stead. They were singularly unprepared.

Until the events of July 5th, Chusan had been the largest of the many islands governed from the walled city of Tinghae. Technically a *xian* or 'county', the smallest administrative district in which the civil magistrate was invested with all the powers of governance, Tinghae had been subordinate first to Ningbo prefecture forty miles away across the waters of Kintang Sound and then in turn to the provincial capital Hangzhou and then Peking. For the maintenance of public order, every family had been registered under an ancient system of mutual security called the *baojia*: ten households had formed what was termed a *pai*, ten *pai* had constituted a *jia*, and ten *jia* had gone to make a *bao* of 1,000 households whose good order had been the responsibility of an elder who answered to the civil magistrate.[12] But now Yao Huaixiang had taken his own life, and the invaders' alternative scheme was inevitably somewhat less thorough.[13] Karl Gützlaff, the Chinese-speaking missionary who just seven years earlier had recommended the invasion of Chusan to Lord Palmerston, revelled in his post as the new magistrate of an island he had long yearned to convert to Christianity. Major Thomas Stephens of the Hertfordshires and Captain William Caine of the Cameronians were sworn in as military commissioners to collect and take care of Tinghae's public property. The top post, that of Governor of Chusan, fell by default to one Brigadier George Burrell, the liverish old commander of the Royal Irish Regiment. But the sixty-four-year-old lieutenant-colonel was a military man, not a colonial administrator, and certainly no diplomat. It was only the unexpected death at sea of the expedition's senior officer, the respected and well-liked Lieutenant-Colonel Oglander of the Cameronians, that had propelled George Burrell unwillingly into the post. He was out of his depth, lacked any knowledge of local law and custom, and readily admitted himself far from happy in the role of governor of Queen Victoria's newest possession; it was, he complained, 'a situation most harmfully unpleasant.'[14] Oglander's untimely death, and the unforeseen appointment of Burrell, would prove to have terrible consequences for the men of the expedition and ultimately for the very conduct of the war.

Governor Burrell (he was suffering from chronic dysentery, which only made an onerous role harder)[15] began by formally addressing what remained of Tinghae's populace in a proclamation that was translated and pasted up around the city. It vied incongruously for wall-space with the Chinese proclamations denouncing opium as a great evil and threatening severe punishments for sellers and users.[16] The British intended them no harm, he explained; the occupation of the island would simply redress the injustices practised by the Chinese at Canton, and their two nations would recover the peace and harmony which had previously existed between them. Few of the Chinese who now remained were literate. Those who could read must have been struck by the sheer impertinence of these barbarians, for it was no more conceivable that they could demand redress for injustices at the hands of Chinese mandarins than a dog could demand redress over a beating from its master. When a copy was peeled from its wall and found its way to the mainland it was condemned as a usurpation of power. The barbarians, coming from so far away, must understandably have been ignorant of their rightful place.

For want of a better plan, Governor Burrell decided upon non-compulsion to prove to the islanders that he meant them no harm. But with a population which had already largely fled to the island's interior or across Kintang Sound to the nearby port of Ningbo, it rapidly became clear that this open-door policy was simply allowing thieves to plunder the city and escape with impunity. Only after a long, sultry day of unchecked looting were sentries placed at the four gates, yet still Burrell gave no orders to prevent the removal of property, preferring instead to make it known that there would be free access and no coercion to remain.[17] It was easier to ignore what the sentries suspected — that the rightful owners of the valuables being removed were not the same as the ragged Chinese removing them.[18] The sentries, who of course had not a single word of Chinese between them, could only look on in exasperation as anything that could be moved — furniture, clothes, cash, food — was carried out before their eyes and with a smiling disregard for their flintlocks.

A flurry of orders emerged from Governor Burrell's office in the coming days, notice succeeding contradictory notice on the streets until it seemed that only the governor himself understood the regulations in force.[19] It was a full week before a system of bilingual transit permits was settled upon: Chinese were only permitted to enter the city on production of a pass issued by

Gützlaff, the intention being to allow only law-abiding citizens to return.[20] When leaving they were restricted to taking with them 3 lbs of fish, 4 lbs of rice, and $2 in cash. Nothing else could leave the city, and soon piles of confiscated goods appeared beside the guardhouses at each of the gates.[21] Honest and dishonest alike, Gützlaff soon found scores of petitioners beating a path to his magistracy to argue the case for the return of some — in fact *any* — property. In the east of the city, sandwiched between two branches of the canals that watered the rice fields of an otherwise undeveloped corner, sat the Confucius Temple. Here were stored goods that had been confiscated, along with valuables rescued from the city's pawnshops — clothes, furs, silks, ornaments, polished copper mirrors and dozens of gongs — and grain and property requisitioned from the public buildings.[22] In the weeks and months to come, regular auctions of the booty would be held (they raised some 6,000 rupees for the public purse, some £600 at the time),[23] while gangs of robbers, undeterred by the risk of capture, tried to break in through the temple's rear walls.[24]

'The Chinese people are quiet and inoffensive; they like anything better than hard blows; but a more subtle, lying and thievish race it was never my luck to live amongst,' complained one correspondent of the *Chinese Repository*, telling of the ruses Britannia's unwilling subjects were employing to circumvent Gützlaff's system.[25] One man had arrived at a city gate with a coffin, a huge piece of solidly made joinery in the traditional style, requesting that he be allowed to take his late mother for burial. Thinking him a fine example of filial affection, and presumably not wishing to insult the locals' religious practices, he was let through. A suspicious number of coffins began to leave the city uninspected until one sentry, less considerate of the dead or perhaps just more suspicious of the living, forced a lid open with his bayonet to discover not a corpse but a cache of silks.[26] Another time, the same observer was approached by a man who claimed that sentries had confiscated his wife's and mother's clothes at the north gate and that the poor women would freeze come winter. When the two reached the gate there was indeed a large pile of women's clothing, from which the man selected a choice number.

Only later, when the real owner came to claim the clothes back from the magistrate's safekeeping, was the trick realised. The next time a Chinese tried to hoodwink our man he had learned his lesson: passing the east gate he saw somebody carrying two large pannierfuls of ashes. Sure enough, under the ashes were the most beautiful silk and fur clothes and a hoard of cash. The goods were returned to their owner and the thief was given twenty-four hours' confinement.[27] Unavoidably, homeowners returning to rescue their property crossed paths with others trying to steal it. They did not feel obliged to conciliate the likes of these common burglars with such very liberal punishments and dealt out summary justice to those they caught in the act.[28] One thief was found drowned, having been trussed up and tossed into a ditch in the city, another tied to a post with such force that his wounds bled and his eyes started from their sockets. A third, caught stealing from the house of a literary graduate, was brought to the magistracy bound in the most excruciating manner. 'It was two hours before he recovered the use of his speech,' a witness recalled with horror:

> The learned character seemed much astonished, and could not at all understand why he should be accused of cruelty, having, as he stated, merely executed an act of justice.

It seemed that many islanders were willing to take these risks for the sake of riches. A popular ruse was to drop plunder over the city wall for accomplices to make away with over the moat. One, loaded down with far more than he could carry, sank and died in the mud. Two more lost their lives to the vigilance of a Scot who shouted at them to stop when he saw them descending the walls. One was shot squarely through the heart as he ran off — incredibly bad luck considering the inaccuracy of a flintlock musket. The other, being taken to Gützlaff under arrest, took advantage of a moment's lack of attention on the part of his guard to throw himself into a canal where he drowned.[29] The guard was court-martialled for not trying to rescue him, and a macabre rumour circulated in camp as to how he had defended his inaction: 'My orders was that I was not to lose sight of the man,' the bemused private had apparently explained. 'I seed him jump in and I seed him stick fast, and I knew he could not get away.'[30]

But despite the lawlessness, there were indications that, given time, the two sides might be able to get along on a human level. Soon after the landings, the ship's surgeon of HMS *Rattlesnake* went ashore to look for food. It is this man, Edward Hodges Cree, that we have to thank for so much of the detail of life on Chusan under British rule.

Edward Cree was twenty-six years old at the outbreak of the Opium War. He had graduated in medicine three years earlier from Edinburgh University and, against his father's wish that he become a country surgeon in Cornwall, had straight away joined the Royal Navy with a posting as assistant surgeon aboard HMS *Royal Adelaide* in his native Devonport. His began on his very first day in the Navy to write his *Journal*, a day-by-day account of his life in prose and watercolour sketches full of vitality and wit, a labour which only stopped in 1861. In 1887, by then in his seventies, he edited and bound his work into the twenty-one volumes which are now in the National Maritime Museum in Greenwich, London.[31] Less than a week after the invasion, on Friday, July 10th, Cree wrote a typically warm and humane account of the day's events:

> As we were bargaining for some food and eggs, a well dressed Chinaman came up and gave us to understand that he would take us to a place where we could get plenty, and at the same time put some eggs into our basket and took the bundles of fowl we had purchased. We followed him through the city gate, where he turned around and gave the fowls to our boy, thanked us and took his leave and, laughing, pointed to the large paper parcels that he had under his arm and walked away as fast as he could. We had inadvertently passed him out by the sentries but we did not think it worthwhile to betray the poor fellow.

When Cree landed on Trumball, the nearest of the inhabited islands in Tinghae's inner harbour, he discovered a farmer and his family who had not fled:

They were very civil to us and sold us some ducks for which we paid a dollar for six, for which they appeared well satisfied. In one house we encountered three or four with their tiny little feet and broad flat faces. They were sitting down drinking tea of which we took some, very hot and very weak, no milk or sugar, and of a very fishy flavour, for I find they dry their tea on the same mats on which they dry their fish.[32]

Another officer had a delightfully close encounter.[33] While out walking in the near-deserted town, he spied a pair of eyes peeping at him through a window. Inside a well-to-do house he found a young woman who by gestures intimated that she had sneaked back into Tinghae under the cover of darkness to find her family had fled. She had tried to leave the city again but had been terrified by the sentries then being posted at the gates, and had ever since been hiding out alone. She showed the officer around her den, pointed out the dried fruit and cakes she planned to survive on for as long as was necessary, offered him a liqueur from a filigreed goblet, and swore him to secrecy. Elsewhere, a musician was caught stealing instruments from one of the regimental bands. Brought before Gützlaff, he begged to explain himself:

When I listen to the music of your troops, the sound of my own instruments appears to be harsh and grating in my ears. I lose all pleasure in them. How could I then presume to enter any longer into competition with its strains? Besides, to me, it appears you have quite music enough; and as the voice of mirth will be heard no more in this city, of what use is my abode amidst the afflicted? I can carry on my profession only amongst joyous parties.[34]

For this consummate piece of emotional manipulation he was allowed to go free.

Those early days of Chusan's occupation were the first time in history that so many Britons had roamed freely on Chinese soil without mandarins forever looking over their shoulders. In previous encounters — Allen Catchpoole's time spent in the Red Hair Hall, Lord Macartney's progress to Chengde in 1793, and of course the years spent in the cramped Canton factories — watchful eyes had noted the aliens' every move, had carefully prescribed what they could see and do. Now, by contrast, Britons had the opportunity to observe without hindrance, to survey, analyse and classify a tiny corner of this enigma. It was a pastime the Victorians excelled at.

Encircling Governor Burrell's little fiefdom were Tinghae's walls, thirteen feet thick, eight yards tall, and two miles long, built of granite and iron-hard blue bricks to protect against piratical raids and with hulking, square bastions.[35] Great stone gatehouses defended by iron-bossed doors commanded the cardinal points, and a moat provided extra protection. Within the walls, the British found Tinghae's main streets on the whole admirably well-built, paved with close-fitting granite slabs (many have survived into our own day). Two main thoroughfares ran crooked courses from the south gate to the north, and from the east gate to the west, each six yards wide, but most were less than half that. Awnings stretched out over poles shaded passers-by from the fierce sun. Running the length of the larger streets were covered sewers which discharged into winding canals, crossed by high-arched stone bridges, all eventually meeting to exit the city by a watergate.[36] From those larger streets descended side streets, and from these branched out alleyways into an unfathomable maze of tiny courtyards and abandoned rooms. Everywhere the British looked they found filth.[37] It was something they had not expected, given the European Enlightenment's general impression that China was a willow-pattern paradise. Great earthenware jars stood on every corner, receptacles for all kinds of discarded animal and vegetable matter and human waste, rapidly fermenting in the summer heat and writhing with maggots.[38] Before their owners had been scared off, sampans could be seen each morning at dawn leaving the city with these jars of ordure that now stood uncollected and putrefying.[39] The masonry sea-gates that prevented Tinghae's fields from inundation with saltwater also held the waterways above them in a state of torpor, and besides, the British had arrived at the height of summer when rain was scarce. The level of the canals had dropped markedly, and their inky-black water was all the more offensive for it. The unsanitary conditions that even the late civil magistrate had been prepared to put up with sickened those who saw them; 'The smell in the rooms,' as one eye-witness put it, was 'as bad as that arising from mouldering graves':

> Even the ladies' apartments, which had only a few hours previously been abandoned, were so uncleanly that a Chinese coolie actually fainted on entering them…. It is difficult to understand how people could live in such damp and infected places, unless they possessed something of the amphibian nature of the toad.

Such hyperbole aside, Tinghae's houses were — and indeed a few survivors still are — typical of Zhejiang's vernacular architecture: those fronting the streets were, in that province's mercantile tradition, predominantly shops, two storeys high, of brick or timber and with a frontage of wooden panels removed by day to reveal the stock. A counter separated the inside from the bustle of the street, and a till sat at one end. A reel of twine would hang from the ceiling, close by wrapping paper cut ready for use. Windows were unglazed, but shutters or lattices of wood and paper kept the cold out tolerably well for Chinese sensibilities. The poorer homes in the back alleys did not display the extravagant curving eaves of public buildings and temples, having just a gently sagging roof covered with a jumble of black tiles. The more opulent homes exuded exclusivity, their public persona a high, whitewashed wall surmounted by a dark strip of tiles, with below a scarlet door in a stone surround. The local name for the style was *fenqiang daiwa*, 'powdered walls and tiles like blackened eyebrows', as though each presented a carefully made-up face to the world. Behind those plain walls were discovered ornate balconies and luxurious woodcarvings — bamboos and birds, red-lacquered bedsteads, tables and gilded chairs.[40] The sheer amount of crockery and reading matter impressed people. Around every door were strips of paper with beautifully drawn Chinese characters, some of them gilt and glittering. They had been pasted there at the start of the Chinese New Year in early February, but the irony of such prayers for wealth and good fortune for this particular Year of the Rat was lost on the British.

Other subtleties similarly escaped Tinghae's conquerors, who were almost to a man blind to every meaning encoded in characters and landscapes. As the common soldiery worked its way from house to house looking for valuables, soon their floors were strewn with books, poem scrolls, hanging couplets and paintings cast aside as worthless.[41] A stone's throw from the east gate, the granite crests of Red Sky Hill were crowned by a pagoda and by a strange structure on a plinth that to the unknowing eye resembled a squat flagstaff. Nobody seemed much interested in what they were, or noticed, when it rained, that water ran down the slope to collect in Inkstone Pool, or that the curious monument was carved like a writing brush so that the god of literature might take it up, dip it in the pond, and form his mighty characters on the vast canvas of the empty fields beyond.

Tinghae, which like every Chinese city was home to its share of Confucian scholars, was found to have a number of libraries, academies and schools, their walls bearing row after row of pigeonholes crammed with books.[42] Appreciating their value to governance and scholarship, Gützlaff issued orders that all be brought to his magistracy. Before he could be heeded, though, they were stolen as souvenirs. Elsewhere were found the accrued archives of the local administration. The damp maritime air had got to them long before the British, who discovered to their horror that any attempt to move them only created a pall of noxious mould. The only people to show an interest turned out to be a posse of agents from the mainland, sent to steal them back from under Governor Burrell's nose.[43] One was caught red-handed, and so the archives were burned in great bonfires to preclude their theft.[44] Just a few scraps — a map salvaged by an officer, some pages bearing the emperor's vermillion script rescued by a doctor — survived an act of vandalism that left a permanent gap in the county's records.

Worse still, when the Madras Engineers began the vital work of fortifying Josshouse Hill against any Chinese counterattack the rocky eminence was found to be swathed in a centuries-old accretion of burials.[45] Chusan's geomancers having long since divined its excellent *fengshui*, each coffin in turn had been placed on the hillside and slowly covered over with soil until it became one with the slope. Finding the ground strewn with bones and funerary clothing weathered out from these graves, the British can be excused for concluding that the Chinese, whatever was said about their punctilious ancestor worship, honoured their duties more in the breach than in the observance.[46] Digging out the caskets proved a distasteful job, and the Engineers turned to conscripting any passing Chinese at bayonet-point.[47] The officer in charge of the work, Captain Pears, simply could not fathom the islanders:

> The fellows are an odd set, with their long tails, broad-brimmed hats and straw shoes. They jabber and scramble and resist at first, then take to their work most kindly, and ultimately receive their pay with every demonstration of pleasure and gratitude.

It was not a pleasurable task. As each burial was uncovered it was heaved down the slope, its boards breaking open to scatter human remains. For days, the exposed contents rotting in the summer heat threw a choking miasma over the scene until a great pyre was made of body parts, burial clothes and splintered wood.[48] No more shocking means could possibly have been designed to alienate the islanders. Even the culturally illiterate barbarians could see that.

The Fortress of Terror, Ting-Hai (Thomas Allom). In the distance to the left is the temple fort on Josshouse Hill.

6

An idle dream

HAVING TAKEN steps to secure the harbour against a counterattack, the question arose as to where the British would live. Elsewhere in China this had never before been addressed: they had simply been confined to their factories. The better-informed members of the expedition were aware that even here in Chusan, as in Canton still, English merchants had once lived ashore, and the Red Hair Hall was known to have stood on the waterfront beneath Josshouse Hill.[1] It is possible that somebody even saw the black humour in a residence built to welcome the English having been fired upon by them on July 5th. The decision in Catchpoole's day had been stark: here or nowhere. Now, for the first time, there were choices to be made.[2]

Governor Burrell himself moved into the late civil magistrate's residence, a range of low, ramshackle buildings around a courtyard overgrown with grass and provided with tanks of stagnant water against accidental fires.[3] In the innermost rooms a final meal lay uneaten on the table, an opium pipe set out ready for a leisurely postprandial smoke that had been forever postponed by the *Wellesley*'s broadside.[4] (Had he lived, he might have been downhearted to learn that Burrell without further ado banned the landing and sale of the drug on Chusan under British rule — not that it did anything to stop the trade at anchor.)[5] Magistrate Gützlaff moved into the former magistracy in the very heart of Tinghae, right beside the Pool of the District Granary, a lagoon that festered with mosquito larvae. Alongside him lived the expedition's other interpreters. One, Robert Thom, was a Glaswegian who as a merchant's clerk had by 1834 found himself working for the Canton agency house of Jardine, Matheson & Co. (they dealt, amongst other articles, in opium). A self-effacing man with a fascination for China, he had married a Chinese woman, had a sound knowledge of Chinese, and had accepted an official post with the expedition.[6] The other interpreter, John Morrison, had six years earlier succeeded his father in the post of chief interpreter to the superintendent of trade in Canton, and was now always on hand to translate for Captain Elliot. Military Commissioners Stephens and Caine took rooms in a lavishly decorated building nearby. Space was found in the city's larger houses for commissioned officers, who were not expected to rough it with Tommy Atkins, while the Pay Office was set up (presumably with no humour intended) in the temple of a Buddhist saint sworn to free tormented souls from hell. Finally, with an all-but-deserted city of some 4,500 houses at his disposal, Governor Burrell might have seemed spoilt for choice over where to shelter his 4,000-strong land forces, but a problem arose in his mind: his ongoing policy was to tempt the inhabitants of Tinghae back, a policy that would be exposed as a lie if returnees found a platoon of Irishmen or Indians billeted in their bedroom. He pondered the matter for a while, then ordered that no private residence should be broken into or occupied. Religious buildings, though, abounded. Some Scottish troops had already been billeted in the largest of them, the Buddhist Zuyin Temple in the heart of the city, others in the temple of the city god (where Sir George Staunton had stopped to escape a thunderstorm forty-seven years earlier), while the Royal Irish were billeted in their entirety in the fortified temple on Josshouse Hill. Its walled precincts stretched for most of a furlong along the flat crest, a great ceremonial square strewn here and there with enormous incense burners and stone lanterns. Men who took the time to look around inside this and the Zuyin Temple were in equal measure impressed with the craftsmanship and disgusted by the idolatry.[7] Through successive halls, one met with the pot-bellied, laughing Maitreya Buddha, the twenty-foot-tall heavenly kings of the four directions with their scowls and their bulging eyes, and finally Sakyamuni Gautama, the Buddha himself, backed by golden halos, attended by bodhisattvas, and protected by four dozen statues of saints each standing yards high. Everywhere there was gilt and the brightest of colours.[8] Officers occupied what had been the priests' quarters, while privates slept in prayer halls under the gaze of the idols. Yet the very first act committed ashore had been the public desecration of just such an idol. Burrell, mindful of giving offence, ordered that no more temple buildings be entered. And so, with shelter denied to them, most of the rank and file remained encamped in their tents on the paddy fields between Tinghae and the harbour, which in places were knee-deep in mud.[9] The 49th Regiment of Foot, the Hertfordshires, landing again after their drunken re-embarkation of the first day, pitched camp on the heights overlooking the harbour a mile west of the wharves (the Chinese called it Dawn Peak Ridge, for it was the point first illuminated by the rays of the sun). Soon the scrub-covered slopes of what became known as 49th Hill were speckled almost from top to bottom with white canvas.[10] The 900-strong Cameronian Regiment pitched their bell-tents on the steep but lightly wooded slopes of the high ground that overlooked Tinghae from the northwest. This 'Cameronian Hill' was dry, well ventilated, and enjoyed a marvellous view across the city and the vale of Tinghae to the ships at anchor.[11] The dark-skinned sepoys of the Bengal Volunteers and the two native Madras regiments set up camp amid the paddy and canals outside the city walls.[12] Burrell's failure to house his men properly would ultimately prove disastrous.

But if the invading armies were finding it hard to get decent shelter, across the waters of Kintang Sound Tinghae's erstwhile inhabitants were in an even worse situation. Rapidly inundated by refugees from the captured city, the prefect and magistrate of Ningbo together devised a strategy.[13] First, Ningbo's men of means were invited to contribute to a relief fund (an invitation they could presumably not refuse). Then the refugees were questioned. Those who had money to live on or friends and relatives to lodge with were granted temporary residency until such time as Tinghae was recaptured. The rest were asked if they were willing to travel to neighbouring districts to take their chances. If they agreed, they were given travel expenses and sent on their way. Close on 3,000 refugees were relocated in this way, leaving 2,000 elderly, disabled and destitute to be housed in Ningbo's temples. As the weeks passed, townsfolk who had at first hidden out in Chusan's villages began to make the short sea crossing to the safety of the mainland, and many who at first had taken their chances elsewhere drifted back to Ningbo. Thousands were facing starvation in the city, the young and old especially so, and the prospect of hordes of young men resorting to crime was terrifying. Even the provincial governor Urgungga 100 miles away in Hangzhou wrote to Peking admitting that the problem was giving him sleepless nights. An additional headache for the Chinese authorities was how to root out the bogus refugees ('these treacherous bandits!' the emperor labelled them)[14] who had arrived in droves hoping to claim the meagre daily allowance of thirty copper cash. A system was devised, whereby a Tinghae native would listen out for their local accent to confirm their *bona fides* before they were placed on a register of genuine refugees. Temporary straw huts were built on waste ground to shelter those whom the temples could not house, door-plaques were nailed up to identify households who had taken islanders under their wing, and food rations were doled out once every five days. As autumn of 1840 drew in, most of Tinghae's 20,000 displaced citizens were living in internal exile. With growing apprehension it was realised that if the British could not be ousted from Chusan then permanent arrangements would have to be made for people who might never be able to return home.

Despite the eerie stillness in Tinghae in the shocked aftermath of the invasion, there were glimmers of hope in the increasing number of shops opening for business and in the farmers who had started to bring food to sell on the streets. In these small ways at least, Magistrate Gützlaff's permit system seemed to be working. As the people of the surrounding villages got over much of their initial alarm, there was food to be bought in Tinghae's markets — meat, fowl, vegetables, eggs, sugar candy and more.[15] The Chinese' love of money, it appeared, might soon overcome their fears and bring in sufficient supplies for the garrison. But it was not just the British whom the Chinese feared. Even as hopes grew that greed would quickly repopulate Tinghae, they were as quickly dashed, with rumours beginning to circulate of spies from the mainland tightening the screws on those shopkeepers who had dared to reopen. One by one they were seen to draw the planks across their shop fronts, click the padlocks shut, and leave with their takings. By the middle of July, the few farmers squatting behind cages of scrawny chickens knew it was a seller's market, and prices were sky-high. For months at sea the garrison had been surviving on salt rations — heavily brined pork or beef boiled until flaccid, along with coarse bread or hard tack, some dried peas, and perhaps flour, raisins and suet for a boiled pudding. Once ashore, it had fallen to an army office called the commissariat to buy the fresh meat that made up the bulk of a soldier's reliable but monotonous diet, and for a few days before the traders had been warned not to deal with the invaders this had indeed been achieved. Now, with little to eat once more beyond salt rations, an armed foraging party was organized.[16] Two dozen Cameronians passed through the north gate with a band of Bengali camp followers to carry the anticipated haul of food. It was the first time the invaders had dared to venture beyond the city walls into the island's hinterland, and at each little hamlet they made sure to paste up a proclamation claiming the island for Queen Victoria. The party's interpreter Robert Thom betrayed a surprising degree of antipathy to the people he encountered:

> The ignorant peasantry, the regular clodhoppers of the land, gaped and stared and laughed as Chinamen laugh, and then went to hoe their fields again. The country people didn't seem to care, or, more likely, they did not understand what we were about.[17]

But while the villagers merely hid their fear behind smiles, the village gentry were patently unhappy:

> They offered no opposition, as it would be inconvenient to come to blows, but in spite of my most honied expressions, and of my most persuasive arguments, I could plainly perceive that they were dissatisfied. I do not now hesitate to call the idea that the Chinese are displeased with their own government, and would join us from choice the moment that the British flag was unfurled, an idle dream.

It is a sentiment just as familiar from the conflicts of more recent times. Besides a few chickens and some eggs, that first attempt to find fresh food for the hungry soldiers ended with the Scots spending the huge sum of $50 on one water buffalo, one cow, and her calf—enough meat for a few days. Other foraging parties inevitably followed. Only by arriving in a village in force, heavily armed and unannounced, could they hope to find food, but such tactics succeeded only in alienating and terrifying the population. As time passed and the garrison resigned itself to living on salt rations, hopes came to rest on one man, Bu Dingbang.

Bu Dingbang was a great asset, an English-speaking merchant from Xiangshan near Canton who had worked for the trading company of Jardine, Matheson & Co. in the south and had sailed with the expedition to Chusan as a comprador—a native go-between, as it were. Alone, Bu Dingbang and his Bengali followers had consistently proved capable of returning from a day's foraging carrying more food than they had set out with, and their success was reason to be optimistic. So it was no surprise that morale amongst the half-starved garrison sank when one day one of Bu's foraging party, a butcher from Tinghae who was likewise working for the British, arrived out of breath in town with news that Bu had been abducted. A stroke of luck on the part of a group of Chinese Green Standard soldiers who had been hiding out in the interior, this was the last thing that was needed. The butcher, fearing for his own skin having seen a fellow Chinese seized, promptly vanished, leaving the British with no idea where to start looking.[18]

Correctly assuming that Bu would be spirited away to Ningbo as soon as possible, armed search parties set out into the mountains—terrain that had changed overnight from a reservoir of potential allies into a hostile world of possible ambush—in the hope of learning something of his kidnap.[19] As the sun rose higher, the soldiers in their heavy woollen coatees began to wilt. Some, already suffering from fever or dysentery when they left out, turned back sick, and in their stead islanders were pressed at bayonet-point into carrying supplies. But invariably a warning cry would ring out, and the search parties were greeted only by a succession of deserted villages. As one party began to despair, a trick was devised: half of the men went on ahead to the next

82

village, while the rest quietly doubled back to take the occupants of the last by surprise when they had returned to their homes. Surrounding the jubilant villagers, who thought they had outsmarted them, the British at a shout charged into their midst, firing into the air to terrify them.[20] And so, in the summer heat, Celtic soldiers, Indian camp followers and reluctant Chinese coolies slogged from village to empty village by day and slept in commandeered temples by night. When the parties straggled back empty-handed and depleted by sickness to Tinghae, all they had to show for their exertions was a few village elders arrested in the hope that their incarceration might reveal Bu's whereabouts, and a hostage who had been shot while attempting to flee and who had been carried back on a makeshift stretcher.[21]

Captain Elliot himself, meanwhile, had been brought up the coast by steamer, but had lost his way while trying to retrace his steps to a rendezvous. Late at night, after an age spent wandering the fields, Her Britannic Majesty's plenipotentiary in China along with a party of officers and men stumbled into a cove where they happened upon the steamer at anchor. Most were rowed over, but, as the tide turned, Elliot was stranded on the rocky shore. To make matters worse, the only bottle of wine had preceded him aboard. Forced to pass the night on the wet rocks, he was heard to comment that the stones were 'very good stones in their way, but a bad substitute for a feather bed.'[22]

It had been just three days since Bu Dingbang's disappearance, but even that short time had made a terrible difference to Tinghae: word had got out that collaborators were being seized, and hardly a shop was left open. Magistrate Gützlaff at least was unsurprised: his essay to Lord Palmerston five years earlier recommending the invasion of Chusan had contained an uncannily prescient warning on just this score: the Chinese, he had predicted, would attempt to cut off supplies of food, and unless the British treated the islanders well and won them over they were in a position to do them severe harm simply by denying them the essentials of life. The British had done anything but, and they were starting to pay the price. Even the persuasive and amiable naval surgeon Edward Cree found there was next to no food to be had without compelling its owners to sell. Assembling a party of sailors hungry enough to risk a foraging trip, and engaging an armed marine in case a kidnap attempt was made, he rowed out one day from HMS *Rattlesnake* to the islands in the harbour. On the first they visited, the Chinese simply fell on their knees in terror. Landing on a second, Edward and his armed guard found a village a mile or two inland. He recorded in his journal what they found there:

> The natives came out to meet us in a crowd and made signs that they had no pigs, goats or poultry and wished to direct us to a village farther on. We tried to make friends with them and went into some of their houses and took tea. We picked up a pig, a goat and some fowl for which we paid them a fair price but they evidently did not wish to have any dealings with us. But hungry men were not to be driven away from food.[23]

Passing on through the island's hamlets, the band scraped together a few more chickens and pigs while the villagers traipsed a short distance behind them in the forlorn hope of getting their animals back. That very same day, the emperor in distant Peking demanded a complete end even to such unwilling fraternisation. The policy of cutting off all sustenance was given added weight by a suggestion from Lin Zexu, the same imperial commissioner who a year earlier had sparked the war by destroying British opium stocks in Canton:

> The barbarians speak and dress differently to us, they have different eyes, noses and hair, and so if we unite we can eradicate the foreign species with no chance of accidentally killing a Chinese. Tinghae has only recently been occupied and, even if all the citizens have fled for their lives, there cannot be fewer than one hundred thousand people in the villages. Everybody should be ordered to eradicate the bandits. Whether soldier or civilian, anybody able to kill a barbarian should be rewarded according to the number of severed heads they can present to us. Once word gets out we shall need only to wait the blink of an eye and not one will be left. And once they are all dead, their boats and cannons will be all ours.[24]

Word did get out, and soon it was understood amongst the garrison that a severed Indian head commanded $50, a white head $100, and an officer's even more.[25]

By early August of 1840, life in the few square miles of Chusan over which the British ruled was falling dreadfully short of expectations. On the first of the month, the joint plenipotentiaries Captain Charles Elliot and his cousin, Admiral Sir George Elliot, sailed north for the mouth of the Peiho River to open negotiations as Lord Palmerston's instructions required (as had been the case for Lord Macartney in 1793, this was the closest they could get to Peking without journeying overland). The sick lists meanwhile were daily increasing: a particularly pernicious form of dysentery was by now affecting fully half of Governor Burrell's men, and the symptoms of malaria were widespread. Even Burrell himself was suffering from violent attacks that sapped his strength. Tinghae was devoid of all but the most desperate Chinese, and there was no fresh food to be had save 1 lb of fatty pork per man per week. The subalterns of the Royal Irish were forced to choose between milk and goat-meat, and elected to kill their animals one by one rather than starve. There were, they complained bitterly, stores aplenty on the merchant ships in harbour, but prices were so high that it was ruinous. Instead they went hungry.[26] Fowls bought, borrowed or stolen on the occasional foraging trip provided soup for the invalids, but otherwise the British were living on salt rations, the Indians on rice, dhal, ghee and mustard seed.[27] Even the ragged beggars were finding life difficult now their almsgivers had vanished. Some were seen fishing in the canals, only to be pounced upon by soldiers if they caught anything. Cockerels, it was observed, only crowed once.[28] A junk taken prisoner proved to be of scant use to a garrison suffering from bloody fluxes and intermittent agues, its cargo — deer horns, tortoiseshell, ivory and tiger skeletons — beautiful but inedible.[29] The only person to draw a grain of comfort from Tinghae's emptiness was Gützlaff. As magistrate he had at first been assailed by rival claimants to property, but by late July he had ceded his post to the military commissioner Captain William Caine in order to focus on his translating duties and on writing religious tracts. 'I had much trouble at first,' he was heard to joke in his German accent. 'But now it is *vary nice*; all de litigious people have left de city!'[30]

Anxious to break the stalemate, Governor Burrell ordered proclamations to be posted around Tinghae informing its wholly absent citizenry that their shops would be broken into if they did not return to trade within the week. The next day a counter-proclamation was posted by an unseen hand, warning nobody in particular not to heed Burrell and predicting an assault that would drive the barbarians into the sea.[31] His every ploy, it seemed, was sidestepped by invisible mandarins across the water, gently tugging the strings that controlled the island.

For Edward Cree at least, from the relative safety of HMS *Rattlesnake*, trips around the harbour in search of food continued to offer opportunities to win over the natives with his personable charm. A fortnight after Bu Dingbang's kidnap, Cree and a friend rowed out to one particular island where they felt safe from the soldiers rumoured to roam Chusan. They bought a litter of piglets, though it was worth the money just to catch them.[32] Despite the edict banning fraternisation, some of the islanders rowed over to the *Rattlesnake* to pay a return visit while Cree was at breakfast and amused themselves at Western table manners.[33] But finally the flurry of proclamations and counter-proclamations convinced even Cree that there would soon be no food to buy at any price. One day he rose early, took coffee, and with a number of followers landed on Chusan armed with pistols for any Chinese soldiers they might meet and with fowling pieces to bag game for the pot. The party found the villages peaceful but the farmers unwilling to sell their livestock — what use was a fistful of silver dollars when it was proof of having disobeyed the emperor? Still, by herding goats and pigs before it and leaving sufficient silver to broach any argument the party soon resembled a walking menagerie.[34]

Just as Cree and his Bengalis were driving their animals back to Tinghae with panniers of live chickens slung over their shoulders, Governor Burrell received a worrying report of four hundred enemy soldiers landing at Sinkong on the west coast of Chusan.[35] Two hundred infantrymen hastily boarded a steamer but found just some junks carrying raw sugar. The entire garrison was on edge. From informants on the mainland were arriving illicit copies of Chinese communications: fiery memorials naïvely promising the emperor that the barbarians would be destroyed; reports detailing a troop build-up on the coast; orders for the casting of cannon and the requisitioning of junks for an invasion fleet. Governor Burrell had no choice but to follow up any word of the threatened invasion, but it was agreed that the Chinese had neither the stomach nor the means to retake Chusan by force. Even a modest plan to install a fifth column in Tinghae came to nothing:[36] a spy sent into the city in the guise of an opium smuggler reported that Burrell was running a tight show, and that a few men at most might make it past the sentries. Besides, in a city peopled by beggars and housebound old women, strapping young guerrillas would stand out like a sore thumb. But leaving the barbarians in peace was unthinkable. For the Chinese, the sole glimmer of hope was that the British were unable to protect their own: Bu Dingbang had been kidnapped within sight of the city walls. The memorial recommending rewards for severed heads had been circulating for a fortnight, and despite the friendly efforts of individuals like Edward Cree the atmosphere of tension between invader and invaded was palpably hardening. Just as in the foreign wars of our own age, the average soldier knew not one word of the local dialect and minor misunderstandings quickly flared into violence. Beatings and worse were meted out to recalcitrant villagers, with the wiry Indian troops, considered social and physical inferiors by the Europeans, especially liable to lord it over the natives. The Muslims among them tended to look upon the Chinese with contempt for their habitual diet of pork, the Hindus for their use of the cow as a beast of burden. More than one soldier had been injured in a spate of attacks on foraging parties, a Bengali had died after a stabbing, there had been numerous Chinese civilian deaths, and a constant trickle of islanders was reaching Tinghae seeking treatment for gunshot wounds and sword cuts.[37]

In mid-August the tension broke into open revolt. One morning, six hungry infantrymen entered a village a few miles from Tinghae.[38] They were heavily armed and, while hardly expecting the streets to be strewn with flowers, were not expecting a confrontation. Hearing a noise from outside the farmstead they were searching, one of the soldiers went out only to find a crowd of some two hundred villagers clearly intent on a fight. A shot was fired over their heads, but far from scaring the mob off this only caused them to charge the man down before he could reload, grabbing and punching him. The fracas alerted his comrades, who fired a volley into the mêlée. Before they could fire a second volley, the Chinese had fled. One had been so badly hurt that he reappeared in Tinghae, carried by his friends, to demand medical treatment. The incident was typical of the standoff that had been allowed to develop: on the one side was a garrison slowly starving to death, on the other a population terrified of these red-haired foreigners who devoured its livestock and killed its menfolk.

But violent resistance and even the threat of beheading could not dissuade starving men. One scorching afternoon two blonde-haired, blue-eyed boys from HMS *Blenheim* — a fourteen-year-old midshipman and a clerk's assistant just two years his senior — decided to land on Chusan to buy some fresh goats.[39] They took a few silver dollars from their mess caterer, and the older boy procured a double-barrelled pistol. Reaching a farm, the two were greeted by the farmer, but he would not part with his animals. As they turned to leave, there began to assemble a group of farmhands clutching rakes and hoes. One approached the older boy offering to sell the goats, and the boy, relieved, crooked his pistol and rifled his pockets for the cash. It was then that the man grabbed his weapon while another pinned him by the throat against a hedge. As the man fumbled at the mechanism, the fourteen-year-old midshipman sprang forward to seize it, put it to the man's temple, and fired, blowing the side of his face clean away. Unfamiliar with firearms, the other villagers were clearly dismayed when the clerk's assistant now took the gun and discharged it into his captor's stomach. The boy made no pretence at reloading, pointing the gun instead at the incredulous farm workers who seemed to think it somehow fired endless rounds. The stand-off, so it was reported, ended when a party of Royal Irish who had been digging for sweet potatoes nearby came to investigate the shots. When the boys reached the safety of the *Blenheim* they were examined as to what had occurred, and the news spread quickly:

> But the innocent little creatures could not tell whether they had killed them or not. All that clerky could say was that the one he fired at had one ear and the side of his face blown away, but he hoped that he was not *much* hurt, as he left him kicking a *little*. Middie was rather bolder, he said he supposed his chap was dead, but was not *quite* certain. He fell down, but did not speak or move, and he had a big hole in his belly. And as Sir Humphrey Senhouse, their Captain, said, I think, 'It is rather presumptive evidence that he was killed *dead*'.[40]

On another occasion, an officer commanding a foraging party was seized while alone in a farmhouse looking for food. Wrestling a hand free he shot one assailant with his pistol, while a soldier alerted by the report shot a second and peppered a third with buckshot. More soldiers arrived and bayoneted the would-be kidnappers.[41]

The island fought back against the invaders in more insidious ways, too — or was it nothing more than paranoia projected onto the blank canvas of the abandoned city that maddeningly hot summer? When a dog apparently dropped dead after drinking from a well, it was whispered that spies had poisoned Tinghae's water supply.[42] Refugees passed on rumours, and by the time their stories reached the emperor in Peking the facts were seemingly incontrovertible: concoctions of noxious herbs had been placed in the springs, and now the barbarians who drank the water were falling ill and dying without respite. There were claims that psychological warfare was being used against an enemy army on the edge of its nerves. One report claimed that:

Men were sent under cover of darkness while the rebels slept, to steal away their valuables or to throw stones about, so that day and night they were ill at ease, their nature much distressed.[43]

His subjects, the emperor could be sure, were fighting back, yet on a pragmatic level it seems not to have struck the Chinese that they were in a pretty fix if this was the best they could boast. The island's population, after all, amounted to some quarter of a million people. From a British point of view there was no hint that poisonings and petty annoyances, if they ever happened, were having an effect on morale. The sad truth was that the troops were going stir crazy and slowly dying of disease without the Chinese needing to lift a finger.

By late August of 1840 there were close on 5,000 foreigners living ashore on Chusan, including public camp followers, private servants, soldiers' wives, and even some children. Aboard the dozens of warships, store vessels and transports in the harbour there were even more. Only one of that great number, the fearless Karl Gützlaff, now dared to venture alone out of sight of the walls, ignoring the solemn warnings, guffawing and insisting that no Chinese would dare touch him as he distributed his Christian tracts.[44] God, he insisted, would preserve him. Others though were being forsaken; there had already been three dozen deaths amongst the soldiers, and cases of dysentery were rising. Fully one quarter of the Cameronians were in hospital, and not one of them was well enough to carry his standard-issue kit for ten miles.[45] Scurvy had killed at least one of the regiment, so bad were the salt rations and so scarce fresh food.[46]

'England knows how to conquer,' observed one officer, 'but never yet has she learned the secret of turning to advantage the successes in many cases earned by a lavish expenditure of blood and treasure.'[47] *The Englishman & Military Chronicle* back in India was just as scathing:

The powers that be seem never to adopt prompt measures, and by their shilly shally are destroying the 26th Regiment who might have been comfortably housed a fortnight since in the town, and many a fine fellow's life saved.... 'Tis too bad!![48]

Even the Chinese seemed aware that the British situation was so precarious as to put the invaders off their guard. One balmy August evening, Captain Pears of the Madras Engineers was in his mess tent on 49th Hill after a busy day improving the escarpment below the temple fort. Relaxing in his favourite lacquered chair (one of many looted from the city) he happened to look south. One of the war junks captured a month earlier, and now used as an ordnance store, was heading out of the harbour of its own accord. Quickly he assembled a boatful of sepoys to discover that five Chinese in a sampan were towing it away. The thieves were taken prisoner, led to gaol tied together by their pigtails, and the next day were spread-eagled and 'introduced with the usual forms to the boatswain's mate,' with two dozen lashes apiece.[49]

But it simply ought not to have fallen to an officer of the Engineers to prevent a magazine ship being stolen from a British harbour. Something radical had to be done to turn the occupation to Britain's advantage before the Chinese and the Grim Reaper together stole away any hope of success.

Mrs Noble on her way to Ningpo, from *The Cree Journals*
(image © Webb & Bower; original watercolour © Henrietta Heawood)

7
Go to hell!

A FTER ALMOST two months in charge, George Burrell finally decided that the islanders should be officially informed of British rule. 'Not before time!' it was murmured around the officers' mess-tables: so far the aged governor had proved himself to be 'a man without ostensible authority, and incapable of exercising real influence.'[1] His staff, too, were thought 'a remarkably slow set', and the men of the expedition had begun to despair of achieving anything creditable under their command:

> With the want of interpreters, want of knowledge of the people, and want of sense, the whole affair has been hitherto as beautifully mismanaged as the warmest admirer of British blundering could wish.[2]

Governor Burrell's plan to win over Chusan's population consisted in a show of military strength and a series of public announcements on how the Chinese were expected to behave from now on. On day in late August, the Indian Navy's paddle-sloop *Atalanta* steamed out of Tinghae harbour with ninety infantrymen, several dozen marines and Karl Gützlaff aboard. It was Burrell's intention to have her touch at various points along the shoreline with a carefully worded proclamation.[3] A few miles along the coast, a party was rowed ashore to a village and Gützlaff began to read aloud his translation in Chinese:

> Magistrate Caine of Tinghae by this proclamation notifies the elders of the city, the villages and the valleys, and all the inhabitants! Having received the command of the general in highest authority, desiring the suppression of disturbances and the protection of law-abiding subjects, patrols will be dispatched to the villages and valleys. The details of how the people are to behave when soldiers pass through a village or a valley are hereby explained. Receive and understand these instructions![4]

Whenever British soldiers appeared, the proclamation went on, elders were required to arrange bearers and workmen, who were promised high wages for their labour, and a daily market for the sale of goods at a fair price. Islanders with grievances were promised the full protection of the law, but in return they were expected to turn over any spies or militiamen to the custody of the British authorities on fear of severe punishment. It was hinted that houses used to harbour Chinese soldiers would be burned down.

> Elders and villagers, where previously respect was paid to the civil and military authorities of the Celestial Dynasty, will now pay respect to those of Great Britain. Let these articles be understood! All who carry on their occupations in peace will be protected by the law, but those daring to disturb the peace or cause obstruction will be suppressed. It is for each individual to choose between calamity and good fortune. Beware contravention!

To the British soldiers who witnessed Gützlaff's speeches, the curious villagers displayed a mixture of ignorance and incredulity, as though incapable of conceiving any other power than that of their emperor. They had, so it appeared to Captain Pears, 'not the remotest conception of the manner in which they are capable of being transferred from the mandarins' rule to that of foreigners and barbarians.'[5] Simple incomprehension might have been as good an explanation: Gützlaff, though a gifted linguist, had had less than two months to adjust to the islanders' dialect, and his German accent cannot have helped their understanding of his perplexingly formal translation of Governor Burrell's words. When toward the end of the year the emperor himself added his personal opinion to a copy of the proclamation, he simply pronounced it 'Abominable in the extreme!'

But most villagers did not even wait around to listen to Gützlaff. Each time the *Atalanta* was sighted, her deck crowded with the red jackets of infantrymen and her paddles thrashing the water, the shout would go up and so would begin the exodus into the hills. It quickly became clear that, where the British had for eight weeks proved unable to assert themselves, the local gentry had stepped into the vacuum left by the suicide of Tinghae's civil magistrate. In one village a notice was found. Under the authority of the village constables, it said, the community had assembled in the temple and voted unanimously for the extermination of the foreigners. It had been resolved that, on the English being sighted, gongs would be beaten as a signal to band together for protection and to attack them. The British had left the safety of Tinghae planning to establish the *pax Britannica* in an ungoverned interior. Instead they found the islanders governing themselves. With just five Chinese speakers, the task of maintaining order in Tinghae had been difficult enough. If the British hoped to govern the entire island they would need the help of local men willing to act as policemen in Governor Burrell's pay. And so with Gützlaff translating as best he could, one respectable-looking gentleman was made to accept, before a large crowd, a lithographed commission to serve Her Majesty Queen Victoria as a British constable.[6] It is likely that the ranks of British troops spurred him to accept, but doubtful that the commission continued to have any effect once the red jackets had marched on to do the same in the next hamlet.

On the last Sunday of August, the *Atalanta* landed a shore party at the fishing community of Sinkamoon on the south-eastern tip of Chusan. Ominously for the health of the garrison, one of the soldiers dropped dead. He had been in fine spirits just a moment before. His body was re-embarked, and his comrades continued inland. Reaching the head of a valley, two old women were spied tottering along on sticks, carrying a basket between them. When they saw the British they turned and ran, 'scared as much as they would have been by a couple of Bengal tigers,' reflected one officer. 'It makes one question one's own real character, we look and feel so like barbarians and robbers.'[7]

The neighbouring Buddhist holy island of Putuoshan too was officially informed of the change of rule, but its monks proved characteristically philosophical and were very little moved by the news.[8] A few miles further, and the *Atalanta*'s approach was met with the familiar gongs and the sound of animals being herded into the hills. Some of the villagers though stood their ground, and one handed Gützlaff a piece of paper with a defiant message: 'We know and care nothing about your comprador. We want none of your money. Nor do we wish to have anything to say to you.'[9] The same quiet, contemptuous refusal to interact was met with at every anchorage. When the next day two elderly men were made to stand and hear Governor Burrell's proclamation read out, they just looked around uneasily and in the end simply walked off. At another village, Gützlaff found a prominent house and stood on its verandah, the proclamation held aloft for all to see. Eventually an educated man walked up, read it in silence, then without a word retreated into the crowd and disappeared.[10]

The *Atalanta* arrived back in harbour after her circumnavigation of Chusan to find the food situation worsening, if indeed that was possible. Other than a sparsely stocked tobacconist's stand, there was nothing to be bought in Tinghae.[11] Come September there was still preserved food in abundance, but much of it had been badly packed and was all but inedible. The regiments which had travelled from Madras and Bombay — the Royal Irish and the Madras Engineers and Artillery — had brought British-cured meat, but the Bengal regiments — the Cameronians, the Hertfordshires and the Bengal Volunteers — were relying on meat dried and pickled in Calcutta. This Bengali meat seemed to have been hastily pickled, and some had turned green, while the Bengali biscuit was so hard and maggoty that some men had stopped drawing their ration.[12] Governor Burrell knew that the average British soldier would readily exchange his ration for a bowl of rice, and for a time considered supplementing their diet with rice confiscated from the county granary, or at least the portion that had not been auctioned off. He decided instead that the Indian troops needed it more. Many thought his decision incomprehensible; after all, there was rice to spare standing ripe in the fields (though in the Vale of Tinghae much of it had been trodden into a malarial swamp)[13] and a large proportion of his land forces had been agricultural labourers before taking the king's shilling. But with so many men now seriously ill, the governor would not contemplate such a time-consuming and labour-intensive undertaking as a harvest.[14]

At anchor in the harbour and not looking to the army's commissariat to provide their food, the men of the Royal Navy at least were faring better. Edward Cree for one was dining well, if expensively, on woodpeckers, fowl, and duck eggs. A one-man diplomatic mission, Cree's friendly demeanour had won over a farmer on one of the harbour islands.[15] On a near-daily basis he had begun to row over from HMS *Rattlesnake* to sit and share a pipe of tobacco with this man, whom he had cured of ophthalmia, for which kind deed he now got his ducks at a discount. The Chinese trusted him. One day, an old man was waiting for Cree in the farmhouse. He wrote him a note, which Cree took for translation. It transpired that Ching Wang, a farmer from a village across the harbour, had had a water buffalo stolen. It now being the season to plough his fields, he requested its return. Cree, suspecting it had long since been made into beef tea for the sick, promised to make enquiries nonetheless.[16] The farmer's youngest son meanwhile, a bright boy of nine, had begun to learn English from Cree and from the coarser naval men who visited his island. 'Go to hell!' he shouted when one day the surgeon took him playfully by the pigtail.[17] But the farmer, one of the few now remaining, knew what he was risking by fraternising with the barbarians. Soon after he began to consort with Cree, his home was visited by Chinese soldiers who had managed to escape the notice of the garrison. His two older sons were robbed and beaten, and could be grateful not to be carried away to Ningbo and executed as traitors.[18] To the mandarins there such peasants were small fry, worth only the attentions of bullying soldiers who could shake them down for a few dollars. Far greater prizes were being groomed on Chusan, prizes whose capture would bring matters to a head and ultimately decide the island's fate.

Like many of his fellow officers, Captain Philip Anstruther of the Madras Artillery was bored to distraction by life in a city which felt like an open prison.[19] Come September, he had turned his skills as an artist to mapping the hills around Tinghae — if

Chusan was to become a permanent addition to Queen Victoria's colonies, such work would be necessary. He would be seen leaving the city each morning with his surveying equipment, his elderly Indian servant close by. They would pass the day walking the paths and mounting the hilltops, measuring angles and calculating distances and heights. The locals, their fear of this well-built, full-bearded redhead waning with every portrait he drew for their amusement, would follow him as he worked, taking turns to peer through his telescope. With time, Anstruther began to leave his pistols behind, satisfied that, like Edward Cree, he had reached his own friendly entente with the islanders. One morning he left his tent as usual with his old servant and, passing through the city, climbed a suitable hill to pitch a flag and take bearings.[20] Presently, he became aware of a crowd following them. One man began to attack the defenceless servant, but the enormous Anstruther managed to drive him off. Soon more villagers appeared and pelted them with stones. The servant, downed by a rock, was set upon and beaten to death. Anstruther too was given a severe beating, bound, gagged, and slung beneath a bamboo pole. At midnight a boat took him to Ningbo where he was thrown into a cage.

At first his comrades paid no regard to his disappearance, as he would often lodge overnight with friends in other regiments.[21] But when he was again absent from mess the following day the alarm was raised. A worse turn of events could scarcely have been imagined. The Royal Irish and the Cameronians were too wracked with dysentery to spare any men, but when Lieutenant Balfour of the Madras Artillery wrote to the Madras Engineers and the Hertfordshires asking for help, troops were unquestioningly got under arms. Anstruther was a bright and popular officer, the life and soul of the party (a school friend remembered him as 'a little, red-haired boy' who grew into 'a great, hulking, noisy, drunken but clever fellow'[22] who only days before had celebrated his thirty-third birthday in the mess. Captain Pears of the Madras Engineers, who was busy fortifying Josshouse Hill, had been a close friend during their training at the East India Company's military seminary at Croydon in South London.[23] Search parties were sent out in clear defiance of Governor Burrell, who feared a harsh response might upset the islanders. No house, he had ordered, was to be entered during the search without good cause for suspicion. It was an order that might have been issued in hunting for the Governor's pet donkey![24] A squadron of boats weighed anchor in the hope of catching any vessel that might whisk Anstruther off the island. Later in the day, two Chinese witnesses confirmed British fears: they had seen the captain being carried away in the direction of Sinkong harbour, the shortest sea route to Ningbo.[25]

By evening, Sinkong was awash with soldiers incensed at the dastardly kidnap of an officer and intent on retribution.[26] They slept in a temple and at first light took hostage the richest-looking man they could find and marched him back to Tinghae in the teeming rain. The other search parties meanwhile were discovering that the islanders were in no mood to submit meekly to British rule. In the valley of Lahoo, which had so far remained unvisited by troops, a mob of more than a thousand men armed with farming implements dogged a search party of just sixteen soldiers, beating gongs and making threats.[27] With just three hundred rounds of ammunition between them, it looked as if the party might simply be overrun and massacred if they dared open fire. After a tense stand-off outside a temple it was agreed that the villagers would draw back if the British left come dawn. It was only by a hair's breadth that a great deal of blood was not shed on both sides.[28] Two weeks had passed since Gützlaff had read out Governor Burrell's proclamation to the coastal villages, time enough for word to filter through to farmers like these in the interior. The governor, utterly unfamiliar with Chinese ways — he had been serving as a commandant in Ceylon for the past four years, and the Sinhalese were such different people — had not expected such a flat refusal to obey him. The suggestion that a warship be sent to shell the prefectural capital Ningbo into rubble if Anstruther were not released was turned down: while HMS *Blenheim* was quite capable of such a feat, the governor did not have the authority to wreak such destruction while the Elliots were in the north negotiating with the emperor's representatives.[29] Yet still, despairing of winning over the islanders by peaceful means and with a growing realisation that his shilly-shallying lay at the root of their defiance, Burrell decided it was time to show force. In a sudden change of mood he abandoned his policy of conciliation and opted instead for what he understood best — military muscle.

And so a force of more than one hundred armed men set out for Lahoo that evening, and by four the next morning they had possession of the villages where the Chinese had been in open revolt.[30] A headquarters was established in a temple while the inhabitants slept. When they awoke to find their valley under British occupation, they began to sound gongs as had been agreed. The buglers in reply sounded the call to action, and as the villagers emerged with their hoes and rakes the British viciously beat them to the ground. After an hour or two, some sixty prisoners had been taken and were sat tied together by their pigtails. A notice was read aloud accusing the bemused Chinese of having rebelled against Queen Victoria, and the ringleaders were whipped. The most important-looking were marched off to Tinghae as hostages, the detachment marched to a nearby village which had similarly dared to resist a search party looking for Captain Anstruther, and there it continued the muscular assertion of British rule.[31]

As Tinghae's prison began to fill with insurgents awaiting interrogation, far away in Peking the emperor was reading reports from his mandarins on the Zhejiang mainland gleefully boasting of their very own haul of captives.[32] Besides Captain Anstruther and the comprador Bu Dingbang, there were two dozen Indian and European soldiers and sailors and a white woman whose name the mandarins could best render as *Annanabu*. To her friends on Chusan she was Anne Noble.[33]

Anne, a captain's wife, had sailed from Tyneside a year earlier aboard a brig named the *Kite*, stopping at Bordeaux to pick up a cargo of wine. The ship's mate was one Mr Witts, and the sailors beneath him revelled in suitably Dickensian names — Henry Twizell, Pellew Webb, William Wombwell. The rest of the crew was typically cosmopolitan for the time — an Italian, a Filipino, ten lascars, and an Indian cook. In Madras the *Kite* had been requisitioned as a transport for the China expedition and had dropped anchor in Tinghae harbour the day the city fell. There she had lain until September, when she was sent to accompany a survey of the Yangtze estuary, carrying a dozen marines and ship's boys from all over the British Isles. Anne herself — a gaunt, Scottish redhead[34] just twenty-six years old — had given birth at sea, was now nursing a five-month-old son, and was once more pregnant. Two days' sailing from Chusan, dysentery had struck the *Kite* with a vengeance, and soon a third of the crew was either dead or seriously ill. Maybe this contributed to what happened next. Instead of making port, the *Kite* struck an unseen sandbank with frightening violence. Turned sideways now to a strong tide, she keeled over. Anne heard her husband's last words, warning her to hold on, but saw no more of him. Both were thrown overboard along with everyone else on deck before they could fetch their child, asleep below in his cot. The others, many weak with dysentery, scrambled into the rigging or clambered onto the masts and yards. Anne caught hold of an iron bar, Mr Witts' little pet dog quivering on her breast. 'But at last I was obliged to put it off,' she would recall. 'Oh! had it been my child I would have died rather a thousand times.'[35]

Somebody managed to right a lifeboat, and it was into this that Anne was dragged by the leg. For hours she shouted and screamed to the figures on the masts to find her husband and baby, and when the wreck vanished from sight she just sat like a statue, unable to cry any more. Her husband had become the third of his family to drown at sea.[36] The tide turned in the afternoon and brought the lifeboat back within view of the wreck. She was submerged but for one mast. Three times in all the boat drifted back on the tide, her crew unable without oars or sail to manoeuvre her. The third time, there were no more figures clinging to the yardarms. Anne was wearing only the thin gown she had had on that morning and was unshod. They had no food or water. So even when the boat that spotted and picked them up turned out to be Chinese rather than British they were grateful for their deliverance. Soon, though, they were handed over to a patrol of the humiliated Green Standards. The soldiers beat Anne, put a chain around her neck, and force-marched her and the others to a town where her wedding ring was stolen from her hand. Separated from the men, she was made to walk in the rain filthy and barefoot past jeering crowds, her only comfort an unshakable faith that God would not forsake her: even if she were to be killed, she could look forward to seeing her husband and child once more. One week after the disaster, she was put in a bamboo cage. It was so small that her nose touched her knees. When eventually it was shipped to England to be displayed at the United Service Institution,[37] the *Devonport Telegraph* reported its dimensions: 2'8" long, 1'6" wide, 2'4" tall.[38] In this, Anne was carried to Ningbo.

Although she was unaware, the *Kite*'s crew had all been picked up by passing junks — all, that is, but her husband and baby son. At first the survivors were treated tolerably well, but one by one they too were handed over to the local soldiery. Alone or in small groups, these twenty-six half-naked men were led in chains across the flat farmland, spat at by crowds during the day, tethered to posts at night, and exhibited in cages. Well-to-do men and women in silks came to look at the prisoners as if they were a freak show. Two marines were beaten to death by their guards, their corporal left near insensible, while townspeople acted out how their eyes, tongues and noses were sure to be cut off.

Reaching the prison attached to the city magistracy in Ningbo, Anne met with Bu Dingbang, the kidnapped comprador, who interpreted and acted as an unofficial *maître d'hôtel*, and with Captain Anstruther who as the senior officer took responsibility for the prisoners' welfare. Clearly regarded by the mandarins as a man of some import, Anstruther arranged clothing and food, and doctors for the sick (though he could not help the badly beaten corporal of marines who lay in his cage soiled from dysentery, maggots crawling about him, until he was blessed with death). Anne was given two women to attend her (one brought a little boy who cried incessantly, the other a dirty little girl)[39] and a room beside the captain's, albeit just a small dirty cell with scarcely a roof above the open rafters. Besides the tiny cage, in which she was still forced to sleep, her furniture consisted of a stool, a table and an oil lamp. Soon she was honoured with a bedstead. The mandarin who oversaw her incarceration would sometimes ask her to dine with him, pressing her to tell and retell how she lost her family and asking how closely she was related to Queen Victoria.[40]

As the weeks passed, a secret channel of communication was opened between the prisoners and Chusan by 'an ugly vagabond' of a Chinaman whom the British dubbed Blondel de Westa. Causing a diversion by splashing water at his gawping onlookers, Anstruther would pass Blondel letters which would find their way to Tinghae. By and by, parcels began to arrive: clothing for Anne and for her baby son (of whose death the British had yet to hear), shoes, a Bible, wine, ale, a case of gin and $300 to buy food from the guards. A gift of soap never arrived, and it was wondered sarcastically whether the Chinese had eaten it, given that they did not blush at eating far worse. Anstruther asked for a copy of Gibbon's *Decline & Fall*, some shirts, a concealed knife and a steel pen and paper, and soon he was bartering drawings for improved conditions.[41] At his captors' request he sketched a steamship, drew portraits of Queen Victoria, maps of England, and of London with all its famous sights.[42] One day, a savoury stew was sent to him as thanks for a portrait of a local mandarin. It was delicious. Not knowing what was in it, Anstruther looked at the servant who had brought it and asked 'quack, quack, quack?' to which the man shook his head and replied: 'bow, wow, wow.'

Shuttling incognito between Ningbo and Tinghae, Blondel de Westa briefed the British on the situation in the gaol. Of the guards, most were friends of his and could be bought over. The prison sat close by a river, and the boat owners were poor and easily bribed. Even Ningbo's magistrate had a price: he owed a vast sum to the government and was known to be near bankruptcy. In return for rescuing the prisoners, Blondel asked only that a kinsman of his be allowed to remove his remaining stock from the family timber-yard in Tinghae — cold weather was by now forcing the garrison to burn any fuel it could find, even to the point of dismantling houses and temples.[43] But Blondel de Westa was, after all, a Chinese and a turncoat, and Captain Anstruther's opinion was sought by secret letter. He wrote back, vetoing the plan: he himself might easily escape, but this would mean severe privation for the others and possible retaliation against the pregnant Anne Noble. Her condition would make any escape attempt exceedingly dangerous. Even if the expendable Indian sailors were left to suffer whatever fate awaited them, the captain wrote, either all the Europeans needed to escape or none. Blondel's plan was out of the question. To console himself, Anstruther requested some brandy and cheroots, the *Artillerist's Manual* and Hutton's *Mathematics*, and took to using the prison walls as a chalkboard to advance his study of ballistics.[44]

As letters from the prisoners and communiqués from their captors began to arrive in Tinghae, the British were provoked into responses guaranteed to infuriate mandarins trained in more circumspect language. An official reply to a communiqué from Urgungga, the governor of Zhejiang province, began in no uncertain terms:

> You call yourself a great nation, yet it is truly unworthy of the name to behave like this. If so much as one hair of the prisoners' heads is harmed, then officers and men of this nation shall pour forth a righteous vengeance, wiping out the guilty and the innocent alike![45]

The sentiment was understandable, but the British had unintentionally shown their hand with their frantic insistence that Anne, Anstruther and the rest remain unharmed. The Chinese for the first time knew they had a weapon as powerful as any naval broadside — white hostages. Urgungga answered swiftly, spelling out his new demands: if the British wished to see their countrymen released, the emperor's mercy might be petitioned on one condition — the British must leave Chusan. With autumn drawing in and living conditions in Tinghae worsening, such an offer was beginning to sound reasonable.

8

We live among the dead

B Y LATE September of 1840, the fine body of soldiers that had landed in victory only in July had been reduced to a mere shadow. As one naval surgeon recalled: 'Even those we do see under arms have more the appearance of animated corpses than any other thing to which I can liken them.'[1] Of more than 3,500 fighting men only 800 could be mustered. From amongst the Cameronians, scarcely a single man was fit enough to go foraging for food. Some of the high-caste Hindu troops were actually starving to death, unable to cook when weakened by disease and incapable of eating anything prepared by a man of lower caste.[2] The lack of fresh food had got so bad that the spongy gums and bruises of scurvy had begun to show. The cure was understood in the navy, but the army had no tradition of supplementing its land diet with lemon juice and no army had ever starved to death like this. Already more than one hundred soldiers had been buried on an acre of muddy ground below Josshouse Hill. The Royal Navy had taken to burying its dead on the tiny Grave Island in the harbour (rather fittingly, the Chinese called it 'the Rat', after its rodent-like outline). Bodies were forever being rowed over to the sound of *The Dead March*, but funerals were now so frequent that firing parties had been forbidden and ceremonial curtailed.[3] 'Graves are forever open,' wrote one Scot. 'And those who assist in paying the last duties to their ill-fated companions look as if they would soon follow.'[4] 'I would rather spend five years in Bengal on half *batta* than as many months in this most accursed place,' wrote another.[5]

The regimental hospitals set up in Tinghae's public buildings were a heartrending scene as the life of the garrison ebbed inexorably away. Standing in the southeast corner of the city, the former pawnshop that was now a hospital for the Cameronians was crowded with row after row of soldiers, from young drummer-boys to old warhorses, all of them at different stages of dysentery, typhus and cholera[6] and many lying beyond help in their own filth.[7] Men suffering from bloody fluxes did not die wracked with convulsions or with much screaming out in pain. They lay of their own choice close by the open privies, too debilitated to walk far at the constant whim of their bowels. Their glands would enlarge, their feet and abdomen become swollen. Their face would become pale and puffy, with bloodless lips and sunken eyes. If primitive treatments such as calomel, opium, leeches or blood-letting could not tip the balance in favour of the patient he would become emaciated, and his stomach would retract.[8] With a crystal clear intellect he would finally sink and pass away in silence, as if he had fallen asleep from weariness.[9] The results of post-mortems were shocking: the flesh of men's intestines was so perished that they practically fell apart in the surgeons' hands.[10] This was not a matter of *dulcet et decorum est, pro patria mori.* The regiment's Color Serjeant John Henderson wrote to his parents in their Lanarkshire village with palpable sadness:

> We are all tired of war. It might read well in a newspaper at a fireside in Biggar, but what a lot of misery and desolation in this city.[11]

Governor Burrell grumbled that too many of the Cameronians who had died had been allowed to join up underage — they were scarcely out of childhood.[12] In return, it was pointed out that he had long had it in his power to billet them in the many empty houses in the city instead of in tents upon a hillside exposed to drenching dews by night and broiling sun by day.[13] For all the regiments, guard duty and parades were carried out in heavy, woollen uniforms in temperatures nearing one hundred degrees.[14] But for the Cameronians especially, encamped on a hill over a mile from the harbour and with too few Indian camp followers, the daily strain of fetching supplies from their transport ships — theirs alas was the rotten meat and the maggoty biscuit — had taken its toll.[15] By the time the regiment left Chusan barely one of its teenage soldiers would be left alive, and there was anger that they had died through sheer incompetence, sacrificed for fear of inflaming Tinghae's residents. Back in Calcutta, where in Fort William the Cameronians had been stationed before leaving for China, *The Englishman* adopted a scathing line: the policy pursued at Chusan was inexplicable. Burrell had asserted authority over deserted streets, had encamped his men in unwholesome marshes, and seemed to prefer that they fall victims to disease 'rather than that the enemy should suffer any injury!' Chusan, *The Englishman* suggested sarcastically, ought to be rechristened 'Walcheren Secundus' after the Dutch island where thousands of British troops had died of disease during the Napoleonic wars.[16]

There was urgent debate as to what was behind the unprecedented death toll. Nothing was known of bacteria, viruses or amoebae, and it would be half a century before the riddle of malaria was solved. Even officers, who were better nourished than the rank and file, had died, so poor diet alone could not explain the deaths. Many of the top brass, including Governor Burrell himself, were chronically ill. Gützlaff, even with God's protection, was suffering from fever, perhaps because his residence backed onto the stagnant lagoon. It was noticed by the more keen observers that the islanders had a strong aversion to drinking unboiled water, preferring instead a weak infusion of green tea, but few drew the now-obvious conclusion that it was mostly bad water that was to blame.[17]

For the British fighting man of the 1840s, drinking water was pumped for preference from rivers and streams, but if none were to be found then other sources had to do. With few suitable springs on the island, the garrison had no choice but to drink stagnant water pumped by hand from the paddy into storage butts. Even the wells were no better, being mere receptacles for surface run-off rather than sources of clean groundwater (the men of the 1793 embassy had noticed as much). The unexpected invasion of July and the flight of the valley's farmers had cut short the annual draining of the rice fields in preparation for the harvest, and then thousands of army-issue boots had trodden the maturing crop into something resembling marshland. This liquid, contaminated with human faeces that had been spread as fertiliser, was drunk unboiled. Men dehydrated from diarrhoea had only more of the same to slake their thirst. From the first pangs, the surgeon Edward Cree attributed his chronic sickness to the 'dysenteric fluid' he was obliged to take — 'it stinks and is white and flatulent' — but there was nothing else to be had.[18] Sixteen years later in the Crimea, still suffering from the dysentery he had contracted on Chusan, Cree would eventually be invalided out of the Royal Navy. Even the Chinese were suffering — by unhappy coincidence, the summer of 1840 was, after 1822, the worst year for epidemic disease in recent memory.[19]

As for malaria, it was surmised with some justification that exhalations from marshy ground and stagnant water were responsible. Some suspected invisible parasites exposed when soil was excavated; others pointed to Chusan's granite rocks, to the filth on Tinghae's streets, to lightning, to rotting timber, to the mudflats exposed at low tide, the imperfectly buried dead of the Chinese tombs, the stench of the bodies burned below Josshouse Hill, even to the *samshoo* the men drank to dull their senses for a while.[20] Those few officers who enjoyed the luxury of a mosquito net did not do so because of any insight into the transmission of *plasmodium* parasites but solely to spare them the pain of being bitten by the island's giant insects: 'The animals at Chusan are from Brobdingnag!' joked Captain Pears in a letter home,[21] while another officer complained that they were so numerous at night that he awoke looking like a man with smallpox.[22] With no understanding of malaria's true cause, the garrison knew it simply had to await the arrival of winter before cases would begin to fall.

As the weather closed in there was still little prospect of fresh food. The medical advice reaching Governor Burrell was now unanimously in favour of moving the men out of their tents, which were not up to keeping out the cold and damp. At long last, Burrell decided it was time to act on his threat to requisition empty houses.[23] On the first day of October, the Cameronians finally moved down the slope of their hill and into the city. Soon the Hertfordshires too had occupied deserted houses on Tinghae's main street, and the Bengal Volunteers followed.[24] Window-glass being almost unknown in China, men had to be content with paper soaked in oil, a substitute which rapidly dissolved in the rain to allow the cold north wind to blow in.[25]

Once word got out that the British were finally breaking into their homes, a trickle of claimants found its way to the magistracy to complain. Plenty of warning, they were reminded, had been given but they had chosen to forfeit their properties. With many officers deciding that the houses allotted to them were simply unfit to live in — some were little better than tumbledown shacks — some of the more opulent property owners were lucky enough to receive rent of a few dollars each month. Under orders from Governor Burrell, subalterns were limited to renting a single room, and captains a maximum of two, to prevent the wealthy from enjoying better accommodation than their superiors.[26] Yet with grim determination disease went on killing even after the regiments were moved out from under canvas. It was a cruel disappointment. By the end of October a dozen men or more were dying every day. With palpable sadness, on November 6th Karl Gützlaff recorded a grim nadir: fifteen more men had passed away on a single day: 'Indeed we live among the dead,' he wrote.[27]

The Chinese practice of having one's coffin made while still alive, and then stored without a trace of ghoulishness in one's own home, had at first provided the garrison with plenty of hefty firewood.[28] Then, as deaths mounted, orders had been issued not to burn them. Now, when the coffins ran out, bodies were placed in grave pits with a minimum of ceremony. The islanders watched these hurried burials, and word reached all the way to the emperor in Peking. 'They showed very little compassion for the corpses of whites,' wrote one witness, 'and just cast aside the blacks who had died of disease.' What more evidence of the inferiority of these barbarians was needed than their disregard for the dead? Transports were requisitioned to evacuate the chronically sick — two to India with the worst cases, and two more to Manila. Conditions aboard were terrible, with many too weak to climb into their hammocks and lying instead on decks awash with excrement. In Manila the authorities refused these plague ships permission to land, and they headed instead for the British fleet in the South China Sea. By the time all four vessels reached suitable ports, half of the 372 Cameronians aboard them had died, and one third of the Hertfordshires. By the end of the year, one in five of the garrison landed in July was dead, to say nothing of the anonymous Indian servants who went to their graves in simple shrouds followed by crocodiles of shivering mourners. Less than one third of the original 900 Cameronians were still on Chusan, and most of these lay sick in the ill-adapted pawnshop that passed for a regimental hospital. When the space allotted in the muster book to the names of men no longer drawing their pay ran out, somebody gummed in a strip of foolscap. When this was full they started to write on its back. The list finally ended at entry no. 208. Under the heading 'Remarks, explaining the cause' was entered simply the word 'died', while below came columns of unbroken dittoes.[29]

9

A Chinese Singapore

ONE MONDAY morning in late September, HMS *Wellesley* re-entered Tinghae's crowded harbour with the British plenipotentiaries aboard. After six hours of talks on the foreshore of the Peiho with Qishan, [1] the governor-general of the capital province of Zhili which surrounded Peking, Captain Elliot had accepted assurances that British demands — these boiled down to improved trading rights and recompense for the cost of the expedition and for the destroyed opium — would be listened to if he returned to Canton. Though Elliot had left satisfied that the meeting would bear fruit, Qishan had in fact conceded nothing — not on the possible cession of Chusan, nor on the sale of opium in Canton, and especially not on Palmerston's wish for a fortune in compensation.

The Chinese man on the street — then as now — was well attuned to subtle shifts emanating from Peking, and word of the peaceful interview at the Peiho soon trickled down to Zhejiang. [2] The refractory barbarians appeared to have become a little submissive. Though deaths from disease still rose on Chusan, the food situation at least began to improve. At the start of October, two transports arrived laden with sheep and oxen. Before the month was out, men who had been surviving on reduced rations of salt meat would be riding buffaloes bareback through the streets of Tinghae. [3] Four dozen head more would arrive in early November, it having been discovered that a small island off the Korean coast was home to vast herds of cattle, which were now stolen by the British despite their owners' protests. [4] Bum-boats began to enter the harbour to sell fowl to the Royal Navy. The arrival of junks from the mainland set the seal on the changed Chinese policy toward the British: they contained thirty head of oxen, eighty goats and six hundred chickens, a goodwill gift from a mandarin named Yilibu, the governor-general of the Yangtze River provinces of Jiangxi, Jiangsu and Anhui. [5]

Yilibu, by all accounts a rather kindly man in his late sixties, had been given a special commission by the emperor to travel to Ningbo to oversee the military response on the Zhejiang station.

At first, he had been full of grand plans to unseat the barbarians. There could be no pitched sea battle, of that he was sure: even the pride of China's maritime provinces — the 'rice boats' of Canton and the 'weaver's shuttle' boats of Tong'an were less than half the size of a modest British warship and could only carry eight small cannon without sinking.[6] His forces would instead have two goals — burn the ships in Tinghae harbour, and massacre the troops in the city.[7] He would launch feints to distract the British, he boasted, place fifth columnists in Tinghae, pick off their outposts, and then 'tear open their belly'.

On first reaching Ningbo, Commissioner Yilibu had ordered the casting of enormous new cannons. The men at his disposal amounted on paper to 2,000 infantry and 3,000 marines, which was certainly too few to launch his planned attack, but he was still awaiting the arrival of regular Green Standards from the inland provinces. So many thousands of soldiers might at first appear to have been a formidable force, but it is doubtful that the numbers were at all accurate, and even the translations 'infantry' and 'marines' are misleading: the Chinese called them *yong* and *shuiyong* — 'braves' and 'water braves' — and they were mostly farmers or fishermen conscripted from among the Tanka boat people who lived along the coast. The Qing practice of paying such men to fight had its risks: the local mandarins were, after all, arming people who in peacetime they would have thought of as undesirable vagabonds, and thus creating a pool of potential rebels for the future. But it was at least a cheap option, and one which avoided the need for Peking to fund a regular military response, always a slow and expensive process.[8]

As luck would have it, news had just at that moment reached Commissioner Yilibu that Elliot was prepared to talk peace in Canton, and he was spared the ignominy of certain failure. His gift of oxen, goats and chickens was the kind of generous treatment one could expect when one submitted to the emperor's wishes. As for the mandarins who delivered this little fleet of Noah's arks, they had been specially chosen for the task. Headed by Yilibu's most trusted aide, and including a military man to cast an eye over the British force, they sailed back to Yilibu with their impression of the island and its occupiers. On November 1st, Yilibu addressed a proclamation to the natives of Chusan assuring them that the barbarians had been ordered to repair to Canton to have their complaints 'soothed'. Once that little matter was concluded, he told the islanders, the barbarians would not tarry in Tinghae. For their part, the islanders should forget all about the rewards promised for severed heads. Instead, Yilibu insisted, they ought to go back to quietly ploughing their fields and studying their books: 'If the barbarians do not distress you, you must no longer hunt out and seize them!'[9]

Comforted by the news that the rebels were being pacified, Tinghae began to return to something approaching normality. Though the weather took a turn for the worse, with heavy rains turning unpaved roads to mud, a renewed sense of confidence settled on the city. The number of refugees returning increased daily, and people moved about amongst the troops and confidently opened up shop without fear of arrest. But however positive the news of a possible agreement at a political level, the ongoing detention of Captain Anstruther, Anne Noble and the other prisoners remained unresolved. Just days after returning to Chusan from the negotiations in the north, Captain Elliot crossed Kintang Sound for a face-to-face meeting with Commissioner Yilibu to demand their immediate release. His optimistic offer to swap for Anstruther some one hundred junks that had been captured in Chusan's waters was turned down, though a delegation of the junks' captains themselves travelled to Ningbo to argue the case.[10] Yilibu restated the Chinese position — if Elliot wished his friends back he must leave Chusan — while Elliot restated his — release the prisoners and then talks on Chusan could start. But Yilibu quite understandably did not trust the British, and the willingness of their highest officer to negotiate in person only convinced him of the importance of holding tight to his hostages: 'This Anstruther,' he informed Peking, 'must be a man most intimately related to the barbarian chiefs for them to have no choice but to demand his release like this!'

Both sides agreed to observe a truce along the coast (though it proved somewhat wary) pending the Elliots' sailing to Canton to continue the negotiations. The communications now arriving from the Chinese subtly changed: the word 'barbarian' disappeared, and Britain became an 'honoured nation'. The price to be paid for such respectful addresses was the obligation to consider Yilibu's proposal. On November 6th a memorandum was issued on the details of the truce. Occupied territory was defined as comprising all of Chusan and its nearby satellites [11] (this technically included the Buddhist holy island of Putuoshan!), and it was from this provisionally British archipelago that Captain and Admiral Elliot sailed south a week later, bound for Canton.

For the officers and men who remained on Chusan, the truce seemed a bit one-sided. The wily Chinese looked to have duped the Elliots just as they had once palmed off Lord Macartney with blandishments. Gützlaff wrote describing the situation to his good friend and confidante, the trader James Matheson:

> It is a queer truce. There is no open market for our troops on the main, no security to anyone on this island, no release of prisoners, in fact nothing at all except the mere word, and that seems to satisfy our great men. Our soldiers are dying in immense numbers, and the returns daily made of the dead are awful.... My heart grieves at this mere show, I can tell you. [12]

Within days the steamer *Atalanta* was once more circumnavigating the island. Parties were landed along the coast march from village to village, hunting out suitable places for outposts. There was a flurry of construction work around Tinghae. An observatory built on Harbour Point at the foot of 49th Hill allowed the city's position to be established with accuracy and the first scientific survey of the harbour to be completed. [13] The Engineers restarted work on the Josshouse Hill fortifications, repaired bridges destroyed by the retreating Chinese back in July, and raised watchtowers and batteries. [14] Gangs of local men were paid to dredge the city canals. Only now that Elliot was preparing to negotiate the return of Chusan, it seemed, did the garrison make the least show of wanting to keep it. [15]

As Tinghae's population slowly returned it brought not only improved supplies to the markets but also, to Captain Elliot's mind, 'the *dramatis personae* of a thieving, roguish inhabitancy.' [16] 'I have never lived amongst any race of people so addicted to thieving and petty larceny,' complained Gützlaff. [17] Mr Waterhouse, an agent for the trading house of Jardine, Matheson and Co., agreed — all the Chinese did was rob him and pass bad dollars. [18] Having landed his goods, Waterhouse had since been burgled no fewer than five times. Police stations were set up in response to an epidemic of nightly thefts, their patrols regularly arresting thieves who would swiftly be brought before a military court. [19] If found guilty, they would be tied to a wooden frame erected in the city and publicly flogged before having their pigtails cut off close to the head. [20] This last indignity was far worse than the flogging, since the queue, a symbol of Chinese submission to the ruling Manchus, was compulsory for all men and its absence was severely punished by any mandarin who subsequently came across the criminal. 'We are always able to pick out the bad characters afterwards,' wrote an officer of the artillery, unaware perhaps that such convicted men were obliged for their own safety to remain skulking about Tinghae until their hair grew back. [21]

It was not only the Chinese who needed to be kept under control: the British and Indian troops, their numbers terribly depleted, still faced the strain of endless rounds of guard duty, and many looked for temporary escape. Though Governor Burrell had outlawed its sale, smuggled *samshoo* was not hard to come by and courts martial for being drunk on duty were common. [22] Though sentences of 150 lashes were often meted out to the soldiers, their camp followers were quite at liberty to drink themselves insensible if they wished. As the weather worsened, men who had never left the heat of Madras and Bengal felt the cold terribly. Many drank *samshoo* just to keep warm and pilfered padded-cotton uniforms from the captured arsenals, the Chinese character *yong* — 'courageous' — emblazoned incongruously across their slight chests. [23] But for the Chinese who had smuggled the *samshoo* into barracks, the punishments were truly harsh: one man who was caught red-handed with clay jars of *samshoo* hidden inside his voluminous sleeves was given twenty lashes, had his pigtail cut off, and suffered the burning down of his home.[24] The uncomfortable comparison with the British trade in opium must have been quite apparent.

When in late October a fire broke out in a magazine near the beach, the Chinese were blamed, it having been forgotten that drunken British soldiers were quite capable of setting light to the wharves without outside help.[25] Three dozen barrels of ball-cartridge were rolled out by men of the Royal Irish Regiment despite the roof having caved in. Some of the barrels had already been charred, and the Irishmen responded to the fire-drum in the full knowledge that if a single one had exploded they would all have been blown to Kingdom come.[26] Chastened by the near disaster, the regiment moved its powder store to the fort on Josshouse Hill, shrouded it in a heavy tarpaulin, and guarded it around the clock. While no cooking stoves or braziers were allowed anywhere near the magazines, the regulations governing billets were less strict. Almost to a man, the garrison was living in wooden buildings illuminated by candles and warmed, if they were lucky, by coal fires. In early December another blaze burned the Hertfordshires' hospital to the ground.[27] By then, greater numbers of Chinese had returned to live amongst the garrison than at any point since the invasion and, far from the finger of suspicion being pointed at them, they were praised for turning out to help extinguish the flames.[28] Their reaction though was rooted more in self-interest than in concern for the patients — it seemed the fire had already spread to nearby houses. The sick were all carried to safety, and nobody was harmed. Within the month yet another conflagration had destroyed part of Governor Burrell's residence. A near disaster so close to home spurred the governor into action: there was a ban on open fires after curfew, an alarm post was established with a commanding view across the city, and an impromptu fire brigade raised.[29] While rank and file huddled around their braziers and sought ways to escape the tedium as the temperature dropped below freezing, a group of senior officers converted a house on the wharves into a branch of London's fashionable United Service Club.[30] Though it can never have hoped to match the Regency splendour of John Nash's clubhouse on Pall Mall, soon it was at least decently furnished, with carpets and looted ornaments to make it more homely. Here gentlemen would gather to exchange the latest news and to enjoy a rubber of whist over brandy and a cigar. 'But we miss ladies' society very much,' grumbled one.[31]

November of 1840 marked a turning point for Chusan. The weather had started out rainy, the wind swinging between a mild southerly and a bitter northerly, but the drop in temperature had not put an end to the fever.[32] By the end of November, by contrast, the sickness had peaked and provisions were so abundant that soldiers and sailors were eating fresh meat every day. Officers, who were expected to make their own arrangements without the help of the commissariat, were able to hunt game unmolested in the interior or purchase supplies from a Parsee shop in the main street or from the city's thriving markets.[33] There, native copper cash bearing the emperor's name fell out of general use, to be superseded by silver coinage from India and Spain — the Chinese called them the *loopee* and the *tolah*.[34] Tinghae was so crowded as to have earned a bit of a reputation for debauchery,[35] and the arrival in town one day of a man requesting a licence to marry his daughter to an Englishman hinted that not all Anglo-Chinese relations were being conducted at arm's length.[36] Karl Gützlaff was in buoyant mood at the upturn in fortunes, anxious only that calculations were being made far above his head which might yet lead to the evacuation of the island he had for so long been promoting as a colony. He exhorted his close friend in Macao, the influential trader James Matheson, to argue the case for Chusan's retention when the Elliots reached Canton:

> If your opinion is ever asked, do never, on any account, consent to give up our footing in this quarter of the world. How small soever the portion may be, that we are going to possess, you may rely upon it, that a Chinese Singapore will soon make its appearance.[37]

If they decided to surrender such a perfect island, he predicted, the British would 'rue it to the last'.[38]

The celestials wish to measure their strength

WITH A sizeable part of the British force having sailed south with Captain Elliot to make a show of strength on the Pearl River, the truce gave Commissioner Yilibu an excuse to demobilise some of his troops to save money. By mid-November, the number of men defending the Zhejiang coast had been halved to just 5,400. Still, this was twice the strength of the British regiments now facing them across Kintang Sound. There on Chusan, it was only now that the men were in somewhat better health that Governor Burrell found it worthwhile to inspect the Royal Irish, who went through their drills on an extemporised parade ground. He praised their appearance and their healthy condition; the disease that had ravaged them for the past four months, he said, was no longer to be dreaded. Next the Bengal Volunteers and the Madras Artillery were inspected, and the Artillery opened fire for the first time since July 5th, causing a mass panic amongst the several hundred Chinese who had turned out to watch the spectacle. The sight of the smart red uniforms and the roar of the guns must have helped to convince the islanders that the British, though weakened, were still more than capable of holding on to Chusan.[1] Across the water in Zhenhai, the fortified town commanding the river approach to Ningbo, Yilibu was bound to hear of the military manoeuvres, but he wrongly concluded that the barbarians were sabre-rattling over the negotiations in Canton. Though months of hardship had left both sides too weak to go on the offensive, neither trusted the other not to break the uneasy truce. On the mainland, newly-cast iron cannon were broken out of their moulds and test-fired. The first proved to be so badly honeycombed that its breech burst, killing its gun-crew and some mandarins who had assembled to watch.[2] Frustrated, Yilibu ordered a conscription of all Zhejiang's available metalworkers and had them sent to Zhenhai.[3] There they were commissioned to produce sixty guns of some four-and-a-half tons apiece, heavier even than the cannons the Royal Navy had brought to China and, without the technical expertise of the Royal Arsenal at their disposal, sure to fail. From a now bitterly cold Chusan, Gützlaff followed their progress through his network of informants: 'They are completely puerile,' he commented acidly, 'but still the celestials wish to measure their strength.'[4]

One celestial especially wished to do so. On being sent to Zhejiang as a commissioner, Yilibu had handed over his governor-generalship of the three Yangtze provinces to the care of an erudite Manchu named Yuqian, then the governor of neighbouring Jiangsu.[5] Yuqian, a man high in the emperor's personal favour, was said by his contemporaries to be proud and overbearing. By forty he had been a provincial judge, famed and feared for his strict application of the law. The archetype in British eyes of a cruel, scheming mandarin, he was thoroughly convinced of China's cultural superiority and eager to show all barbarians their place. Like Commissioner Yilibu he was unnerved by the military manoeuvres in Tinghae but trusted the British even less. They were to him 'mere bulrushes' to be scythed down. Soon, he boasted, they would be like moths to his flame, fish caught in his nets.[6] He disapproved of the conciliatory approach Qishan and Yilibu were taking, and he set about formulating a plan to retake Chusan by force.

Yuqian might have underestimated the difficulties to be faced, but he knew his history. Japanese 'pirates' had held the island for over a year against Ming troops, and remnants of the Ming had in turn held out for seven years against the Qing. Key to both those protracted occupations had been the village of Sinkong, sitting in its easily defended valley on the west coast. Yuqian proposed ferrying thousands of crack troops there, hidden in the junks which were a common sight on Kintang Sound. From Sinkong they would wage a guerrilla war, attacking by night only to melt away at dawn. The British, he predicted, would get no rest and within a fortnight would up and leave.[7] Yilibu was no less given to bluster, but five months of getting nowhere had dampened his enthusiasm for such fanciful schemes. Yuqian's maritime invasion and guerrilla campaign, he knew, were patently unworkable. Yilibu wrote to Peking with an alternative suggestion: by mid-February he expected to have new cannons with enough range to hit the enemy ships and keep them from approaching the Zhejiang coast. 'But defences can only frustrate an enemy, they cannot break him,' he admitted, and went on to outline a suitably low-key plan of attack. Boats were being prepared, firewood bought up, and local water braves conscripted to burn the British at anchor. 'If my plan fails, we shall not have lost much,' he consoled himself.[8]

It was essential that the British remain totally unaware. Yilibu began giving directions to his underlings face-to-face rather than by the normal system of written orders — he could not risk Governor Burrell getting wind of his incendiary plans. But there were ever Chinese like Blondel de Westa willing to talk for the right price. By late January the whispers in Tinghae were of an imminent fire-attack, and within a week of his committing it to writing in a memorial to Peking Yilibu's plan had been leaked in its entirety. Soon everybody in Tinghae knew that the attempt to burn the fleet was set for January 27th, that divers had been trained to bore holes in the ships' hulls, and that junks were being readied to land a force on the north coast. What sounded like the boom of gunnery practice from across the water only added to the sense of threat.[9] The *Rattlesnake* was sent out to look for signs of the anticipated invasion, and the navy kept its guns shotted in readiness. But the attack never came. Spies reported that press-ganged sailors had run away rather than face the British.[10] The plan had scarcely been more than a way of keeping the emperor happy, and one might doubt whether even Yilibu himself had believed in it.

The arrival of 1841 had been celebrated in rather low-key fashion in Tinghae's United Service Club,[11] but Chinese New Year was meant to be an altogether more joyous occasion. Only then the rumours of a fire-attack had coincided with the annual New Year migration to the ancestral villages to leave the city as desolate as it had been for months.[12] Shutters were pulled across the shopfronts, homes were locked up.[13] For ten days the markets were bare. Soldiers exchanged anxious glances, fearful that the privations of the autumn might return. Cold and hungry, they set about pulling down empty houses with renewed vigour to provide fuel for their braziers. The Chinese who did remain began the celebrations on the last day of the old Year of the Rat, sending it off in a riot of gongs and firecrackers. The atmosphere must have turned sombre when later that evening each family sat down around the hearth to welcome the spirits of their ancestors to feast with them. How could they apologise enough, when they had suffered their graves to be desecrated? At midnight, while the British slept, doors and windows all over Chusan were flung open to allow the old year out and the new one in. Spring couplets were pasted up, those great strips of red paper proclaiming a new season of hope. Words and deeds on New Year's Day would set the tone for the rest of the year, and this year more than ever demanded punctilious observance. Perhaps somebody twelve months ago had absent-mindedly uttered the word for 'four' and brought its homophone — death — to bear on the household? Had somebody swept the coming year's good fortune out of the front door? Could the accidental stroke of a knife on the first day of the first month have cut short the family's luck? Maybe, by an unprec-edentedly lavish celebration, the gods of heaven and earth might banish the barbarians in this Year of the Ox. February 6th saw the end of the festivities, when the full moon in the heavens was mimicked on earth with spherical paper lamps. The British paid little heed to the heathen customs. Even the observant Edward Cree managed just a short entry: 'Chinese feast of lanterns. At night all round the islands hundreds of lanterns and plenty of crackers.'[14] The very practices of the Chinese New Year in all their superstitious detail showed the yawning cultural chasm between the British and their nominal subjects to be as wide as ever it had been. Though none of the Tinghaenese sitting down before the family hearth that New Year's Eve yet knew it, it was events in distant Canton rather than their own religious observances that would decide their island's fate, for Captain Elliot's patience with Qishan had by that time run out.[15]

In the decades before diplomacy could rely on intercontinental telegraphy to brief its men in the field, and at a time when a fruitful exchange of letters with Whitehall might take seven or eight months, a plenipotentiary acting for Her Majesty was given written instructions and granted the freedom to negotiate within certain parameters. Lord Palmerston's instructions to Elliot had required compensation — for the destroyed opium, for the cost of the expedition, and for all debts due from bankrupt Chinese merchants while he was about it — and the throwing open of ports in Eastern China to British trade. As for Chusan, the island was to be kept at least until the compensation had been paid and, if Elliot could manage it, permanently retained just as Gützlaff had recommended. Palmerston had granted Elliot the flexibility, if the Chinese steadfastly refused to give up Chusan, to swap possession of it for a grant of territory on the mainland. Yet when negotiations got underway on the Pearl River below Canton, the opening bid from the Chinese — $5,000,000 in compensation for the opium, official intercourse on an equal footing without the constant implication that the British were inferiors, and improved trading conditions — was far below Palmerston's bottom line. As the talks progressed, it struck the plenipotentiary that only by a resumption of all-out war might the Chinese be forced to meet Palmerston's demands in full. It would be better, Elliot was convinced, to take what he could than to restart the conflict and so throw trade with China once more into turmoil. Might not improved trade quietly and with time win for Britain the advantages Palmerston desired? By the start of January 1841 Elliot had resolved to lower his demands for compensation if the Chinese would agree to cede Chusan, yet still the right even to trade there was jealously refused. Nothing seemed to have changed since the days when Allen Catchpoole and the East India Company had been sent away with a flea in their ear. For the Celestial Empire, the evacuation of Chusan was to be a symbol of Britain's status as an obedient vassal.

On January 5th, tiring of Qishan's prevarication, Elliot ordered the Royal Navy to flex its muscles by destroying the forts commanding the entrance to the Pearl River. Believing these to be impregnable, the Chinese were stunned when they were effortlessly shelled into rubble and captured by infantry. The next day, as Elliot's warships moved against a second line of forts, the shocked Chinese called for a ceasefire. Deploring the slaughter, Elliot agreed to restart negotiations. Now that his willingness to use force could not be doubted, it took less than a fortnight for a settlement to be agreed: the sparsely populated island of Hong Kong, strategically placed at the mouth of the Pearl River and long appreciated for its excellent harbour, would be ceded to the Crown as a trading station; a $6,000,000 indemnity would be paid for the opium; official intercourse between the two nations would from now on be carried on as between equals, and trade would restart in Canton on a secure footing. In return, Chusan was to be evacuated, and the steamer *Columbine* was duly sent north to inform Governor Burrell.

Captain Elliot was aware from the beginning that he had settled for far less than Lord Palmerston had demanded of him. The foreign secretary had stressed to him the importance of the Chusan archipelago: 'It is the intention of Her Majesty's Government,' he had made clear, 'that the Chusan Islands shall be retained until everything shall be satisfactorily settled by the Chinese Government.'[16] One condition of their military evacuation, he had explained, would likely be that some settlement for British subjects be granted, much like the Portuguese in Macao — in effect a permanent extraterritorial presence. Palmerston, of course, had never ventured within 5,000 miles of Chusan, and had based his choice on the informed opinions of men like Karl Gützlaff and his correspondent in Macao, the trader James Matheson, in whom he had great personal confidence. Though the final choice of island would rest with Elliot, Palmerston's express preference had been for the island of Chusan itself rather than one of its smaller satellites (and 'smaller' was a relative concept — half a dozen of those outlying islands rivalled Hong Kong in extent). Before the outbreak of violence, Elliot had wholeheartedly concurred with Palmerston. In February of 1840 he had written from Macao:

For permanent settlement, I still believe an insular station... is the safest course, and the more I consider the subject, the more does the impression fix itself upon me, that one of the Chusan group will present the greatest advantage for that purpose.[17]

From there, British manufactures would flow down the Yangtze to countless millions of consumers. In his mind's eye, even Captain Elliot had pictured the Union Jack flying at the peak of an island he had yet to see:

> With a British possession on one of the Chusan islands, and the Emperor's permission that his people may trade with us there, I am sure that Her Majesty's Government will be satisfied: It will have gained enough. To declare it a Free Port for the ships of all nations, with the establishment of moderate and liberal tariffs, would no doubt be the earliest measure of the Government; and I believe it is not too much to predicate of such a possession on such a footing, that it must soon come to be the very first commercial station in Asia, and very probably one of the very first in the world.[18]

And once he had seen it, Elliot's considered opinion of Chusan was even more positive:

> Nothing can be more delightful than the climate, or more perfectly beautiful than the country. The hills are cultivated with the most exact garden husbandry to the very summits, and the verdure is brilliant. It is not a rich woodland country, but neither is the landscape bare of trees, and taken altogether it certainly is as fair a scene as ever the eye rested upon. If we can but hold this place we will make a second Havanah of it in three years, with the difference that it will be a delightful retreat for mere purposes of change of climate and recreation.[19]

But then had started the messy business of dealing with the infuriating Chinese, and Elliot's naive hopes of simply landing upon Chusan and turning it into a model colony had been dashed. Before he had even left Chusan to negotiate at the mouth of the Peiho, he had privately arrived at the opinion that British interests might be better served by accepting less than Palmerston had wanted.[20] Yes, Chusan's geographical position was perfect, but it had a large native population alienated by the incompetence of invasion and misrule, and, Elliot was sure, 'no country is worth holding against the good will of the peasantry.' Sickness had soon left fewer than 1,200 men fit to defend the island, and Governor Burrell had made it clear that he might find it difficult to repel a concerted Chinese attack. A recourse now to yet more violence to force the Chinese into accepting every last one of Palmerston's demands ran counter to Elliot's compassionate nature. It was, Elliot believed, 'a war in which military success must be dearly purchased.' Victory on Palmerston's terms would only come 'with the slaughter of an almost defenceless and helpless people.' It is hard, after the conflicts of our own time with their 'collateral damage' to civilians, not to feel sympathy for Elliot's decisions. But such humanity was perhaps not the character trait Palmerston had hoped would predominate in a leader entrusted with a costly show of overwhelming strength. Faced with a confusion of assurances and threats, of peace offers and promises of improved conditions, Elliot chose a recommencement of trade and access to Hong Kong over possession of Chusan and the risk of more destruction.

When news of the peace settlement reached Zhejiang, it filled Commissioner Yilibu with relief. As reports of the fighting in Canton had filtered back to Peking, the edicts issuing from the Forbidden City had become frantic, and Yilibu had been presented with direct orders to invade Chusan and unseat the British.[21] No more failures would be tolerated! Yet when Yilibu wrote back to Peking, it was with a tangibly desperate insistence that he was unable to obey — he simply had too few ships and sailors even to attempt a landing.[22] For months he had been sailing perilously close to the wind with his abortive invasion plans, and disobedience now would have guaranteed an appointment with the Imperial Strangler had peace not broken out.

And so it was with palpable relief that Yilibu and Governor Yuqian began to prepare for the handover. In long and jingoistic memorials to Peking they began to brag of how their great armies were putting pressure on the barbarians upon Chusan, ready to destroy them if they tarried. They claimed to have had 10,000 *liang* of silver — some 820 lbs — smuggled onto the island to buy the loyalty of village braves. If the barbarians proved perfidious, they would rise up all around Tinghae to defeat them![23] Anstruther and the others would be paraded before an army of liberation and beheaded to spur them on! It was just what the emperor had wanted to hear.

The *Columbine* steamed into Tinghae harbour, and for a week the city and wharves were a scene of frenzied preparations.[24] The men rolled up their mattresses, packed away their kit, stripped their billets of souvenirs, and soon regimental baggage was piled high on the quayside. The arsenals were emptied and the hospitals decommissioned, their medical stores shared out and their sick carried aboard ship. The observatory was dismantled and the Chusan United Service Club held its last meeting.[25] The Chusan Police Force was thanked for its good work and stood down. The bakery was closed (it had been providing bread baked using wheat freshly ground by oxen upon some dozen millstones), as was the garrison's slaughterhouse.[26] Re-embarkation began in earnest on February 17th, with the Royal Irish boarding the *Rattlesnake* at dawn. The richer officers bade farewell to their landlords, who would sorely miss their rent. And most importantly, a steamer was despatched to demand that Captain Anstruther, Anne Noble and the other prisoners be released.

On February 23rd, a Chinese deputation sailed proudly out of Ningbo port. When its junks reached Tinghae harbour the next day, a general named Zheng Guohong entered the city with a body of junior officers to accept the formal handover in the Temple of the God of Wealth.[27] The remaining guards were stood down (reportedly prompting a riot of looting at the Confucius Temple where confiscated property was still piled high),[28] British troops marched out of the south gate in crimson ranks, and at noon the next day the Union Jack was struck.[29] Anne Noble meanwhile had awoken to her attendant's cries of 'Zhenhai! Chusan!' and an explanation from the comprador Bu Dingbang that she was to be freed. The prisoners were assembled from their places of incarceration and marched by torchbearers between ranks of

Chinese soldiers and past great crowds who had gathered to see them,[30] and then the Europeans were placed in palanquins to be carried the ten miles to the coast. They were breakfasted, and Anstruther was introduced for the first time to Commissioner Yilibu. The old man informed Anstruther that Chusan was to be evacuated right away, and that he had a great army ready to take the island back. At dawn the prisoners, thirty-seven in all, caught sight of an English vessel, and soon Chusan itself became visible through the sea mist. The waterfront had changed dramatically since Anstruther and Anne had last seen it: the acres of white canvas covering the hills and the paddy had disappeared and the wharves had been cleared of rubble. As the bands on the transports struck up *Rule Britannia*, a gig from HMS *Blonde* conveyed Anne, Anstruther and the rest aboard.[31] Anne, despite her bereavement and her frail state of health (she was by now seven months pregnant), rejoiced in her liberty and only expressed her constant thankfulness to God for his mercy.[32] She strikes one as a woman of the most immense faith and courage. Just as they had when HMS *Wellesley* had led the first assault eight months earlier, cheers rang out from the soldiers as they set sail for the south.[33] This time, though, they were cheers of relief.

Soothing the sores and bruises

THOUGH THEY were unaware, Captain Anstruther, Anne, and the other thirty-five prisoners had only narrowly escaped a horrific fate: Yuqian (the mild-mannered Yilibu was less inclined to such barbarity) had been in deadly earnest when he had boasted of plans to execute them to inspire the troops. But Captain Stead of the transport ship *Pestonjee Bomanjee* knew nothing of Chusan's evacuation when a month later he landed at Kittow Point on the nearby mainland, hoping to learn something of the fleet's whereabouts. Instead he was seized and taken to Zhenhai where Yuqian, his ambition to drive the barbarians into the sea foiled by their peaceful departure, declared him guilty of rebelling against the emperor and sentenced him to die by *lingchi*. Tied to a stake, Stead's limbs were slowly cut off before finally he was beheaded. His severed head was displayed in a cage, 'to raise morale and gladden men's hearts' as Yuqian would later boast. When two crewmen from the opium clipper *Lyra* were captured ashore not far away, Yuqian decided on an even more sadistic demonstration of his hatred of these barbarians. The twenty-eight-year-old ship's mate was bound to a stake, the skin from the tips of his thumbs, up his arms, and across his shoulders and back flayed off in a single strip, apparently just to provide Yuqian with a new horse bridle. Slowly dismembered by *lingchi*, his head was then displayed to the troops. The other crewman, an Indian nicknamed 'China' for his knowledge of the language, was already dead from the beating his captors had doled out, but still his head was placed in a cage. For the 'white barbarian', the captors had earned $200; for the 'black barbarian' $100. Yuqian had been looking forward to executing Anstruther and offering his entrails as a sacrifice to the spirits of China's war dead, but Yilibu had hurried the prisoners back to Chusan, foreseeing the devastation that would be unleashed by British warships if this hothead succeeded. Still, the gaol in Ningbo held traitors whom Yuqian might yet make examples of.[1]

One, Yu Guozhen, had been a doctor in Tinghae. He had fled when the British arrived, but in late August had crept back into the city to look around. There Gützlaff had persuaded him to sketch a map of how to reach Ningbo, promising to pay $10 if he would go there and return with news. This Yu had done, consigning what he had learnt to paper. But Gützlaff had in the meantime been taken ill and, on his return, Yu could not deliver the letter. His behaviour had aroused suspicion, and he had been caught red-handed with his accounts of Chinese troop movements. Yu Xiuqing was also a doctor, and come August he too had re-entered Tinghae. Paid handsomely to copy out Governor Burrell's proclamations in Chinese, his unexpected wealth had similarly betrayed him, and he had been bound and spirited away to Ningbo. A third man, Yang Jianting, had been a teacher in Tinghae. One week after Anstruther's disappearance it had been Yang who provided Gützlaff with a lead. Promised $50 if he could produce the suspected kidnappers, Yang had led a party of soldiers to Qingling village. Eleven of the kidnappers' family had been taken into custody, but they themselves had escaped and Yang was given just $12 and a few items of confiscated clothing by way of a reward. Perhaps it was these that cast suspicion upon him. Along with the kidnapped comprador Bu Dingbang, all three were now executed and their heads exhibited beside a placard warning others not to make the same mistake.

Less than a week after Chusan's liberation, a Bureau for Reconstruction was set up in Zhejiang with Yuqian at the reins. Magistrate Shu Gongshou of Ningbo, the man who had successfully managed the refugee crisis as it swept over his city, was made civil magistrate of Tinghae. For his endless dilly-dallying and his failure to recapture Chusan, a disgraced Yilibu was stripped of his position in the emperor's inner circle and of the double-eyed peacock feather which had adorned his mandarin's cap. Impeccable behaviour for eight years, he was told, might see him once more in favour. The island's gentry, in recognition of the resistance they had led, were rewarded with an increase in the annual quota of degree candidates the island could put forward for the civil service examinations — the future prospects for their sons looked bright.[2] For the moment, however, through

Chinese eyes eight months of foreign rule had left Tinghae in a parlous state.[3] The rice in the granaries had been squandered, the city walls were in disrepair, temples and schools had been torn down, fields and market gardens trampled underfoot. The final reckoning was 1,257 houses destroyed. 'There is scarcely a chicken or a dog to be found,' lamented Yuqian, 'and soothing the sores and bruises will not be easy.'[4]

He began to soothe those sores and bruises by commanding the mass reburial of the human remains from the destroyed cemetery on Josshouse Hill:

> The unearthed bones of the island people are scattered in confusion like the stars in the sky, and even the most filial and compassionate of their descendants cannot determine whose are whose.

'I cannot help my heart breaking and my eyes filling with tears of sadness to think of how my innocent children have endured such bitter poison,' the emperor added in his own hand to Yuqian's memorial. As for the barbarian invaders, although some of their graves had been dug barely a fortnight earlier, Yuqian had sent orders that they be disinterred, dismembered as criminals, and tossed into the sea to placate the spirits of the Chinese tombs they had disturbed.[5] When six crates of Christian tracts were discovered in Gützlaff's erstwhile home, they were publicly burned.[6] A final and unintended slight was Yuqian's description of Gützlaff's staunchly Protestant treatises as 'the evil teachings of Roman Catholicism — those wild and fabulous stories not found in the Confucian canon.'[7]

A board of commission sent from the provincial capital Hangzhou assessed compensation claims and distributed funds for rebuilding — from the remains of walls and the number of broken tiles it was estimated how many rooms the vanished buildings had contained.[8] But rebuilding homes was just one pressing task; these particular barbarians now had a history of submitting to their masters only to turn violent: 'If we are not very strenuous in our exertions, they will make of Chusan another Hong Kong,' Yuqian argued in a memorial to Peking, and he began the fortification of the island.[9] Where Captain Pears' Madras Engineers had cut short their work, the fortification of Josshouse Hill was completed. As a matter of urgency Yuqian ordered the construction of a three-mile-long earth wall along the shoreline of the harbour, an enormous undertaking carried out behind a screen of junks for fear that opium clippers might espy the goings-on.[10] As destitute refugees trickled back in the weeks following the British withdrawal, their numbers would reach a staggering 35,000, and it was from these that Yuqian found his labourers. At first, women, children, the elderly and the infirm were all exempted, yet their willingness to toil in the rain and mud in exchange for copper cash and a modicum of future protection was such that Yuqian could soon boast of startling progress.

When finished, the wall dominated the foreshore, a great platform of pounded earth and stone some fifteen yards thick at its base and sixteen feet high, faced with wide battlements that could shelter several hundred guns. Two sally ports — they were optimistically named 'Enduring Peace' and 'Long-lasting Governance' — were now the only means of passage from the landing stages into the vale of Tinghae beyond.[11] The building of this vast rampart left little of the once-bustling commercial wharves, save for a few temples and large houses which now became barracks. To Yuqian's mind, their destruction marked the removal of a community which for too long had offered succour to foreign ships. He explained his actions to Peking:

Under the Kangxi Emperor, the red-haired barbarians were permitted to trade in Tinghae. This long ago ceased, but the quays were still commonly known as the Red Hair Wharf, while the remains of the foreign factory lay close by. For nine years now, their ships have each summer appeared off Zhejiang, selling opium to the boat people who live on the quays in exchange for fresh water and livestock. For this reason, I have torn down the Red Hair Wharf and removed all trace of the factory. If outside the wall they find nothing, this will stifle the barbarians' covetous desires.[12]

As March of 1841 drew to a close, Yuqian set foot on Chusan in person for the first time. A tour of inspection satisfied him that reconstruction was progressing smoothly. Three hand-picked and seasoned generals had arrived on Chusan and were busily preparing their respective regiments for the island's defence.[13] The first, Ge Yunfei, had stepped into the role of general of the Tinghae station left vacant by the death of General Zhang the previous year. General Ge was a native of the ancient city of Shaoxing, just eighty miles distant and close enough for him to feel a local affinity for Chusan. Born in 1789, the son of an officer stationed on the nearby Grand Canal, he was always destined for the army: his family told of how his birth had been marked by a cloud shaped like a military banner descending into the room. One day while out hunting his father had passed him his full-sized bow. Despite its enormous draw-weight, Yunfei had notched up six hits out of six. Throughout his career, if his eulogies are to be believed, Ge remained a man of simple pleasures, dressing and eating like an impoverished scholar, but a strict disciplinarian who had once whipped a soldier so hard for stealing a single taro root that the man's wounds bled. Ge had earned a special reputation for capturing pirates, a favourite trick of his being to disguise a war junk as a defenceless honeypot to entice an attack. Zhejiang's buccaneers, it was reputed, had a saying: 'Nobody encounters Ge and lives to tell the tale!'

The second of Yuqian's three chosen generals was Wang Xipeng. Wang was a northerner, a native of Peking, and an experienced soldier: in 1826 he had been awarded a peacock feather for helping to take the restive Muslim oases of Kashgar, Yengisar, Kargilik and Hotan on the farthest fringes of Chinese Turkestan. By 1832, a campaign to crush rebellious Miao tribespeople in remote Hunan had earned Wang a promotion and the Manchu title of *batulu* — 'courageous soldier'. Called upon to put down a rising of the Yao tribespeople, come 1838 he was a fully fledged general with a reputation for pacifying non-Han rebels. The old warhorse must have relished the prospect of teaching the people of upstart Yingjili a lesson in obedience. The third, General Zheng Guohong, had already dealt with the British face to face, as it was he who had formally accepted the surrender of the island back in February. A professional soldier from the inland province of Hunan, he too had made a name for himself fighting the Miao there. His father had been killed by rebellious tribesmen, and Wang was doubtless eager to avenge his death on these seaborne barbarians.

This trio of generals now set about leading their regiments on manoeuvres across the island until they were intimately familiar with the lie of the land, and were able — so they claimed — to roam the hills from memory in the dark.[14] Their men's uniforms and weapons had been begged and borrowed from across the province and were still too few, but the local commissariat was rushing to provide more. Where Tinghae's arsenals had once been filled with rusty old cannon, twenty newly-cast bronze pieces had now arrived, as had a consignment of gingals all the way from Henan province hundreds of miles inland. More were expected to follow. Native fishermen and skilled boatmen up from Fujian province had been given tabards and commissioned as water braves. Fire-rafts were on standby. Soon the village gentry would raise a militia to rival Yuqian's 6,000 regular troops; the most upright of them would even be entrusted with matchlock muskets.[15] When Yuqian sailed back to the mainland, the irascible old Manchu cast a romantic eye over the scenery:

> I spent the whole of the voyage looking at the sea. The hills and islets were so elegant and beautiful, the merchants and the fishermen contentedly employed.[16]

Though he admitted himself ashamed at having failed to affix George Burrell's severed head to a spike, the barbarians had been duly pacified and everything was in order.

12

We read this with fast-falling tears

EVERYTHING MIGHT have been in order from the vantage point of Ningbo or Peking, but 18,000 miles' sailing away in London there was dismay at the outcome of the Pearl River talks. When Lord Palmerston learned that Captain Elliot had swapped possession of Chusan for Hong Kong (his view of Hong Kong as 'a barren island with hardly a house upon it' had of course been formed not from personal experience and would soon change for the better) he was livid: it was not up to the Chinese to decide which island Britain may have — the Royal Navy might take any it wished! Viscount Melbourne's government had provided a large and costly military force, and Palmerston had made his instructions clear. These had been decided upon not willy-nilly but on expert advice, the intention being to bypass the labyrinth of vested interests that had frustrated British trade in China since the 1600s. Instead, Elliot had allowed the Chinese to wallow in the luxury of their obsolete world view. If British demands had been driven firmly home with gunpowder and shells and had yet failed, then maybe Elliot would have been justified in accepting less. Even then, Palmerston fumed, he ought to have referred home for permission to deviate from his instructions. The army and navy had achieved their aim of taking Chusan without loss, and they were powerful enough to hold on to it as long as they chose. Six million dollars was far short of the value of the opium destroyed, and Elliot had not even bothered, it seemed, to insist the Chinese underwrite the cost of the war. And where was the anticipated treaty, ratified by the emperor himself? Without this, even Hong Kong's status as sovereign territory was uncertain. Palmerston was scathing:

> Throughout the whole course of your proceedings, you seem to have considered that my instructions were waste paper, which you might treat with entire disregard, and that you were at full liberty to deal with the interests of your country according to your own fancy.[1]

Hong Kong might, Palmerston admitted, prove its worth with time, but still Elliot had failed to secure that vital opening for trade on the east coast that had been expected of him. By the end of April he had been recalled, and a new broom had swept through the top rank of Britain's commanders on the China station. There was to be a second military expedition to China, and this time Lord Palmerston did not expect it to return empty-handed.

Captain Elliot's replacement as Britain's plenipotentiary, the man chosen to press Palmerston's demands once more upon the Chinese, was one Sir Henry Pottinger. And where Elliot was a 'tender-hearted avoider of casualties',[2] Sir Henry Pottinger was a blunt Ulsterman of fifty-one with three decades of service in the Bombay army behind him. It would fall now to Pottinger to decide where and for how long talks should proceed, and at what point of deadlock they should be called off and the powder kegs broken open. Chusan, Palmerston offered by way of guidance, was to be retaken before Pottinger sent a communiqué to the Chinese announcing his readiness to negotiate. If negotiations failed and war became necessary, Pottinger had no authority to rein in his military forces until the emperor had acceded to every one of his demands. He could accept nothing less than the permanent cession of an island on the east coast — it was naturally assumed that this would be Chusan — or else its equivalent in the right to live and trade at a handful of ports from Amoy northward. As for Hong Kong, months had passed since Palmerston's first, angry reaction, and the foreign secretary now conceded that it had the potential to be an important trading station — the island should be retained unless Pottinger could wrest from China another, closer still to Canton.[3] But Palmerston's flexibility on the equivalence of possessing Chusan and being allowed to trade at coastal ports was not without its critics: George Eden for one, who as governor-general of India had been closely involved in the military preparations for Elliot's China expedition, was of the opinion that gaining access to northern ports, where the Chinese authorities would doubtless make life difficult, would be scant compensation for missing out on sovereignty of an impregnable island such as Chusan.[4]

In June of 1841, Sir Henry Pottinger left for the Far East with Sir William Parker, now Britain's naval commander in China following the retirement through ill-health of Admiral Sir George Elliot. A new commander-in-chief of Britain's land forces, too, had by then already arrived, despatched when it was learned what a mess the feverish old George Burrell had made of Chusan. Burrell's replacement was Sir Hugh Gough, a white-haired old veteran of Wellington's Peninsular War. His appointment was greeted with applause by the British press in India, whose editorials had sniped from the sidelines as the occupation of Tinghae had degenerated into farce.[5]

Her Majesty's 55th Regiment of Foot ('a wildish set of Irish boys but good fighting men,'[6] they were nicknamed the Westmorelands after the county the regiment hailed from in north-west England) had been hoping to sail home from India after two decades spent serving overseas. Though they had already proved their colonial mettle by defeating the Kaffirs on the banks of Africa's Mtata River and the opulently named Rajah of Coorg in southern India,[7] the widespread sickness on Chusan now meant that their numbers were needed to bolster Sir Henry Pottinger's China expedition. As Yuqian began work fortifying Tinghae harbour, the Westmorelands exchanged their old flintlock muskets for the latest in percussion-cap technology, waved farewell to their wives and children, and in late May sailed down Calcutta's Hooghly River bound for the new British possession of Hong Kong.[8] There they joined the Cameronians, the Hertfordshires, the Royal Irish and the Madras Engineers and Artillery (this last regiment under the command of none other than Captain Anstruther, fully recovered now from his incarceration in Ningbo), all of them veterans of the first occupation of Chusan, along with a body of Madras Native Infantry. On August 21st the fleet sailed from Hong Kong with HMS *Wellesley* at its head and a swarm of transports and colliers at its heels. It was an enormous show of military strength. In Singapore, the *Free Press* newspaper observed confidently that 'Chusan is to be retaken and occupied.

Of course the whole archipelago will fall under our rule.'[9] On the 25th, the most powerful body of China's imperial government, the Council of State, passed an edict to Yuqian and to Liu Yunke, governor of Zhejiang province. It was the emperor's opinion, they wrote, that Zhejiang was now sufficiently well defended.[10] His majesty had been assured that there were 15,000 men and 400 officers in Tinghae and the nearby harbours, enough to ensure that the rebels would not dare to come plundering again.

Northward of the port city of Amoy (where a naval bombardment and a landing by the Royal Irish swept aside the recently strengthened defences) the monsoon faltered, and soon the expedition was struggling its way up the Strait of Formosa, the rain lashing down on the decks and the sails tested to their limits. Creeping up the Zhejiang coast to Kittow Point, landing parties had time to take revenge on the murder of Captain Stead and the unexplained disappearance of the *Lyra*'s crewmen by burning villages scattered along the coastal valleys and putting one town to the torch. When local braves challenged them, they shot and killed two men. Had they known the grisly fates of the *Lyra*'s crew they might not have stopped at that. When word of the violence reached Yuqian, the only reason he could see for a landing at such a remote spot was that the approaches to Chusan were clearly visible from its hilltops.[11] Could the rebellious British, so recently pacified by Qishan in Canton, really be thinking of attacking the island again?

Within a week of announcing its presence with burnings and shootings, the British fleet had once more assembled just fifteen miles from Tinghae. Sailing ahead aboard the iron paddle-steamer *Nemesis*,[12] Captain Pears of the Madras Engineers caught a glimpse of the fortifications his men had begun on Josshouse Hill.[13] They had evidently been 'touched up and beautified' by the Chinese since February. And was that a line of batteries running along the harbour? It grew dark and he could not tell. But no attack could be considered without knowing what awaited the troops, and late the next morning Captain Pears was invited to join Sir Henry Pottinger and the commanders of his sea and land forces, Parker and Gough, to cast an expert eye over Yuqian's work.

From the deck of the steamer *Phlegethon* it took no expert engineer to assess the transformation of the waterfront: on the slopes of 49th Hill two batteries had been built (they were empty but it could only be a matter of time before they were armed), and behind these sat three curious, white, pepperpot-shaped structures — they turned out to be some manner of signalling beacon — and a fortified barracks that might hold 400 men. As *Phlegethon* and *Nemesis* played follow-my-leader into the middle of the harbour, the alarm was sounded and the guns on the earth wall opened fire. Parker counted the muzzle flashes: of 267 embrasures, just 95 held a weapon.[14] It being standard practice in the Chinese military to strap cannon horizontally to their carriages, allowing for no possibility of elevation or aiming, every last shot fell short. The British had openly criticised them for such ignorance of gunnery, yet the celestials, it seemed, would not be told.

The next day was filthy — cold, rainy, and very windy — and the planned recce of the troops said to be encamped at Zhenhai across Kintang Sound was cancelled. The day after that turned out to be even worse, and so the planned razing of the barracks on 49th Hill was postponed, *Nemesis* contenting herself with dropping a few shells into its courtyard instead by way of target practice.[15] Only on the 29th did the wind drop to leave just the cold and the rain. Sir Hugh Gough, his mind on a long and peaceful occupation and acutely aware that Sir George Burrell had a year earlier captured only an empty city with an army drunk on *samshoo*, dictated his orders for the coming assault.[16] This time, he hoped, 'no single instances of misconduct will call for reproof.' As Tinghae would be held for the present by the British 'and perhaps permanently retained', it was essential that the inhabitants be encouraged to remain in their houses and look to his troops for protection. All public property would be secured for the Crown, and all private property was to be respected.[17] The tone of Gough's pronouncement left the men of the expedition in no doubt that British rule was to be quite unlike the charade they had witnessed the previous year.

The fleet stood in closer to Tinghae harbour. All that day and throughout the next night the hills echoed to the sound of cannon fire from along the shore, though not one shot struck home. The British commanders had seen all they needed to, and a plan of attack was finalised. Though the islanders' extraordinary exertions had rendered a frontal assault on the wall too dangerous to consider, they had failed to protect their flanks. Weeks of toil had resulted in an earthwork that was superficially forbidding but militarily useless, just like the cannons strapped immobile to their carriages or the frightening faces painted on the braves' shields. Gough briefed his men: the first column to land would simply scale 49th Hill, turn east, and take the wall from behind. The weather had cleared somewhat when, come dawn, a battery of howitzers was dug in on the peak of Trumball Island, but by then a mist had risen and the skies had again opened. Orders were issued for a landing the next morning, and the defensive works on 49th Hill were pounded with explosive shells: there was no point in risking the lives of the men who would be fighting their way up the slope the following day. As daylight faded, the Royal Navy took up its positions, and at sunset a large body of Chinese appeared on the heights to fire their obsolete matchlocks.[18]

Although the sun rose unseen behind low cloud, Friday, October 1st 1841 turned out to be rather warmer than previous days.[19] The morning mist was soon dispersed by a brisk north-easterly, but still showers moistened the granite slopes and the scrub blanketing 49th Hill. At 8am, *Nemesis* and *Phlegethon* began to embark troops, and soon their decks were crowded with men in their smart uniforms: black coal-scuttle helmets, red jackets criss-crossed with bright white leather, and blue trousers. Each carried a musket fixed with a glinting bayonet. Behind each of the steamers came a train of twenty or more ship's boats, each crammed so full with redcoats that their sailors struggled to work the oars. For two hours while the steamers battled against the tide, the Chinese kept up a constant fire from the shore, but still not a single shot struck home — that much is clear from the military reports sent back to London. At last the rowing boats were cast off. On cue, the howitzers on Trumball opened up, sending shells arcing high into the air to explode squarely in the temple fort 700 yards away.

The Westmorelands were first to land, then the Royal Irish and the Madras Native Infantry, and as they waded ashore and readied themselves to advance a barrage of Congrève rockets from the harbour screeched into the Chinese soldiers gathered above. Viewed from the safety of the harbour, the British soon became just lines of red dots, irresistibly creeping up the slope toward the blue-jacketed Chinese. With the two sides closing, the inaccuracy of the Green Standards' matchlocks was becoming less of a handicap, and as the vanguard neared the summit the British took their first casualty. Ensign Richard Duell had been promoted from sergeant major only the previous night, toasted and wished a long life, and had been delighted to have the honour of carrying the regiment's colours into battle.[20] It was rare for a man who had enlisted as a common soldier to become a commissioned officer like this. Sir Hugh Gough too was hit in the shoulder by a spent ball, though he pronounced himself little hurt.

Just a stone's throw from the Chinese line now, the Westmorelands prepared to charge with their bayonets. Seeing perhaps that the British standard-bearer had fallen, Ensign Duell's opposite number stood unflinchingly before the advance.[21] Shouting to his comrades to press forward, he waved a great banner to and fro above his head as musket balls flew past him. Attracting the attention of the ships riding below, he became an easy target for two gun crews who fired within a split second of each other. One shot ploughed up the earth at the man's feet, while the other, a 32-lb explosive shell from the *Phlegethon*,[22] at the same moment sliced him clean in two 'with the certainty and rapidity with which one cuts a young nettle off with a switch,' as Captain Pears observed.[23] With their flag officer dead, the men of the Shouchun regiment (they had marched 400 miles from their home in Anhui province to defend Chusan) were swiftly driven from the heights and chased down across the fields to the city. As their matchlocks failed, some resorted to throwing stones. Their battle-standard, a

141

yellow silk pennant beautifully embroidered with an undulating dragon of shimmering blue scales, was snatched up from where it had fallen. It remains to this day at the Westmorelands' regimental memorial in Kendal parish church. As the Chinese fled, the Westmorelands' own colours were waved from the peak of 49th Hill for all to see, and cheers broke out on the ships riding at anchor. While Captain Anstruther's artillery heaved its field-pieces over the now undefended hills and began to bombard the city, the Westmorelands scaled the walls and swarmed over.[24] By 2pm, barely three hours after first landing, their colours were fluttering over the battlements. Tinghae had again fallen.

Meanwhile, its flank turned with unexpected speed, the Royal Irish were at liberty to drive the Chinese on the long earth wall from their guns. They advanced steadily from embrasure to embrasure, firing volleys into the utterly unprepared defenders and bayoneting any they overtook. The infernal roar of Congrève rockets exploding amongst them as they fell back only added to the sense of panic. General Ge Yunfei, by now the only one of Yuqian's three generals still alive, rallied his men at the foot at Josshouse Hill but was brought down with terrible wounds to his head and took his own life.[25] His cannons, still pointed uselessly out to sea, were red hot, their barrels split from days of ineffectual firing. Above them, the temple fort had been cleared by shells from Trumball Island, but the battery on its lower slope was still occupied. With cold accuracy, marksmen killed the last of General Ge's men as they floundered knee-deep in mud.[26] The walls of their battery, it was found, were covered with large wooden crosses, in the hope, perhaps, that Christians would not fire upon their sacred symbol.[27] The surviving soldiers fled across the fields, casting off their silk uniforms and blending into the populace. As silence returned, the glowing embers of discarded matchlocks set fire to the cotton-padded uniforms of the Chinese dead. Soon the battlefield was strewn with burning bodies that now and then exploded as the powder-bags tied to their waists caught light.[28] It had been another macabre and one-sided slaughter.

A party of officers assessed the scene of the fighting late that afternoon, but it was impossible to tell how many Chinese had died. Certainly it was in the hundreds. 'Shockingly mutilated' bodies littered the heights, though people emerging from the city had begun to bury them.[29] It was not a task the British considered their own duty. A week after their deaths, the broken remains of Generals Ge and Zheng were dug up by the islanders and ferried to the mainland.[30] General Wang's corpse, the Chinese feared, had been dismembered in revenge for his spirited defence of 49th Hill (they were mistaken — it would in time find its way to the mainland, decomposing but otherwise intact). Many more soldiers had drowned when the boats they took to flee the island had foundered in the dark, and the survivors who had reached the mainland had on Yuqian's orders been beheaded for cowardice.[31]

As reports of the fighting filtered back to him, an increasingly shocked Yuqian provided Peking with a rambling and piecemeal account of events, breaking the news as was his duty but desperately trying to avoid accusations of incompetence.[32] The people of Chusan, he assured the emperor, had been sleeping with spears as pillows, his troops ready at action stations with each high tide. When *Nemesis* and *Phlegethon* had first entered the harbour, General Ge had fired on them, shattering a mast and causing the defenceless barbarians to flee like rats. A great victory had been won, the British repulsed. Two attempted landings — these had in fact been successful attempts to render the fortifications on 49th Hill useless — had been met with musket fire, and innumerable barbarians had been killed. The howitzer battery on Trumball Island had been fired on from the earth wall, Yuqian claimed, killing a dozen more of the enemy. In the early hours of October 1st, General Ge had fired at a prowling steamer, hitting its magazine and blowing the vessel to smithereens. When finally the barbarians had landed in force, General Wang and his regiment had almost managed to drive them back. Yet the more they killed, the more there were to replace them. After four days of fighting on 49th Hill, Wang's 800-strong regiment had been reduced to just a handful, leaving the way clear for the wall to be outflanked.

In all, Yuqian's officers and men had fought bitterly for six days and nights 'until their sinews were exhausted and their strength was at an end.' General Ge himself had manhandled a cannon weighing two and a half tons and fired it into the barbarians, 'whose blood flowed like water in a ditch'. The barbarian chieftain Anstruther had led his troops forward, waving a great banner. When they encountered each other, Ge had personally cut off Anstruther's head. His sword broken by the force of the blow, he had then charged into the British ranks only to be felled. Even in death, the one eye that had not been hacked from his head had stayed as bright as that of a living man's. The barbarians, when at last they dared examine it, could only sigh in wonder. A final factor in the enemy's victory, Yuqian informed the throne, had been traitors from Canton and Fujian who, dressed all in black, had landed in wave upon wave. There must have been more than 10,000 of them fighting for the British! Although Tinghae had again fallen, Yuqian's intelligence indicated that considerably more than 1,000 barbarians had died, one iron steamer had been blown to splinters, and three warships and many landing boats had been sunk. The emperor, reading of what his children had endured, soon added in his vermilion ink: 'We read this with fast-falling tears.'[33] One can only imagine his rage had he known that it had been a fabrication from start to finish.

In truth, the British had lost five men in the day's attacks, a further thirty wounded, but certainly no ships.[34] Still privy through their network of paid informants to many of the memorials and edicts that travelled between Zhejiang and Peking, they shrugged off such exaggeration. The desperate insistence that everything was under control was a telling insight into how the emperor's servants were forever anxious to keep him in the dark. Then, as the Son of Heaven took stock, edicts began to emerge from the Forbidden City. Yuqian and Governor Liu were indicted for their failure to hold on to Chusan despite months of preparation and vast sums of cash. The emperor and his Council of State might have suspected that they were being misled, but still their orders betrayed a naïve assurance that once a new commissioner was appointed in Yuqian's stead the barbarians would be scattered and Chusan retaken. Simply being Chinese was enough to ensure victory.

Foraging Party, from The Cree Journals (image © Webb & Bower; original watercolour © Henrietta Heawood)

13

You have done us incalculable injury

JUST A day after the island's reoccupation, Sir Henry Pottinger announced in a circular to all British subjects in China that Chusan had been retaken.[1] But he had ultimately been sent to China to force the emperor into accepting Lord Palmerston's terms, a task that could not be achieved from the comfort of Tinghae. A week later, all but 400 of his troops were re-embarked and shipped across Kintang Sound to take the fortified town of Zhenhai that commanded the approaches to Ningbo: so long as the Chinese were able to amass men there, Chusan would be under threat. What should have been a formidable stronghold was swept aside — some of the defenders had seen with their own eyes the effectiveness of the assault on Chusan and did not hang around to see it repeated. As the British secured the area, four severed heads were discovered in a cage. They belonged to Captain Stead, the mate of the opium clipper *Lyra*, the comprador Bu Dingbang, and one of the Chusanese kidnapped for helping the British. As for Yuqian, the man who had ordered their beheadings, after a failed attempt at drowning himself in the ritual pool of the town's Confucius Temple he fled to Yuyao (this, coincidentally, was where Anne Noble had been mistreated by the crowds) and there he took an overdose of opium. He had had no difficulty in acquiring a fatal dose: in almost every tent in the Zhenhai encampment Pottinger had seen with his own eyes large amounts of the drug belonging to both officers and men.[2] The emperor, hearing of the suicide, set aside a decree demanding Yuqian's punishment and instead gave him a posthumous title and lavished honours on his family. For his military commander, though, nothing of the sort: with Yuqian's honourable death the blame for this latest defeat rested on one man's shoulders. Commander Yu Buyun was led to Peking in chains and beheaded. It was a pointless piece of scapegoating that did nothing to halt the British advance.

On October 13th, Sir William Parker's steamers made their way south-westward to Ningbo with three warships in tow. When they dropped anchor, the gates of Zhejiang's second city were flung open from within and the barbarians allowed to take possession without firing a shot. The first act of the Madras Artillery was to tear down the prison where Captain Anstruther and Anne Noble had been held. The tiny cages in which they had been forced to live were spared destruction and sent back to Madras and to London as objects of black curiosity.

As Pottinger's men found their feet on Chusan once more, Yuqian's boast to the emperor of having opened graves and dismembered British corpses was, like his other reports to the throne, found to be an exaggeration. One officer of HMS *Blonde* buried on Grave Island had indeed been dug up,[3] and, where the earth wall had cut through the British cemetery, coffins had been disinterred,[4] but most, including the graves of the 26th Regiment on Cameronian Hill, were untouched, perhaps for fear of releasing vengeful ghosts. The living, it turned out, had suffered more on Yuqian's reoccupation than had the dead: a basket filled with Chinese heads was quickly discovered on Grave Island — presumably they had been accused of fraternisation — and Edward Cree's pipe-smoking duck farmer was rumoured to have been executed along with an aged Buddhist priest who had stayed to live with the Irishmen in the temple fort.[5] By contrast, now their immediate goal of taking the island had been achieved, the British saw to it that any casualties they could find were treated humanely.

'My first work was to collect all the wounded Chinese,' surgeon Alexander Grant of the Bengal Medical Service wrote to a friend, 'many of whom were in the most pitiable state, and dying for want of surgical aid and proper nourishment, for their countrymen had entirely deserted them.'[6] Some refused treatment. One man with a maggot-infested bayonet wound to the throat lay under a bamboo mat in the city, sipping from a cup of water but brushing away offers of help until eventually after five days he died.[7] Another tore away his bandages and had to be tied to his bed and guarded around the clock.[8] A year later a letter from Alexander Grant appeared in the *Times*.[9] The man's operation had been a success:

> I placed [the wounded] in a house next to my quarters, amputated their limbs and dressed their sores. Many of them have recovered, and have been sent to their homes; only two now remain; they have each had a leg amputated, and are now quite well. One is a fine Tartar soldier, about six feet two inches in height, who had his leg shattered while fighting bravely at the beach battery. At first he considered my object was to torture him, but he is now the most grateful and pleased being in the city. I am now getting up a subscription for them amongst the officers in the garrison to pay their passage, and enable them to reach their homes, where they must carry with them some remembrance of our humanity.

Perhaps he was right, but such humanity could not alter the fact that both they and the hundreds of dead were victims of what had been a pitiless attack. Captain Anstruther, perhaps less inclined after his kidnapping to treat the islanders as friends, had not shrunk from lobbing explosives into a densely populated city (for General Ge had insisted that nobody leave Tinghae — it was safe, he said, under his protection). One shell had killed a mother and two children in their home and mortally wounded their father.[10] Injured civilians were daily met with, cowering in their houses too scared to seek help (today it would be called post-traumatic stress). One boy of nine or ten was discovered wandering the streets. Young Afah's father, it seemed, had been killed, and of his mother's whereabouts nothing could be learned. William Hutcheon Hall, captain of the *Nemesis*, took him to live aboard the steamer.[11]

The British too needed a roof over their heads. Whereas Governor Burrell had left his men first to bake and later to freeze in their canvas tents, the very day Tinghae fell Sir Hugh Gough moved his men into shelter in the city.[12] Surprisingly little had changed — the street names the British had put up a year before were still there, their billets designated company by company upon the doors, and even old credit bills chalked on the walls were legible.[13] The vast Zuyin Temple, rundown when Burrell had left in February, had been regilt and repainted in the hope of atoning for the first invasion and warding off a second.[14] Soon its enormous halls, crammed with statues of Buddha, his saints and his disciples, once again sheltered men who had no interest in them beyond their worth as souvenirs. A temporary officers' mess — the name hid the fact that here was a frail tenement of lath and plaster that teetered on the verge of collapse — was requisitioned, while a courtyard complex was renovated and offices and kitchens erected to create the first purpose-built barracks on Chusan. Instead of the rank and file turning in just anywhere as they had the previous year, they were provided with trestle-and-board beds. By and by, a better officers' mess was created by knocking through two adjacent houses and converting their rooms to suit British tastes in privacy (though sadly they could not live up to British expectations of comfort, admitting the rain and cold all too readily).[15]

General Ge's insistence that nobody set foot outside the walls turned out to be a stroke of luck for Pottinger: the city, though scared and subdued, had not been evacuated and was filled with people. When pot-shots were taken at patrols and a brickbat thrown at a sentry, suspicions were voiced that many of the young men on the streets were soldiers in mufti. But not everybody was as keen to see the back of the barbarians: familiar faces quickly reappeared to offer their services as servants and factotums.[16] Neither did Gough, determined that not just the mercenary old tradesmen but the island in its entirety would submit to British rule, repeat Burrell's military mistakes. A show of strength began almost immediately, with the Royal Irish marching out to Sinkong and the other villages on the west coast and the Westmorelands showing their presence in the fishing port of Sinkamoon on the east.[17] Everywhere, the reappearance of the British put the lie to Yuqian's assurances, found pasted up at each village, that his defences were impregnable. The harvest was fast approaching, and the rice fields were groaning under a rich crop of paddy. The farmers stopped work and simply stood to watch the regiments pass by, seemingly neither astonished nor displeased at the appearance of foreign troops, though they must have feared a repeat of the thefts and violence of the previous year.[18] Some were willing to sell food to the soldiers; more were quite happy to sell them *samshoo* in abundance.

After resting overnight in Sinkamoon, three companies of Westmorelands marched on in a great loop northwestward to impress the hamlets of the interior — Pishoon, Kanlon and Mowah — before crossing the spine of the island back to Tinghae.[19] Though a long confinement at sea swiftly followed by a forced hike with easy access to *samshoo* meant that many of his men had to be carried through the city gates on their return,[20] within four days Sir Hugh had managed a more visible show of strength than had Burrell in as many months.

Within the week, Pottinger had issued his own proclamation to the Chusanese: their island would be retained as a British possession until such time as the emperor agreed to his demands and carried that agreement into effect. Years, he stressed, might elapse before that happened, and in the meantime they were to go about their lawful occupations as British subjects under the protection of British law. After Captain Elliot's farcical attempts to win over the terrified islanders, Pottinger was determined to make it clear that the British were going nowhere fast, and that they had nothing to fear from co-operating with them. A military government would be formed, he declared

> to protect the well disposed and quiet, and to punish the ill disposed and refractory.... All classes are hereby invited to resume their usual trades and occupations, under the assurance of being fostered and protected, so long as they conduct themselves as orderly and obedient subjects to the Government under which they are living.[21]

The proclamation ended, as was the usual practice, with 'God save the Queen', a sentiment which must have baffled the Confucian islanders.

Major Stephens of the Hertfordshires (he had of course had the arduous but invaluable experience of acting as a military commissioner during the first occupation) was appointed Governor of Chusan. One Captain John Dennis was made military magistrate and given a twenty-strong police force based in posts across the city and the suburb.[22] It was clear now that the British could take Chusan whenever they wished, but to a Chinese unthinkable that the Son of Heaven could bend to their will. Yet if he did not, then Chusan, like Hong Kong, would evidently remain British. Chusan, it must have seemed to the islanders, would from now on forever be under foreign occupation.

The temperature dropped sharply as winter got underway. The fleet's barefoot Indian sailors, whose winter clothing and shoes had been lost in a shipwreck, were surprised when one morning they awoke to their first fall of snow.[23] They said it was salt,[24] and that it 'bit' them.[25] The cold drove packs of wild dogs to dig up the shallow graves on 49th Hill, their scrabbling uncovering the dead soldiers' faces.[26] In the city, the sepoys shrank their slight frames into the corners of their sentry boxes, the philosophical Hindus amongst them muttering that death by cold was simply to be their fate. (There were, aboard the merchantmen in Tinghae harbour, plenty of warm, woollen fabrics which would have made fine winter uniforms for the Indians, but the officers who went to look at them found them too expensive for the regimental purse. In any case, as Edward Cree noted incredulously, the Indian troops' prejudices seemed to prevent them from wearing anything but a thin, white sheet.)[27] As the mercury dropped, the plank walls of the officers' mess shrank and split and the oiled paper that had substituted for window glass was torn out and replaced with heavy calico. Braziers kept the worst of the chill out, but the combination of charcoal smoke and the fug of tobacco drove men out into the cold for fear of suffocation. Labourers were hired to fit a fireplace fashioned from the barrels of captured match-locks.[28] The remains of the wharves were cleared to provide fuel, and soon the barracks faced out past its flagstaff and across the ostentatiously named Royal Marine Square all the way to Yuqian's earth wall.[29] Daily parades were held here as men struggled to keep active and warm. One bright little Chinese boy in particular paid close attention to the drill, saluting like a trained soldier and mimicking the commands — 'Present arms! Order arms! Shoulder arms!'[30]

Though boys could be excused their playfulness, it was a different matter with adults and a well-known fact that many of the people who had so far dealt with the British had ended up with their heads in cages. Pottinger knew he must impress upon the islanders that they had less to fear from British rule than they had from their own mandarins. He issued a proclamation stressing that Chusan would never be returned to Chinese rule without the emperor first signing an amnesty for anybody who had dealt with the British. The islanders, of course, knew that Pottinger simply did not have it in his power to make the Son of Heaven abide by any such agreement, but there was hardly any need to embolden them to deal with the garrison anyway. In spite of the kidnap and beheading of a fisherman who had been acting as a dialect interpreter for Gützlaff, by mid-December Tinghae's shops were all open and the city markets were jammed with men and beasts. Good, fresh bread was being baked; there were plenty of vegetables; Chusan's fishing fleet was landing an important part of the men's diet. True, the epithets *fangui* and *bizi* — 'foreign devil' and 'nose' — were forever being heard on the streets, reported one officer of the Royal Marines, yet

> their ill will, however, did not extend beyond words, and conquerors of islands and cities must not expect to be always welcomed by the conquered, however great may be the forbearance of the victors.[31]

And so Christmas was an altogether jollier affair than it had been in 1840. Divine service was held in a hall of the Josshouse Hill temple that, for the remainder of the occupation, was reconsecrated as a church.[32] The sailors in the harbour enjoyed a day of merry-making (and the master of the ship *Worcester*, after drinking himself stupid aboard an opium clipper, fell into the harbour and had to be rescued).[33] On HMS *Rattlesnake*, Edward Cree enjoyed roast pork and suet pudding (the traditional roast beef and plum duff being unobtainable this far from home).[34] The Westmorelands' regimental mess presented the splendid sight of twenty-five brace of woodcock shot by the officers.[35] Despite the cold, the mood rose yet higher on New Year's Eve. All hands stayed up until midnight when, at a signal of ships' bells, the whole harbour was suddenly illuminated in a blaze of guns and fireworks. Gongs were beaten, bells rung and men cheered until the harbour's great sweep rang with their sound and its very islands echoed the fleet's optimism.[36] It was an auspicious start to 1842.

Positive thinking, though, could only achieve so much. The reappearance of rupees and dollars might have made for an amicable atmosphere in Tinghae and the harbour islands, but in the villages of the interior it was still positively hostile. When the garrison had finished eating its way clean through all the water buffalo that the villagers near Tinghae were willing to part with, foraging parties emerged to look for fresh meat. Friction was inevitable as hungry soldiers confronted farmers who needed their oxen for the spring ploughing, and the average private's contempt for the Chinese meant that violence came easily. Two islanders were shot one day, one of them fatally, after a foraging party tried to lead an animal away. An angry crowd threatened a hunting party, and only dispersed when a boat from a seren-dipitously moored warship came to the officers' assistance.[37] To general dismay, the same old problems that had blighted the first occupation seemed to be arising again. The question was not simply of lost lives and grieving families — it was ultimately a matter of moral authority. In Calcutta, *The Englishman* lamented the ultimate effects of the violence:

> The whole British nation will become a by-word for all that is bloody, barbarous, cruel and avaricious. Can it be forgotten that when a Chinese is murdered, it is most certain that a wife loses her husband, and children their father; and, perhaps, a widowed mother may be added to the list of mourners, or a father may lament for an only son, whose death has robbed him of all hope that his shade shall be, according to their hopes and fears, propitiated and gratified by the observance of the immemorial worship at the tombs and ancestral ceremonies?[38]

There was at least a little comfort to be taken from the fact that some were willing now to make such humane observations.

But while Britons were often guilty of indifference to Chinese deaths, a renewed promise of silver in exchange for severed heads meant that many of the natives on the Zhejiang coast were soon actively engaged in cold-blooded murder. It having been too late in the year to move against the provincial capital Hangzhou, Pottinger was satisfied instead to hold on to Ningbo until the spring thaw. As the city atrophied in the freezing cold, the British stayed active. The towns easily reached by river on shallow-draught iron steamers such as the *Nemesis* — Yuyao, Cixi, Fenghua — were one by one looted and left burning. As 1842 came around, the frozen canals and snow-bound rice fields witnessed almost daily skirmishes between Gough's patrols and an army assembling under the late Yuqian's replacement, a man named Yijing.[39]

General Yijing, an imperial Manchu of the Bordered Red Banner and a nephew to the emperor himself, was the latest mandarin to be encumbered with the impossible task of sweeping the barbarians into the sea. He was said by Pottinger's informants to be a man of leisure, fond of presents and bribes,[40] but his louche persona hid a determination to succeed where Yilibu and Yuqian had already failed. With the grand title of Awe-Inspiring General bestowed on him by imperial favour, Yijing now based himself in Shaoxing, just 50 miles from occupied Ningbo. His army — levies from a swathe of central China, militiamen from Zhejiang, mercenary boat-people and other ragtag forces — massed on the banks of the Cao'e River. Some (witness the weary conscripts who had fled Zhenhai) had retreated before successive onslaughts and were reluctant to give their all in any counterattack. But with the arrival of Yijing a spark of renewed confidence was evident in the Chinese camp. Here perhaps was the man to change the outcome of the war.

To start with, Yijing began to sponsor kidnappings on a scale the British had not yet seen, aware that the tactic had handed his predecessors their strongest card, Captain Anstruther. For private soldiers even more than a listless officer, the endless round of duties was grinding, and there was no shortage of men prepared to risk capture on a promise of *samshoo* or sex.[41] Plied with spirits until they were drunk enough to be slipped some poisonous alkaloid, they would be bound hand and foot, slung insensible beneath a bamboo pole and carried, hidden within a bale of goods perhaps, past unsuspecting sentries, or crammed into the bilges of a boat to be punted away to their deaths.[42] One evening, Privates Toplis and Russell slipped out of their barracks for a nearby inn where they were regular customers.[43] Half a rupee's worth of *samshoo* — some four pints — was prepared just the way they liked it, with sugar and beaten egg added to soften its kick. As the two started upon a second half-gallon, the innkeeper exited without a word. Their suspicions raised, they sneaked back to barracks with the remainder. Before they had gone far, Toplis confided that he felt unwell, his feet cold and numb. Russell, too, felt distinctly odd. They reached their quarters in a few minutes, unexpectedly sober for men who had drunk the better part of a gallon of spirits between them. Toplis reported ill, lay down on his bed, and soon afterwards was sick. He was quiet for a short time before his comrades heard him cry out: 'Oh God, it is creeping up to my heart!' Writhing, he fell from his bed and died in his friends' arms before they could reach the regimental hospital, his only sign of injury a slight graze to the nose.

Private Russell, meanwhile, his skin clammy and pulse slow and a numbness creeping up his legs, had admitted himself to the care of the regimental surgeon. Dr Shanks administered an emetic and kept him vomiting. Soon his pulse was scarcely detectable. The paralysis was inexorably moving up his chest into his face, while his extremities, clenched and stiff, felt as cold as ice. But the worst passed quickly, and by midnight Russell was sound asleep. What on earth had acted so devastatingly upon the constitution of fit, young men? Evaporating the *samshoo*, Dr Shanks recovered a peculiar substance that stubbornly refused to identify itself to any of his reagents. His assistant found himself volunteered to try a tiny amount on the tip of his tongue. He reported that it was intensely bitter and, after a few minutes, of a numbness and partial paralysis of his body which lasted for some twenty-four hours. Dr Shanks' report was full of regret that the state of chemical science was in 1842 not far enough advanced to discover the secret of the Chinese poison, but the 55th Regiment required no more detailed proof than that one of its men had been murdered. Whole villages were being put to the torch for lesser acts of resistance, even suspected kidnappers had been shot without benefit of a trial, [44] and retribution was ruthlessly exacted.

In mid-February the mate of a transport ship landed with eleven Indians at a creek.[45] As the tide fell their launch was grounded and they sat down to await the next. When men approached and made it clear there were prostitutes to be had in their village, the mate agreed to follow them. At dawn a search party discovered his corpse floating in a pond. It was headless, and bore the marks of horrific torture. The sailors took their anger out on the villagers, beating any they found and hauling thirty aboard ship. Eleven who confessed to being on the spot the night before were soon destined for the hangman.

All through spring the tally of kidnappings steadily rose, with headless bodies identifiable only by their insignia regularly being dragged out of rivers.[46] In April, a private of the Hertfordshires was found strangled. Into his mouth had been stuffed a large walnut wound around with hair, a task that had demanded the slitting of his cheeks.[47] One kidnapper was caught red-handed, and when his home was burned a female accomplice was flushed out.[48] Another time, the whereabouts of a missing soldier were rightly presumed to be a favourite *samshoo* den. When his lacerated and headless body was found in a sack the inn was burned though the landlord had already escaped.[49] But Chinese collaborators too remained targets just as before, and they died in even greater numbers. Most simply vanished without the British ever hearing about it, and it was only by chance that the occasional kidnapping came to light. One took place in Ningbo. There, the sampans which by morning transported night-soil and slops out of the city were allowed to pass unsearched through the water-gates.[50] A boatman happened one day to strike the stone archway, knocking himself flat and uncovering a secret compartment that hid a Chinaman of Karl Gützlaff's native police force, gagged and bound (Gützlaff had travelled north once more with the British and been made magistrate of Ningbo on its occupation). The boatman, when he had recovered from a beating that almost killed him, confessed to seven other kidnaps. Though Gützlaff pushed for a summary hanging, Gough was away fighting and had not deputed the authority to pass a capital sentence.[51] On another occasion a Chinese, the servant to a British officer, screamed out his only two words of English — 'police!' and 'mandarin!' — as the night-soil boat he was tied up in passed out of Ningbo.[52] The gang behind his kidnap was quickly rounded up and imprisoned ('A more ill-favoured half dozen I have never set eyes upon,' admitted a correspondent to *The Englishman*) but Gough ignored calls for their summary public execution. Gützlaff, himself almost murdered when a bomb planted in a house exploded a fraction too late,[53] held such men in contempt. They were the dregs of maritime society, he said, ruthless cowards, able to murder with utter *sang froid* but terrified when faced with a single armed Englishman.[54] Yet, just as today, there was little defence against an enemy who refused to engage in battle.

On Chusan, where plentiful food and bracing temperatures had had a remarkable effect on the garrison's health, kidnapping now became the sole cause of British deaths.[55] Dozens of men disappeared, black and white alike, beheaded for the reward money and their superfluous bodies hastily buried or dumped at sea. Others had frighteningly close calls — even the amiable ship's surgeon Edward Cree, who still counted a number of the islanders amongst his friends, had narrowly escaped being taken while out sketching.[56] When a local boy working for Dr Milne of the London Missionary Society was abducted by a kidnap gang based in Hangzhou, its ringleader Mr Le was able to wring from him a picture of the doctor's daily life.[57] Milne, eager to live amongst potential converts, had already turned down an offer to move in with the Westmorelands for his own safety and went on living in an outhouse in a respectable man's garden in Tinghae. Unable to bear the thought of killing a man, even in self-defence, he had locked away the pistol they had given him. He awoke one night amid a thunderstorm to hear the mumble of voices from outside. Leaping out of his hammock he took up an iron bar, struck it against the window frame and shouted the curfew salute of the English sentries — 'Who comes there?' — and the men ran off. At daylight, Milne found a discarded sack and a sword.

It was to be not force of arms but good old military intelligence that finally dealt a body blow to the kidnappers who plagued Chusan. In early May an informant brought word to Governor Stephens that the culprits had gathered to carouse and fritter away their reward money. In the early hours of the next morning a house in a village some seven miles from the city was surrounded and its door smashed down. A cache of matchlocks was found, as were the ringleader Little Babao and his elder brother. Twenty men were bound and taken to Tinghae, another shot dead as he tried to escape. All were spared the hangman — orders only allowed for men caught in the act to be lynched out of hand — and were transported instead to the secure new gaol in Hong Kong.[58] Though the risk of kidnap and murder diminished with the arrest of the Babao gang, others remained ready to risk the noose: the very next day, a servant boy and a ship's boatswain were both kidnapped within a stone's throw of 49th Hill and were not seen again.

When the Tinghae garrison was further reduced to just 300 men as, with the arrival of warmer weather, the fighting recommenced in earnest on the mainland, those who wished to see the back of the British took their chance to plot against them. The heads of Chusan's villages met in secret one day in a temple in the interior. Here were gathered the men — landowners, elders, Confucian gentry and literati — who had most to lose from a protracted occupation, an elite whose social status in Chinese eyes now counted for nothing when they stood before Governor Stephens and Magistrate Dennis. They penned the *Manifesto of the People of Tinghae*, and proclaimed that it would be better to die fighting than face their ancestors tainted by treason.[59] Homes had been burned, people arrested and ransoms demanded, temples had been demolished and the gods desecrated. The native police force was nothing but a band of bullies with a commission from a monarch whose authority they did not recognise. The same went for the quisling directing the cultivation of all land within 5,000 feet of Tinghae's walls: an order from Gough that the malarial paddy be drained and replaced by dry wheat and barley[60] had been received with incredulity — rice was the very foundation of the empire! Seeing the hard life that private soldiers had to endure and believing them to be on the point of mutiny, the elders urged them to make that leap: they were tens of thousands of *li* from home, they were reminded, dying so that their officers could grow fat on spoil. If they died on Chusan they would become hungry ghosts in an alien land, a pitiable fate by Chinese thinking. 'You black and white sons of devils,' the *Manifesto* appealed (though it was a choice of address unlikely to endear it to its audience)

why do you suffer to assist in their tyranny? Kill your leaders now or hand them over, else we shall not differentiate good from bad and shall kill you all!

The black and white sons of devils soon had a copy of the *Manifesto*. From the outset it was suspected that it was a forgery, that General Yijing was behind it,[61] but details of known events on Chusan hinted at collusion rather than outright concoction. And from where the Chinese stood, of course, the *Manifesto* was speaking the truth. Though such a naïve attempt at fomenting a mutiny amongst the garrison never stood a chance, it did encourage yet more kidnap attempts by the islanders. It was complained that, by the end of an unusually wet May, an unarmed European could no longer walk in safety from the seafront to the city walls in daylight. Even beyond that point, the streets were effectively in the hands of the Chinese once a patrol had passed by. Attempts were made to burn the Tinghae barracks, watering parties were fired on, and the essential task of maintaining a presence in the villages soon left the garrison exhausted.[62] In late July three men were paraded out of the south gate to a roadside tree, and there they were inexpertly hanged, leaving one of them kicking and struggling for twenty minutes.[63] They had been caught trying to carry off Indian water-carriers. Perhaps they were gentry, sworn to rid Chusan of the British; perhaps hired indigents, hoping for a reward or for the peacock feather the *Manifesto* had promised. Nobody stopped to ask; they were just glad that these particular men would not be attempting another abduction. 'It ought to be a good lesson for them to leave off the work,' a lieutenant of the Madras Native Infantry remarked in a letter to his wife.[64] But even if the true authorship of the *Manifesto* was in doubt, a letter left anonymously at the foot of Josshouse Hill bore all the hallmarks of the genuinely aggrieved. 'You dwell in the West,' it began,

and your manner, clothes and language differ from ours. You have an ancestor whom you call Jesus Christ, whose doctrine is to save the whole human race. You have for many years been permitted to trade, and go back and forth through our land, yet for good you have returned evil. Ever since the days of the Jiaqing Emperor your vessels have been engaged in trade here and you have been permitted to deal in various merchandise; but all these favours you have forgotten, and have, in return, robbed and plundered the common people. You have in your incorrigible wickedness attacked our cities, killed and wounded our officers, burnt and destroyed wherever you have come, so that your conduct is obnoxious to gods and men. The consequences of your wickedness fall upon *our* unfortunate heads. At the mouth of the Ningbo River you take taxes from all who pass up and down. Perhaps you think we have more than enough for our own support? Within 100 *li* of where you live, bullocks, geese, fowl and ducks are made scarce by your rapacious appetites. You assert your concern and love for the common people, but do your actions correspond with your assertions? On the contrary, you have done us incalculable injury. You know that the sale of opium is forbidden, so why do you not obey? At the same time, you make us attend to yours against *samshoo*, on pain of houses being burned down. Our commander-in-chief knows how to make use of his troops, and that there are thousands who will volunteer themselves to defend their families and country. Even women and children are ready to take up arms. For every one that falls on your side, you lose one, but for every one that falls on ours, two spring up in his place. If we do not do our best to exterminate you, may we for ever be blasted with misery and suffering. You are acting contrary to the principles of heaven. Repent of your wickedness, lest shortly repentance may come too late![65]

The letter was a thoughtful and detailed condemnation of the British, and a stark reminder to Pottinger and the rest of how far there was still to travel before Chusan was at peace with the idea of foreign rule.

14

So ends the Chinese war

THE AWE-INSPIRING General Yijing did not put his entire faith in fomenting unrest to unseat the British from Zhejiang. Fortunately for them, they often knew as much of his wider plans as did his own commanders.[1] Through paid informants, word filtered back to Gützlaff that the army massing near Shaoxing would soon move. The attack, when it did come, only underlined the yawning gulf between a West that had emerged from the Enlightenment into the Industrial Revolution and a China whose every action seemed hidebound by tradition. For as town after town was looted and burned that winter, Yijing's diviner had alerted him to the imminent passing of an uncommon event: three brief windows would soon open up when, by mirroring the machinations of the heavens, he might subdue the barbarians.

By ancient Chinese usage, years were named not with increasing distance from Christ's birth but according to their place in recurring cycles of ten heavenly stems and twelve earthly branches. Every twelfth year — and 1842 was one such — was governed by the earthly branch of *yin*.[2] Months, days and even hours too were in turn assigned one of the earthly branches, and each year's first lunar month too was governed by *yin*. Within that month, three days — by the Western calendar they would be February 14th, 26th, and March 10th — were governed by *yin*, as was the fifth watch of the night, in the hours before dawn. Such a cosmic conjunction of *yin* was of high importance to the superstitious Yijing through another association in Chinese thought: *yin* was the sign of that most martial of creatures, the animal gracing the breast of every military mandarin in China, the tiger. With the harmony of the heavens on his side, attacking when all four *yin* were aligned, General Yijing believed he could not fail.

The attack finally came on the third tiger-day, after which Yijing would have had to wait another twelve years. Of course, the early hours of March 10th held no cosmic significance for the private soldiers garrisoned in Tinghae, Zhenhai and Ningbo. A prohibition on *samshoo* had curbed its sale — one bootlegger had been given twenty lashes and had his home torn down — and unusually harsh punishments for drunkenness on duty meant that the sentries were as watchful as could be hoped.[3] The Zhenhai garrison easily beat back the troops sent to dislodge it, but Ningbo faced a far larger onslaught. As the guard at the south gate fell back, Yijing's men had swarmed into the city. The British rallied, checked the advance, and beat them back. Meanwhile at the west gate a bigger force looked likely to overwhelm the garrison, but discipline and modern weapons won out. An artillery piece dragged into position by Gough's men drove the Chinese back out and into the narrow streets of the suburb beyond, where they were scythed down in their hundreds by grapeshot. When daylight broke, it revealed alleyways waist-deep with bodies. It was just more of the same butchery, the British losing not a single man.

As for Chusan, the man chosen to retake the island when the heavens were in harmony had more reason than most to hate the British. Zheng Dingchen was just a lowly official assigned to a salt transit station, but he was also the bereaved son of General Zheng, who had accepted the surrender of Chusan a year earlier only to die in the second invasion. A week after his hasty burial, what remained of General Zheng had been dug up and secretly ferried to Zhenhai so that he could be given a funeral befitting his Muslim ethnicity in his native Hunan. His son, still officially in mourning and thirsty for vengeance, was entrusted with almost a quarter of a million *liang* of silver (some ten tons — one wonders whether the memorials were exaggerated!) with which to buy the loyalty of Zhejiang's boatmen: no one could be expected to take up arms out of altruism or patriotic fervour. In late February of 1842, a fleet of junks and fire-rafts under Zheng's command set sail from Zhapu on the far shore of Hangzhou Bay. Aboard were several hundred village braves and Tanka boat men, and a good many 'sand people' — those cheaply bought indigents who lived a squatter's life on the foreshores of rivers and lakes. Soon these highly irregular troops were dispersed across the outlying islands in readiness to burn the British at anchor. Others, it was claimed, were sent into Tinghae as sleepers, ready to rise up when they saw the harbour ablaze. The main body of junks assembled on Daishan, the second largest of the archipelago, within sight of Chusan's north coast. But it proved impossible to hide so many masts from Gützlaff's spies, and word of Zheng's preparations inevitably reached his ears.[4] Coupled with intelligence on Yijing's grand scheme, the threat was grave enough to see Gough and Parker steam back to Tinghae on February 23rd to lead any defence in person. No attack came on the 26th, the second of the tiger days, but the sense of relief did not stem the rumours that a force sat encamped on Daishan ready to strike in another twelve days' time.

The steamer *Nemesis* had been in Tinghae harbour for over a month, undergoing repairs after holing herself on a rock (the emperor would have been disgusted had he known that Chinese carpenters were overhauling her boats). On March 7th, just three days short of Zheng's last window of opportunity, Captain Hall received orders to weigh for Daishan.[5] *Nemesis* got up steam and anchored opposite the fishing village of Gaoting. An armed party landed and quizzed the locals, but could wring from them no news of Chinese troops. Gützlaff's intelligence, though, was explicit, and at dusk a second party landed, hoping to spot campfires in the darkness. Instead, a number of braves found the British and threatened to cut off their retreat. Outnumbered, and taking it in turns to fire and so keep the Chinese at a safe distance, the small party edged back to the shore. It was resolved to make an impression. Dawn saw all four of the *Nemesis'* boats row into a creek, packed with marines. Some two miles or more upstream a number of junks were spotted, their braves and crew — there were perhaps 600 in all — in a farmstead on one bank. Shouted hastily to arms, they managed to get off a few weary shots. As they did so, a British officer spotted smoke rising from one of the junks. Thinking it might be a booby-trap, he signalled to his men to land a little further downstream. This they did, and with a fatal lack of insight the untrained Chinese took the move to be a retreat and charged. No match for professional marines, who fired volley after volley into them, the Chinese scattered, leaving behind their dead — each was found to have in his pockets the $4 that had bought a modicum of valour — and a $2,000 war chest. The farmstead and junks were put to the torch and the British rowed back to the *Nemesis*. A week later, Parker landed with a column to scour the island and burn any buildings he came across. He had made it abundantly clear that he would not suffer Daishan to harbour enemies. Even though gentrymen in Tinghae and in the island's hinterland went on passing messages to the mainland, making it clear that village braves were eager to rise up against the British if given firm instructions and a few days' notice,[6] the rout on Daishan proved to be a turning point: March of 1842 would be the last time the Chinese considered an invasion of British-administered Chusan.

General Yijing, on hearing that Zheng Dingchen's forces had been put to flight and Daishan's villages burned, was furious. He ordered a court martial of this prodigal son of such a fine general, but in a memorial to Peking chose to dwell on the one positive aspect of his financial investment: Zheng was still hiding out in the islands with a substantial number of men. Through March and well into April, rumours abounded that these remnants were drifting from anchorage to anchorage, waiting only for favourable winds and tides to move against Tinghae. For Zheng, it was more a matter of keeping his head attached to his shoulders: if he failed to show anything for such a vast amount of silver he could expect it soon to be grimacing sightlessly from inside a bamboo cage. The next time Yijing heard from the Chusan theatre was in late April, and the news was utterly unexpected. Scarcely able to contain himself, he wrote to Peking:

> On the 4th day of the 3rd month, Zheng Dingchen loaded firewood, gunpowder and combustibles onto his boats and sailed them to Meishan, where his fleet divided into three columns to continue northward. Captain Xu Jiabao's fire-boats were tied together to form fire-rafts, and these were launched one after the other against the harbour where three British warships were moored. As they surrounded these ships they were set alight. A strong south-easterly fanned the flames, which lit up the sky. Men's cries were like the boiling of a great cauldron. Our

rearguard arrived in support, firing guns and cannon, attacking the ships headlong and spreading terror and confusion amongst them. Many vessels rammed each other and sank. One tried to flee the harbour, but the chief of the water braves went after it. The rebels fired guns and rockets at the chief's boat but only succeeded in setting its kindling ablaze. As it burned it set light to many ships. The biggest warship, moored in the outer anchorage, was the target of a concentrated attack from over twenty large fire-boats. These set fire to her mainmast and rigging. When her magazine ignited, the smoke and flames shot high above the peak of the nearby island, the mast collapsed and the ship sank without trace. When our braves in Tinghae saw these flames they began to put the rebels' dwellings to the torch, killing dozens of them. A white man and many swords and guns were captured. Others burned buildings outside the city walls to add to the spectacle. Zheng Dingchen, seeing an enemy encampment, landed to attack. The British fled, but our men chased down and killed a dozen of them. Two steamers arrived from the northward and were fired upon. It is calculated that four British warships were destroyed by fire, of which one sank; dozens of smaller boats were burnt or sunk, three to four hundred rebels were burned to death, drowned, or shot in the city. There were no Chinese losses.[7]

The emperor was beside himself. After months of planning, a great victory had been gained over an enemy who had terrorised his coasts for too long: 'How can I express my joy at reading this memorial?' he asked, and awarded General Yijing a double-eyed peacock feather. As reports of the fighting filtered back to Hangzhou, Yijing was able to confirm the scale of the victory from the accounts of local merchants, and added details for the emperor's titillation: the batteries on Josshouse Hill had opened fire in panic when the fires broke out in the harbour below, their thunderous explosions shaking the ground for miles around. One such shot had dismasted a British ship! Many British sailors had died when, the braves having let out a terrifying battle cry, they jumped overboard in terror. Some had scrambled ashore but most had drowned. One of the steamers had been damaged by Chinese cannon, but managed to sail back and forth across the harbour as day dawned, firing to keep the braves at bay. It was only this rearguard action that finally made Zheng's men withdraw, but as they looked back at Tinghae they could see flames and smoke still filling the sky.

Sir William Parker, unaware for now of Zheng's claims, informed his superiors of the very same attack in the drily matter-of-fact way expected of a British admiral.[8]

> An abortive attempt was made by the Chinese to set fire to HM ships and transports in the harbour of Tinghae, and the adjoining anchorage, at Chusan, on the night of the 14th instant. About 10pm I received information from Captain Dennis, the military magistrate of Tinghae,[9] which he had just obtained from his scouts, that fire-rafts, formed of large boats, prepared with powder and other combustible materials, well assorted for the purpose, were supposed to be on their way from Sinkong. An hour had scarcely elapsed when several fire-rafts were discovered in flames, on the eastern side of the harbour, and drifting towards the shipping, while the others approached between Macclesfield and Trumball, on the south side, where the *Nemesis* had for some days been undergoing repair; others attempted to enter the anchorage occupied by the ships of war to the northward of Tea Island, and some even to the southward of that island, in which latter direction the *Jupiter* was moored.

The ships' boats of the Royal Navy vessels and the transports in the harbour were manned, and the whole of the fire-boats — Zheng had assembled some five dozen — were grappled clear of the fleet without doing the slightest harm. Shots had been fired at the sentries in the north gate, but nobody had been hurt. Parties sent the same night as far as Sinkong to hunt out other fire-boats. Finding some thirty moored near one of the harbour islands, they burned them all.[10] When the next day *Nemesis* and *Phleg-ethon* scoured the coast they found even more, the last remnants of Zheng's once-numerous fleet. The attack had caused no more than a night's lost sleep, and the highest-ranking Manchu on the

Zhejiang coast had again failed to make the slightest impression on the enemy. Such was the reality of the imbalance in power.

Despite the celebrations in Hangzhou and Peking over the supposed sinking of the British fleet, one man remained unconvinced by Zheng's boasts.[11] Since Chusan's fall, a Major Zhou Shifa of the now-exiled Tinghae garrison had been receiving regular briefings from his own spies in the city, and these were adamant that Zheng's fire-attack had done no damage. The senior licentiate of Tinghae's Confucian college, whom Zheng's report had credited with having burned buildings during the attack, denied any such involvement. Major Zhou wrote to Zhejiang's Governor Liu with his misgivings, and Liu forwarded them to General Yijing. Major Zhou's doubts put the general in a delicate position: he had told the emperor of a great victory in no uncertain language and now sported a double-eyed peacock feather on the strength of it. Opting for a cover-up, he sent an underling to tamper with the licentiate's statement and ordered that the man resubmit it to Governor Liu. When Liu remained adamant that the first version had been accurate, Yijing appointed a committee of inquiry. Sending it not into occupied Tinghae (where it would quickly have become clear that the fleet was unscathed) but to the safety of Zhapu, from where Zheng's fleet had set sail, he was all the more perturbed when it found the evidence ambiguous. A new committee was set up, one member obediently reporting back that Zheng's story was true, but another daring to bring up inconsistencies. Governor Liu persisted, forwarding a report from an undercover agent on Chusan confirming Major Zhou's original scepticism. But General Yijing of course held the trump card — the Son of Heaven was his uncle. He cut the inquiry short and announced its verdict: Zheng had told the truth all along.[12] As the situation moved from bad to worse, the encouraging myth that a bereaved son had struck back at the invaders was preferable to the unpalatable truth — that the Qing dynasty's bureaucracy was thoroughly corrupt and that the mighty empire was powerless against a few thousand so-called barbarians. The emperor himself was quite certain of what had happpened:

There is no doubt that the British fleet was burned in Tinghae harbour. Major Zhou's petition was not in agreement with the situation as uncovered, and was clearly untrue. Let him be severely punished![13]

Of course, Daoguang's pronouncements did nothing to alter the reality in Zhejiang. The British fleet, far from lying on the bed of Tinghae harbour, was as strong as ever and soon to be reinforced further still. Back in London, Viscount Melbourne had resigned as prime minister to be replaced by Sir Robert Peel and his Tories, and Palmerston had been replaced by the notably less hawkish Lord Aberdeen at the Foreign Office. With a view to concluding the war in China as early as possible — and there was never any doubt in London as to the ultimate success of Pottinger's expedition — an additional dozen warships, eight steamers, and thousands of fresh troops were now on their way to Hong Kong.

In the meantime, Gough and Parker had recommenced campaigning on the mainland. In mid-May of 1842 the *Nemesis* reconnoitred the defences thrown up at Zhapu, seventy miles from Tinghae on the northern shore of Hangzhou Bay. Two days later, after a brief but unexpectedly bloody resistance, the town was taken. Finding Hangzhou's Qiantang River too treacherous (it still regularly claims the lives of people who gather to view its spectacular tidal bore), it was decided not to attack the provincial capital but to head instead straight for the Yangtze and China's heartland. By mid-June the Wusong forts defending the approach to Shanghai had been disposed of and the city had fallen. (With cannonballs whizzing through the air during the engagement, Captain Hall's protégé the Chusanese orphan Afah was spotted on the walkway between the *Nemesis*' paddlewheels. Chastised, he told Captain Hall that he had only come up on deck 'to see the fun and what go on.')[14] In early July, the billowing sails of a 72-strong British fleet began to move upriver, causing little short of panic in the Forbidden City. This was the first time that a foreign war-fleet had dared to enter the Yangtze, China's greatest river. If not stopped, it would in just a few days' sailing have reached Zhenjiang and the junction with the Grand Canal, the route by which hundreds of thousands of tons of grain and supplies were shipped to Peking. The Qing could not hope to cling to power for long once those cargos were denied to them; a British fleet anchored foursquare on the Yangtze across the canal's mouth would act like an embolism to China's body politic. Just fifty miles further lay Nanking, the Southern Capital, China's second city, and it was within Pottinger's power to reduce it to rubble if the whim took him.

In mid-April, with Yijing's dismissal, a man named Qiying had been appointed the latest in a growing list of imperial commissioners who had so far failed to manage the British.[15] Like Yijing, Qiying was a Manchu of the Imperial clan, descended from a brother of the dynastic founder Nurhaci, and he had held top posts in four of the six ministries of central government. He had been sent to Zhejiang in company with a familiar face — Commissioner Yilibu. Yilibu, his failure to retake Chusan forgiven in light of his invaluable experience in dealing with the British, had spent scarcely a year in the political wilderness. By early May of 1842 he and Qiying were in Hangzhou, and there it was that they got word that the British were sailing in force up the Yangtze. Treading carefully, lest it be thought that they were willing to negotiate on anything approaching equal terms, they made overtures to Pottinger. If he should care to call a halt to the fighting and stop harassing the river traffic, they would be amenable to talks. But falling into the same trap as the disgraced Captain Elliot was the very last thing on Pottinger's mind. With his counter-demand of immediate face-to-face talks rebuffed, in late July the British attacked Zhenjiang, the Manchu garrison city that guarded the point where the Grand Canal met the Yangtze. It was precisely the tactic that Gützlaff, back in 1835, had predicted would make Peking sit up and pay attention.

One oppressively hot day, the British landed at Zhenjiang in their thousands — nobody was taking any chances by under-manning the attack — while rockets and shells were thrown into the city.[16] The walls were scaled, the gates blown in, but Zhenjiang's defenders did not flee like they had in every previous encounter with the British. These were no territorial Green Standards but instead hereditary soldiers of the Manchu banners, a courageous breed sworn to defend the dynasty, only they were still no match for the modern weapons and training of a European campaigning army. There was bloody fighting, hand-to-hand and inch-by-inch, as the Manchus were slaughtered. The survivors withdrew into the quarter of the city reserved for their families, and there they systematically murdered them — drowned them, slashed their throats, garrotted them, rather than see them despoiled by the invaders. During the night the city was looted and torched, an unmistakable foretaste of what awaited Nanking if the British were not given what they wanted. By morning the ships at anchor on the river could taste the battle: smoke hung over the city, and corpses bobbed ghoulishly about their moorings. Landing parties hurried to bury the piles of bodies that had started to putrefy in the furnace-like heat. The men of the expedition who went ashore to see the aftermath were sickened by this senseless massacre of the innocents. The Manchus had killed defenceless women, old men, even children and babies. Peking was shaken; but it was not the horror of the massacre that shook the court: such an end was praiseworthy, preferable to capture, and the fault in any case lay with the army whose aggression had precipitated the mass suicide. For all his insistence that he shed tears for his children's suffering, the emperor seemed to Western sensibilities shockingly adept at ignoring their pain. Until, that was, the source of that pain drew uncomfortably close. The difference now was that a 2,000-strong regular Manchu garrison had fought to the death and lost, giving the enemy control of that vital economic crossroads where China's greatest river met its longest canal and leaving the way clear to Nanking. Zhenjiang was no boon-dock Tinghae, its professional Manchu troops no irregular Han Chinese forces or ill-equipped conscripts who fled at the first shot, yet still they had been swept aside. And after Nanking, would the British head for the Peiho and take Peking? That would mean the end of the dynasty, and they had shown that they were quite capable of it.

When a fortnight later the fleet anchored beneath Nanking's ancient, straggling walls, Pottinger was master of the Yangtze. Commissioner Yilibu, rushing to the city, sent his most trusted aide to plead against any attack. Pottinger agreed to wait while credentials were produced, but when dissatisfaction was expressed at the limited scope of Yilibu's negotiating powers the warships were made ready to pound Nanking into submission. More offers were made — of money and of talks — with Yilibu and Qiying terrified that Nanking would be razed to the ground yet still unwilling to grant the British *carte blanche*. On August 13th, the two commissioners were informed that Nanking was to be destroyed the next day. The threat was enough to force the Chinese to open full plenipotentiary negotiations, and a fortnight later the Treaty of Nanking (the Chinese preferred to call it rather euphemistically 'The Yangtze Provinces Treaty for Ten Thousand Years of Peace') was signed aboard HMS *Cornwallis*. Lieutenant James Fitzjames of the *Cornwallis*, who was present at the signing, had been recording the expedition's progress for his messmates' amusement. His pithy summing up of the provisions of the treaty was eventually published in the *Nautical Magazine* of London: [17]

> Dollars twenty-one million by China to be paid;
> Free permission for all British subjects to trade;
> At five ports; *videlicet*, Canton, Ningbo;
> Shanghai, Amoy, Foochowfoo; and to go;
> From Amoy and Chusan (where a force now remains);
> When the money is paid, and then England retains;
> The whole of the island and bay of Hong Kong;
> To show the Chinese we were not in the wrong.
> A Consul in each of these five ports to live;
> 'Native traitors' the Emperor agrees to forgive.

So Pottinger had got his reparations for the destroyed opium, for the cost of the war, and even for outstanding debts owed to British merchants in Canton. He had opened ports on the eastern seaboard to foreign trade, just as Palmerston had asked, had confirmed Hong Kong's status, and had even kept his word over an amnesty for Chinese who had fraternised. Nor were his terms as onerous as they might have been: the $21,000,000 was to be paid in instalments before New Year's Eve of 1845; the opening of ports was an extension of privileges already enjoyed at Canton; and consular representation was not so far removed from the long-standing practice of recognising agents of the East India Company as to be unacceptable to Peking.

But would it *really* be necessary 'to go from Chusan when the money was paid'? The Chinese delegation is reputed, when Pottinger had made his demands known, to have asked with a degree of incredulity: 'Is that all?' It had been assumed by most observers, and feared by the Chinese, that the permanent cession of what was already a *de facto* British Chusan would be at the top of the list. Only with Hong Kong now unquestionably sovereign territory and its commercial advantages becoming apparent, it seemed that Pottinger attached less importance to wresting control of a second, even larger island than he did to securing wider access to new markets. Almost straight away, the first downpayment of $6,000,000 was loaded onto HMS *Cornwallis* and the fleet released its stranglehold on the Grand Canal to sail back to Tinghae. It had taken an unprecedented and permanent cession of territory to achieve it, but the Qing dynasty had finally succeeded in managing the barbarians.

'So ends the Chinese war,' wrote Edward Cree with relief. 'It has cost the lives of many thousands of human beings, and great destruction of property and misery and sorrow to many.' One of those lives was to be the mild-mannered Commissioner Yilibu's. Ordered south to Canton to negotiate the details of trade in Pottinger's treaty ports, in early March of the next year he sickened and died. The tense talks, conducted in the torrid heat of a Yangtze summer under the threat of terrible violence, had in the end proved too much for him.

How muchie loopee?

AS ONE by one the men-of-war and transports returning from the Yangtze rounded Bell Island to enter Tinghae's inner harbour, their crews noticed an unfamiliar vessel lying at anchor amongst the usual press of Chinese bum-boats.[1] The hospital ship HMS *Minden* had been commissioned by the Admiralty late in 1841, when it had looked likely that the war in China would prove protracted and disease-ridden, and she had slipped quietly into Chusan the day negotiations had begun at Nanking.[2] (She had, incidentally, been Captain Charles Elliot's first posting as a midshipman in 1816, though he was no longer in China to greet her.) Her cannons had been unshipped and her decks scrubbed and painted white to create wards. Iron bedsteads had taken the place of hammocks, hygienic water-closets replaced the age-old heads (which were essentially holes in the deck), boilers provided hot water on tap and a laundry clean bedding, the galley stove baked nutritious bread, and Dr Reid's Ventilation Apparatus worked to replace the malignant air from the lower decks. Especially to be welcomed by the men of the China expedition, she carried large stocks of *buchu*, a plant which, it had been discovered, the Hottentots of the Cape used to treat dysentery. A decade before Florence Nightingale would open her doors in Scutari, the *Minden* was the largest and most efficient hospital ever to leave English shores. Whispers soon reached her expectant ward-decks of a terrible strain of malignant cholera gripping the Yangtze fleet. It had taken a man, they said, 'from full health to Davy Jones' locker' in just eight hours.

On Michaelmas Day 1842, the troopship *Belleisle* became the first of the Yangtze fleet to drop anchor in Tinghae. She had left Plymouth a year earlier to brass bands and bunting, with 862 soldiers of Her Majesty's 98th Regiment of Foot, 300 sailors, 41 wives and 75 children aboard.[3] Her lower deck alone housed over 700, with families sleeping behind sheets strung between the hulls. Below the waterline in her orlop deck were squeezed 272 men, on hammocks set just a foot apart at their clews. No hint of a breeze reached to those foetid confines, where the mercury was forever in the nineties. Every spare inch was crammed with chests, crates and casks. The cows and horses in their stalls and the sheep, pigs, ducks and chickens that lived below with the passengers rendered the *Belleisle* a squalid ark. At Zhenjiang the 98th Regiment had been landed in full battledress despite roasting temperatures.[4] On that first wretched day of fighting and suicides, thirteen of the regiment had died of heatstroke. Fifty-seven more would swiftly follow, of cholera, malaria and dysentery made fatal by confinement on ship. By the end of July the *Belleisle* was a floating lazaretto, and when she slunk into Tinghae harbour only seventy men were still fit for duty. On October 1st, the anniversary of Chusan's recapture and what ought to have been a day of celebration, fifty of the regiment's worst cases were admitted to the *Minden* for treatment.[5]

Though the expedition had been buoyed by the successful conclusion of the Treaty of Nanking, the winter of 1842 was gloomy. The hospital lists rose (this was mainly the result of hard drinking over the festive season)[6] and the clouds now and again opened to release truly torrential downpours. It grew cold. A mile away, the island seen through the *Minden*'s glazed portholes was a strip of white hills sandwiched between a black sky and a brown sea, a most depressing sight.[7] Then a week passed without a single death aboard. Then another. And by the end of March, for the first time since 1840, the whole squadron was in perfect health. Bracing weather, good food, plentiful medical supplies, and an end to the strain of subjugating a restive population had improved life no end. In early May the *Minden* discharged the last of her patients to a purpose-built military hospital ashore and left Chusan for Hong Kong where tropical diseases were still devastating the British garrison.[8]

By October 1842, the victorious British high command had all safely arrived back in Tinghae. Mandarins came from the mainland, and with much ceremonial handed over soldiers and sailors who had been kidnapped before the treaty. In Hong Kong, the Babao brothers who had kidnapped some of them were set free.[9] Upriver in Canton province, three of the executed comprador Bu Dingbang's family had perished in gaol. His mother, widow, and daughter, their property and money now forfeit under Chinese law because of his crimes, were obliged to survive on a British charitable handout of $15 each month.[10] The public hangings of July had drawn a line under the kidnappings on Chusan, and the Treaty of Nanking had rendered any more superfluous. But still there occurred one last, singular episode before the two empires could put the unpleasantness of the last few years behind them.

In early October while out walking scarcely half a mile from Tinghae's north gate, Ensign Lawrence Shadwell of the 98th Regiment and a friend named George Wellesley were ambushed by a gang armed with bamboo poles.[11] Though George managed to escape back to the city, Shadwell was gagged, bound, and dragged away. Despite the blows, he contrived to work a hand free to shoot one assailant with his pistol. The others ran off, and when George returned with an armed sentry they found Shadwell badly beaten but otherwise safe. That the attack came after the promulgation of the treaty was put down to ignorance, but what really caused a stir was the identity of Shadwell's friend: the kidnappers had come close to capturing the nephew of no less a person than the Duke of Wellington.[12] The youngest son of the Duke's brother Gerald, George Wellesley had arrived in Chusan in late June as the fighting still raged in the Yangtze. Granted a discharge from his ship, he had landed to await a passage to his next posting. If Captain Elliot had been tactically wrong-footed (and the British public scandalised) by the capture of the otherwise unknown Captain Anstruther, the disappearance of a member of one of England's highest families can only be imagined. The Duke of Wellington was commander-in-chief, a cabinet minister without office, and leader of the House of Lords to boot. His nephew's kidnap or death would have demanded a ferocious backlash, but against whom would it usefully have been directed? It is intriguing to ponder whether the sanctity of Pottinger's hard-won treaty (it had not yet even arrived in England to be signed and ratified) would have withstood the clamour for retaliation had George been beheaded, or whether the Chinese camp might have felt emboldened to sell his release only at the highest diplomatic price rather than hand him back as a token of peace. As Yilibu had rightly surmised, the close friends and relations of barbarian chiefs were the most valuable pieces in games of such high stakes. But George's quick-thinking that afternoon, and Shadwell's assuredness with a pistol, left all such questions forever in the realms of supposition.

The greater part of the troops who had fought in the Yangtze campaign now left Chusan for Hong Kong, and a field force dominated by the Westmoreland Regiment was left to garrison the island. Their commanding officer Sir James Schoedde accepted the insignia to become the latest British governor. The ineffable Karl Gützlaff, who had thoroughly enjoyed his time lording it over the Chinese as magistrate of Ningbo, was pleased to take up the reins once more as magistrate of Chusan. As harbour master and marine magistrate, one George H. Skead RN was sworn in to oversee the anchorages for international shipping and to bring some kind of order to the countless skiffs, sampans and junks that plied the waters.[13] Like Hong Kong, Tinghae was for the first time declared a 'free port' — so long as Queen Victoria ruled here there would be no customs charges, port duties or taxes levied on ships of any nation.[14] In the coming years, the French tricolour and the Stars and Stripes would be a common sight in harbour. For the time being at least, things had finally turned out as Allen Catchpoole had wished when, 142 years earlier, he had sought from a humble *zongbing* the right to live and trade freely on those shores. As Cree had said, it had cost the lives of thousands and great destruction to achieve. Would it in the end be worth the price?

Peace between the Chinese Empire and Great Britain had breathed a rare confidence into Tinghae. It was the emperor himself who had permitted the British to live and trade here, and there was no question of the islanders being punished for having dealings with them. Sir Henry Pottinger had reiterated his promise that, if Chusan were ever again to be returned to Chinese rule, it would only be on the stipulation that the emperor grant a signed amnesty to any Chinese who had had dealings with the British. They could, he stressed, live and trade on Chusan assured of their impunity.[15] What the islanders thought of Pottinger's assurances is unclear: Sir Henry was a mere barbarian officer, while the emperor was the very Son of Heaven. Of what import was the emperor's signature if it bound him to act in a way dictated by the barbarians? Such insolence was outrageous. Yet they had seen with their own eyes that the emperor's armies were quite unable to dictate terms to the British, and they were a pragmatic and commercial people.

Soon Tinghae was a scene of bustle and activity, all its shops open for business, and the words 'How muchie *loopee*?' were everywhere to be heard.[16] They were neat and clean now and would have done honour to any London grocer.[17] Pastry-cooks were naturally selling mostly Chinese dainties made of ground rice and sweet red beanpaste, ill-suited to Western tastes, but already some had learned how to bake English biscuits for their captive market. Others had memorised the English names for their goods, and one cobbler had begun to make shoes in the European style.[18] A fertile source of confrontation between traders and soldiers would soon be removed by the enforcement of standardised weights and measures.[19] Guttersnipes tailed the officers in the hope of a few rupees' fleeting employment, squawking away in pidgin English.[20] There was a great number of merchant vessels in harbour, and prices were lower even than Hong Kong.[21] On October 11th they decked themselves out with flags for the Chusan Regatta.[22] As for opium, the drug that had lain at the root of the war, it was, despite the best efforts of the British commanders on Chusan to stem its trade on the China coast, readily available. Determined, as ever, to walk the thin line between condoning and condemning the trade, the British government was most careful not to give the Chinese the mistaken impression that they were able to stop the trade if they wished: that was in the lap of the opium traders themselves. Two years into the second British occupation, in fact, one Charles Hope, captain of HMS *Thalia*, would even be rapped over the knuckles by the foreign secretary Lord Palmerston for attempting to exercise control over British opium vessels: how could the Chinese, if Hope were to be successful in stopping the opium trade, come to any other conclusion than that the British had been lying all along when they had insisted that they had no authority over private merchants?[23] How ironic, that Captain Hope's conviction that the actions of British merchants were bringing both Britain's flag and her national reputation into disgrace were outweighed by fears that stopping the opium trade would cast the British as perfidious. And so the trade went on.

Edward Cree for one was thankful to swap the miasmas of the Yangtze for the sea breezes of Chusan. His arduous caseload during the river campaign was forgotten now the *Rattlesnake* was once more surrounded by sampans full of babbling farmers eager to sell their produce. Word of the treaty had reached Trumball Island, where during the first occupation Cree had often visited the pipe-smoking duck farmer. This man, Cree found to his delight, had not after all been beheaded for fraternisation. True, he had been in trouble for selling food to the barbarians, but it was nothing the old rogue could not worm his way out of. His name, he was now prepared to tell Cree, was A-Tin, and he began to take in ship's laundry to wash, helped by a youngest son whose English was becoming quite passable.[24] His take on that summer's denouement was that the British 'were beaten away from Hong Kong, so went up to Nanking, where the mandarin said "What do you want?"' The British had answered 'Six million dollars', and the mandarin had given it to them to keep them quiet.[25] Already, the indemnity was being referred to by the Chinese as *fuyikuan* — 'the sum paid to soothe the barbarians'. From the rarefied confines of the Forbidden City to the islands of Tinghae harbour the understanding of the war was the same — only by the grace of eternal China, the one civilisation around which All Under Heaven revolved, had the British been suffered to carry on their grubby trade. There had been no admission of Chinese inferiority. Far from it, the peaceful withdrawal of the Yangtze fleet could only be construed as a Chinese victory.

As the damp Zhejiang winter drew in, Cree resumed his butchery of the local wildfowl. His *Rattlesnake* became more roomy with the departure of the Royal Irish for Amoy, and he spent Christmas of 1842 dining with the remaining officers while the ship's crew drank themselves into a disgraceful state. On New Year's Eve, Cree and his army friends played whist and celebrated the coming of 1843 with anchovy toast, whisky punch and cigars. For the first time since 1839, it looked likely that the coming year would bring nothing but peace.

16

Tabula rasa

UNDER THE Treaty of Nanking the Chinese had agreed to open ports other than Canton to foreigners, but it was only after the details of tariffs and trade had been hammered out that merchants could begin to live and work in them. It would be almost two years, the summer of 1844, before goods were freely flowing through Amoy, Fuzhou, Ningbo and Shanghai alike. Even then, for security and companionship foreigners found themselves confined in the main to enclaves outside the walls, their travel officially restricted to the distance of a day's journey. In Amoy and Fuzhou they lived upon the islands of Gulangyu and Nantai, in Ningbo upon a spit of land at the confluence of two rivers, and at Shanghai in a concession bounded by water. On a still sparsely populated Hong Kong, Britons restricted themselves to the community that was fast growing up at Victoria, where the Chinese population was dominated by shady individuals eager to avoid the attentions of the authorities across the bay in Kowloon. (As the missionary George Smith put it, Hong Kong with its theft and violence had become 'a receptacle for the most abandoned desperadoes of the continent.')[1] Only on Chusan did Britons find themselves living squarely among a large and thoroughly indigenous community. Never before had so many men and women from every class and calling found themselves free to roam towns and villages in complete safety, without the mandarins forever looking jealously over their shoulders, deciding what they saw, insisting they turn back. Through their writings, published in the newspapers, magazines and books of the day, detailed information on every aspect of life became available to readers back home, and Chusan became for a number of years the most familiar of Chinese place-names.

Britain's understanding of China was set to change beyond recognition in the years after the Union Jack was raised over Tinghae. Until that point, what the West thought it knew of distant Cathay had still owed as much to the social agenda of the Enlightenment as it did to reality. Even the most easily reached province,

Canton, was for most Europeans an unimaginably long journey, and almost all knowledge had arrived through the distorting prism of those missionaries who since Matteo Ricci in the 1580s had penetrated the emperor's court. Even the eighteenth-century Jesuit Père Du Halde, compiler of the authoritative *Description de la Chine* which had been essential reading matter for visitors such as Lord Macartney, had never in fact visited the country in person. The *philosophes* of the Enlightenment especially became enchanted with the Jesuits' stories. These thinkers, who like the Jesuits were themselves a product of the religious chaos of the Reformation, insisted that reason was superior to the irrationality of revealed faith. Seeking to replace Christianity with humanism (or even with thoroughgoing atheism), they saw in Confucianism a model to emulate. Working at best from second- or third-hand accounts, they thought they had found in China an ideal example of morality without religion. Men like Voltaire, an outspoken propagandist for China (though of course he too had never ventured within 6,000 miles of the Forbidden City), lauded it as the perfect example of enlightened government. The Chinese, though, would not have recognised his description of their world.

By the end of the eighteenth century a more realistic view of China had begun to oust the idealisations of the Enlightenment, and it had been mercantile Britons rather than continental theoreticians who had led the way. Fruitless attempts to reason with its Manchu ruling class over trade and diplomatic ties — the failed embassies of lords Macartney and Amherst were a perfect case — had made it clear that these were a people in thrall not to rationalism but instead to a conservative and inward-looking despotism. Yet old stereotypes are slow to change, and publicly available accounts of even the Macartney embassy had persisted in painting a willow-pattern scene of Tinghae as though it were a smaller version of Venice. What little remained of that myth of a beautiful and orderly Celestial Empire began to dissipate along with the smoke of battle on July 5th, 1840. If familiarity did not quite breed contempt, eye-witness reports of the reality of China were disdainful of its once-vaunted culture and tinged with disappointment that the Chinese had fallen short of the high ideals that had been ascribed to them. 'Some writer has compared Tinghae with Venice,' one scornful observer wrote of Sir George Staunton's description. 'If that's true, then the straw hovels of Mongha near Macao are like the Tuileries, for both are the habitations of men.'[2]

On closer inspection it struck one that the nation once lauded by Voltaire and his kind was technologically backward and politically bankrupt, that its supposedly comfortable peasantry lived for the most part exploited by landlords in abject poverty, and that a supposedly utopian system of farming was nothing but a myth. As for Chinese towns being kept clean by refuse collectors, as the *philosophes* insisted was the case, the British invaders of 1840 had been almost overcome by the filth. Gradually the mirage of an oriental Arcadia began to be replaced by a more businesslike view of China and its people. The process was inevitable, and no bad thing: Britain's projection of the Enlightenment onto this distant canvas had led to centuries of trying to reason with the Chinese as with an idealised self, and that profound misunderstanding had ended in war.

In the hiatus between mirage and reality came a great deal of exasperation and prejudice. The breathtaking bluntness of one Henry Monk, who like Edward Cree had arrived in Chusan as a naval surgeon, was typical. He would one day write a note to accompany some ladies' dresses he had sent back to his wife in Guernsey:

> The thing I fear is that some of you will be taking up the cudgels and cracking my pate when I get home for having dared to enter and violate the sanctity of the boudoir of a Chinese *she* to get possession of the same; I made a mistake above when I called them ladies, they all smell very strong; and they appear to me to find greater favour in the eyes of their lords as this peculiar quality predominates, they choose their spouses as our epicures do game, the more they stink the better.[3]

Captain Pears, the same man who had quarried away the graves on Josshouse Hill with little thought for the relatives of the dead, was even less circumspect: 'The Chinese are a mean, dirty, stinking, low, cunning, villainous, abominable, never-too-much-to-be-hated set of *bêtes*,' he wrote, having at least the decency to add: '(oh dear! I am better after that!)'.[4]

Amongst the educated elite there was a great deal of frustration with a reputedly civilised people the British had hoped might be more, well — *British*. Doctor Duncan MacPherson, who had arrived on Chusan to look after the health of the Madras troops, held similarly one-sided views:

> Haughty, cruel and hypocritical, they despise all other nations but their own; they regard themselves as faultless…. They style all foreigners barbarians, and they tell them, "We can do without you, but you cannot do without us; if your country is so good, why do you come here for tea and rhubarb?" No argument will induce a Chinaman to adopt a different style of reasoning.[5]

MacPherson and the rest seem not to have reflected that the islanders had every reason to despise a nation that had bombarded its city and slaughtered its people just to force the Cantonese to open their markets. Even Sir John Davis, who would soon take over from Sir Henry Pottinger as governor of Hong Kong and who might have been expected to temper his views, admitted that he thought the women of Chusan unattractive (they went bald early, he said) and their men faithless thieves.[6] A correspondent of the Protestant missionary magazine the *Chinese Repository* did manage a modicum of faint praise: he found the islanders 'talkative, thievish, troublesome, but tame — wanting little to hold them in subjection — and inquisitive.'[7]

As to their eating habits, correspondents on Chusan confirmed to readers back home many of what even today are enduring stereotypes. One wrote to the *Englishman* magazine with his first experience of Chinese food:

> Picture to yourself one of our men bringing me the hind quarter of an evidently well-fed rat, all ready for a Chinaman's breakfast, and you may imagine our horror at a Chinaman showing us the

same a quarter of an hour afterwards, and very civilly asking us to allow him to dress it for us.[8]

Another reported that dogs, cats, rats and frogs were all being brought to market: 'tabby cutlets and bow-wow sausages are I understand rather delicacies.'[9] One lieutenant let his imagination roam freely:

> They don't use the milk from the cows for butter or to drink, but they use that what comes from the pigs, a very curious set of people, and they consider an ass's head with frog's sauce or young puppies with rats, mice or cat soup the greatest dainties they can have — what next will they eat?[10]

The islanders, needless to say, did not drink pigs' milk nor eat ass's head with frog — or any other — sauce. But they did indeed eat dog (they hung puppies for sale in cages in the markets), and a preference for black, white or light brown ones was noticed, as was the upper classes' predilection for animals having a black palate and tongue, and which had been raised on a vegetarian diet.[11] Many British officers employed Chinese cooks. They probably ate a lot of dog without knowing it, it was wrongly surmised:[12] it is far more likely that any man willing to try the delicacy would have been palmed off with a less costly substitute than *vice versa*.

Yet other, more thoughtful, men did reflect seriously on their new home. For a start, Tinghae, though it had its seamy side, was a far remove from the claustrophobic environment of Canton, to which port British merchants had been restricted for almost a century. One Lieutenant Forbes of the Royal Navy put that place into context:

> No-one could think of searching the back streets of Chatham, or the purlieus of Wapping, for a fair criterion of British society, or specimens of the yeomanry of merry England; yet from such data as these we have hitherto drawn our ideas of Chinese morality and civilization, but, as the country opens, and we become better acquainted, I trust that both parties will find that they are not the barbarians they have hitherto mutually believed each other to be.

His trust was to be well-founded. In October of 1842, as peace settled on the Zhejiang coast in the wake of the Treaty of Nanking, the *Times* published a letter which cast Chusan in a positive light: [13]

> The people of this island, and those in the other parts of China which have come under my observation, are a fine class of men, well-formed, intelligent, and in many points highly civilized; the lower orders muscular, healthy, and to all appearances happy under their government, which is not certainly so oppressive as is generally supposed in Europe. In agriculture and in native manufactures they are far advanced, and in most of the mechanical sciences they possess great genius.

The reason many looked down on this conquered race, the letter's author Dr Alexander Grant of the Bengal Medical Service argued, was that they were measuring its worth by the wrong yardstick — that of military power. Pottinger's great successes on the Yangtze were unequal, dishonourable, akin to buccaneering:

> Of the art of war, as practised among Europeans, they know nothing, and they are at once appalled with the effective power of the mighty engines of death which we bring against them. There has, indeed, been nothing like fighting upon this expedition, and those who have mingled in the various actions would scarce recognise them in the flaming despatches in which they are described.

The *Times* printed another long letter, written six months later in May of 1843.[14] Prolonged peace had transformed the Zhejiang coast, and there had not been a single case of robbery or assault on Chusan since the kidnap attempt on Lieutenant Wellesley. Peace, so much was evident, was now doing more for British interests than conflict. 'Physical force,' the *Times*' correspondent was certain, 'is the worst instrument for destroying the prejudices of the Asiatic. That there is something innate in mankind to resist force, all history and experience prove.' British opinions of the Chinese too had mellowed with exposure to their everyday lives. Their harshest critics now, in fact, were said to be Western missionaries:

> These men of God, carried away by their enthusiasm, can see nothing fair in God's people, because it is their lot to be heathens. Hence one cause of our despising the Asiatic, of our treating him as possessed of no feeling — as indeed an inferior being, fit only to be governed. I have seen no reason to change my former opinions — on the contrary, I now lean more to the favourable side of the Chinese character. Their worst features are perhaps inattention to personal cleanliness, a universal addiction to the filthy habit of tobacco smoking, and the cruel practice of compressing the female foot. Still these are not crying sins, and are only hurtful to our prejudices…. I do not include opium smoking, for that vice they owe to Europeans.

Other Britons examined Chusan with all the taxonomical exactness of the Victorian age, for the garrison consisted of educated officers and men who were well qualified to make scientific observations. 'The Government,' observed the *Englishman*, 'ought to encourage those gentlemen to avail themselves of every opportunity to contribute to the extension of knowledge, and the result of their observations ought to be entrusted to the Learned Societies of Great Britain for criticism and publication.'[15] In the fields of language, literature, astronomy, meteorology, botany, mineralogy, zoology, philology and statistics, the *Englishman* was sure, even given what the British had learned from the Jesuits, China was a '*tabula rasa*'.

Perhaps the most famous, in subsequent years, of all the gentlemen who turned an educated eye to Chusan was a botanist, Robert Fortune.

'When the news of the peace with China first reached England in the autumn of 1842,' recalled Fortune, superintendent of the Horticultural Society's Chiswick gardens, 'I obtained the appointment of Botanical Collector… and proceeded to China in that capacity in the spring of the following year.'[16] He had been provided by the committee of the Horticultural Society with 'a fowling piece and pistols, and a Chinese vocabulary.'[17] And so Robert Fortune embarked upon *Three Years' Wanderings in the Northern Provinces of China*, (stepping into the shoes of one Mr Douglas who had accidentally perished in the Sandwich Islands at the bottom of a pit dug to catch wild boar).[18] Born on the banks of the Tweed, Fortune had by his twenties made a name for himself in Edinburgh as a gardener of prodigious talent. His reputation placed him squarely in line for the job when China's opening up convinced the Horticultural Society that it ought to despatch somebody to bring back hardy plants (and flowers, but only 'exceptionally beautiful' ones, it was specified) for propagation. Yet after a four-month passage Fortune was disappointed by his first view of China.[19] After the lush forests of Java, the outlying islands of the Gulf of Canton were all barren, sun-scorched granite dotted with stunted pines, and not at all like the glowing descriptions of a land of camellias, azaleas and roses he had read. Although this first impression of Hong Kong stayed with him, he did grow to find much of merit there. It had a fine natural harbour, and he expected that the settlement at Victoria would make a pretty enough place, given time. The lush vegetation of the Chusan archipelago, on the other hand, was a perfect delight, its hills and glens reminiscent of the Scottish Highlands. Its inland valleys were beautiful, watered by clear mountain streams, and some of them were as yet untouched. 'Did our island of Hong Kong possess the natural advantages and beauties of Chusan,' Fortune mused, 'what a splendid place it might have been made by our enterprising English merchants in a very few years.'[20]

Governor Schoedde provided Fortune with a house in Tinghae and an introduction to Dr Maxwell of the Madras Army, a keen botanist who had already catalogued and sketched the more striking of Chusan's flora, saving Fortune months of work.[21] Fortune became familiar with the island over two years of meanderings in every season of the year, watching and making notes as the inhabitants flooded their fields, transplanted their rice, hoed their hillside rows of sweet potatoes. He admired the elegant simplicity of their ancient waterwheels; recorded the planting of wheat, barley, beans, peas and sweetcorn; watched as the farmers sowed the spent paddy with clover to use as manure. Spring on Chusan would see fields of wild mustard come into blossom throughout the island:

> In April, when the fields are in bloom, the whole country seems tinged with gold, and the fragrance which fills the air, particularly after an April shower, is delightful.... Chusan in spring is one of the most beautiful islands in the world. It reminds the Englishman of his own native land. In the mornings the grass sparkles with dew, the air is cool and refreshing, the birds are singing in every bush, and flowers are hanging in graceful festoons from the trees and hedges.

Springtime in Chusan is just as lovely today. The climate, Fortune discovered, nurtured an abundance of beautiful plants that would thrive back in England. In the torrid south, azaleas confined themselves to cool mountaintops, but here in Zhejiang they grew wild on the lowest slopes:

> Few can form any idea of the gorgeous and striking beauty of these azalea-clad mountains, where, on every side, as far as the vision extends, the eye rests on masses of flowers of dazzling brightness and surpassing beauty. Nor is it the azalea alone which claims our admiration; clematises, wild roses, the honeysuckles, the Glycine and a hundred others mingle their flowers with them.

Great shell-burst splashes of quivering bamboo reminded Fortune of the young larch forests back home. The long waxy leaves of the Chinese bayberry drew the eye toward the clumps of juicy red fruit at their centre. Groves of kumquat bushes speckled the green hillsides with orange during the season. For trees there were the ubiquitous fir and pine, and the wind-tortured cypresses and junipers ever to be found crowding around the graves of the wealthy like stooping mourners. He painstakingly dug up specimens of scented lilac daphnes, of buddleia with its long, purple spikes, of the most eye-catching of rose-coloured weigelas found growing in the garden of a mandarin near Tinghae, of peonies, clematis, honeysuckle, japonica, hibiscus and more, and sent them all back to London.

When Robert Fortune turned his eye-glass toward the details of everyday life on the island he found two cultures tentatively exploring one another — if Chusan's social fabric was not of Chinese warp and British weft, perhaps it resembled a little an oriental silk sparsely decorated with Western embroidery. For a start, the inhabitants of this place struck one as a 'quiet and inoffensive race, always civil and obliging.'[22] Like the flora of their island home they were mercifully different from the Chinese of Canton, whom outsiders found avaricious and xenophobic. British government, thought Fortune, was keeping the inevitable bad elements amongst them in check. The proximity of a large British garrison had geared much of the island's agricultural production toward supplying its needs, and the city markets were filled daily with fruit and vegetables, with fowl and oxen. A great variety of fish was landed — sole, mullet, pomfret, seer fish, mandarin fish, mackerel, sea trout and more.[23] From the interior came wild game, hog-deer, and the many species of birds Edward Cree found so delicious. Before the British landed, the islanders (who had no access to firearms, these being forbidden to all but soldiers) had left the wildfowl in peace, artificially hatching and raising all the ducks and geese they required. But now the hills swarmed with trappers who harvested their bounty to feed the hungry foreigners. Tartar sheep were imported from the mainland, thrived, and ended up on British dining tables.[24] The Chinese quickly learned that Europeans preferred baked bread to steamed buns, and brick-built ovens sprang up to meet the demand.[25] Several pastry shops opened up, selling sweetmeats.[26] Bespoke tailors set up near the wharves. Curio shops sold mass-produced souvenirs for officers and their wives to impress family and friends back home — gods carved in wood or stone, incense burners, bronzes, dragons and kirins, porcelains, paintings, silks and satins, endless fans, and the most elaborate and beautiful embroidery fashioned into scarves and aprons in quite the style of an English lady.[27] Reading the descriptions of Tinghae in 1843, it is impossible not to picture the alleyways around the popular

Chinese tourist sights of our own day. These shopkeepers had the confidence to extend credit to these valued customers, and each of them thought it *de rigueur* to have an English shop-sign above his door, chosen under advice from the men who formed their clientele:[28] 'Stultz, tailor, from London', read one, 'Buckmaster, tailor to the army and navy' another, 'Dominie Dobbs the grocer', 'Squire Sam, porcelain merchant', 'Tailor to Her Most Graceful Majesty Queen Victoria and His Royal Highness Prince Albert, by appointment'. '*Ici on parle Français*' was one unlikely boast.[29] Testimonials from customers were in great demand, many of them florid to the point of ridicule and clearly the result of an escalating joke played on the poor Chinese. They, ever suspicious, would forever be showing them to other customers for advice, and so ever more extravagant touches would be added by way of correction.

Many of the Chinese having dealings with the British seem to have understood a little English, plus a smattering of Malay and Indian words (a large part of the field force throughout the occupation remained sepoys).[30] In a Babel of tongues, they classed foreigners as *mandalee*, *siensang* or *a-say*, depending on rank. A *mandalee* (an attempt at 'mandarin', which is a Portuguese rather than a Chinese word) might be *bulla bulla* or *chotta chotta* — the islanders' best approximation of 'big' and 'small' in Bengali. *Siensang*, used to address merchants, was the local equivalent of 'mister'. *A-say* was used for everybody else, a misunderstanding that apparently arose from the Chinese hearing the English hail one another with the words 'I say!' and taking it to be a form of address. The British in turn called the Chinese *fokee*, a Cantonese term meaning 'friend' or 'boss', the name one might use these days to fetch a waiter. It would have meant nothing to the Wu speakers of Chusan, who presumably thought it an English word. In the markets, Robert Fortune reported, there grew up an onomatopoeic vocabulary of animal names:[31] *boo* for cow, *kake* for chicken, *his-wak* goose and *kwak* duck, though why simply pointing did not do, heaven only knows.

Between lengthy peregrinations across eastern and southern China, Fortune visited his favourite Chusan archipelago on many occasions through 1843 and into the following year. As the heat of summer waned he headed back to Hong Kong. When he sailed for home on the *John Cooper* there travelled with him glazed Wardian cases filled with quite the most beautiful plants from Chusan, whose descendants ornament our gardens today.

Doctor Alexander Grant of the Bengal Medical Service, a correspondent of the *Times* newspaper back in London during his time on Chusan, was another man who found himself just as fascinated with his island home as was Fortune.[32] With his Westmoreland Regiment now facing only light duties, with plenty of fresh meat and (now that they were in proper barracks) no undue exposure to the elements, throughout 1843 Dr Grant had plenty of spare time to devote to his hobby, a systematic study of Chinese husbandry. The time had been ripe for a reappraisal of the subject: following the theories of continental polemicists such as Voltaire, writers like the French economist François Quesnay (he too had never visited China) had insisted that there was no uncultivated land near Chinese towns, nor even trees, hedges or ditches for fear that the smallest plot of soil would be wasted. Hills and mountains, he said, were cultivated to their very summits, an image of fertility, while China's towns were kept clean by the practice of collecting refuse to fertilise the land. Quesnay's descriptions had become such a cliché that the British had been perplexed to find on invading Chusan that much of the island was covered with scrub. Far from living in an agrarian utopia, it swiftly became apparent that the Chinese were quaintly medieval and inefficient in these matters, that they relied for irrigation upon man-powered waterwheels, and were insistent that the time-honoured ways of planting, transplanting, weeding, reaping and threshing were not to be altered. More objectionable to British sensibilities, the islanders insisted upon leaving coffins unburied on the hillsides, with bones and skulls left strewn about the place by wild animals, and rotten lids forever a trap for unwary feet.[33] One officer wrote of his days spent wandering the hills, that:

in the tenanted graves which curiosity induced us to open, the body appeared dressed as in life, the pipe and tobacco lay on the breast, and loaves and rice at the unconscious head.[34]

After a decade of major advances in sanitation back home, Britons could not fathom the islanders' irrational attachment to such traditions over advances in public health. Knowing from experience that malaria was linked to stagnant paddy, still they refused to raise wheat instead! Sir Henry Pottinger had tried and failed to convince Tinghae's farmers of the benefits of dry cereals, though he in his turn had failed to appreciate the central — even mythic — role that rice played in the imperial Chinese system. The inquisitive Dr Grant, however, not satisfied with merely sniping at the Chinese from the sidelines, trekked across the island with his notebook to record age-old practices that aimed to eke every last drop of worth from the soil.[35]

Chinese agriculture proved to be different in many and unexpected ways from how it was portrayed in Europe. To begin with, their lives bound to the turning of the year, farmers divided each of the four seasons into six fifteen-day periods called *qi*, and each *qi* into three *hou* of five-days each. The cycles of rural life closely followed the predictable path of those twenty-four annual *qi*, whose names like ancient mnemonics encapsulated two millennia of observations — Winter Solstice, Slight Cold, Great Cold, Start of Spring, Rainwater, Insects Awake, Spring Equinox…. Come the *qi* of Clarity and Brightness in early April, the island's rice fields were ploughed up. Flooded using hand-powered chain-pumps, the mud of the seed-beds was raked until, as smooth as a billiard table, exactly one inch of water lay on them. Rice seeds that had been steeping in water and urine were now sown in nursery beds. By the middle of the month, the fields were being manured with a mixture of cow dung, fermented night soil, and slurry dredged from the canals (it had been this lethal concoction that Burrell's men had been obliged to drink after the invasion of 1840). The green seedlings pushed through the water of their nurseries during the *qi* of Grain Rains, and when in early May they reached six inches the back-breaking task of transplanting could begin. Having set the seedlings in bunches one foot apart in their flooded fields, the farmers' attention turned to other crops.

Once the mustard had blossomed in a splash of yellow, the mustard fields were planted with sweetcorn seedlings. The mustard seed was dried and winnowed. As May rolled over into June, a succession of foods came into season. British officers found that the peas their Chinese cooks served up to them were replaced by green beans. There was anxiety during the *qi* of Grain Fills over a drought that threatened the rice crop, though the same dry spell saw the wheat and barley harvested and winnowed. The countryside was dotted with sheaves of drying straw; roadsides and cottage gardens were full of fine cucumbers and melons; the aubergines bore a lustrous purple tinge. As the canals dried up and the soil of the paddy began to crack, though, the farmers prayed for rain, 'the aged and experienced anxiously scanning the setting sun for the indications of the blessed shower.' It worked, and the heavens opened for three days. Come the arrival of Slight Heat, the streams and canals were again full.

July of 1843 was just as sultry as when the British had first landed three years earlier. As the last of the wheat, barley and mustard was got in, the bare fields were turned over to the next crop of rice and vegetables. Young boys would set about weeding the paddy, pulling each up by the roots before burying it to rot down at the foot of the rice plant it had tried to usurp. From dawn to dusk they scrabbled in the mud, bent double. But the main occupation in summer was tending the fruits and vegetables. The aubergines, cucumbers, melons and pumpkins were plump and juicy, the sweetcorn and millet were in seed, and the sorghum promised to make good *samshoo*. Tinghae's markets were filled with apples and pears, peaches and plums.

Through Autumn Begins and Limit of Heat in the month of August, the reaping and threshing of the first rice crop overlapped with the weeding and irrigating of the next. Tender lettuces and hot chillies appeared on British dining tables. A typhoon damaged farmhouses early the next month, but the harvest went on regardless. It was a fine time to be at mess, with sweet potatoes, limes, chestnuts and walnuts making an appearance in town. The last plantings of the first rice crop were brought in, making way for more wheat, mustard and other vegetables. A second typhoon struck the island during the *qi* of Autumn Equinox, on the second anniversary of Pottinger's invasion. The low-lying valleys were flooded, trees were uprooted, houses lost their roofs, and bridges were swept away. The whole western part of the island, in fact, was a sheet of water out of which the hills now rose as islands.[36] Over one hundred Chinese drowned, but still the survivors doggedly gathered in the harvest once the waters had subsided. Clover was planted for brewing into a nitrogen-rich fertiliser, and the cotton the villagers grew to make their clothes was picked. By the end of a tumultuous month the second rice crop was being reaped and threshed. Fields of soy were ripening, the turnips were fat, clumps of radishes were ready for digging up on the hillsides.

The face of the island by Slight Snow in late November was very different to its summer appearance. Most of the paddy had been drained and ploughed and farms were cropped with mustard, clover, wheat, barley and beans. With the second rice crop now harvested, labour was directed toward digging up the last of the sweet potatoes and drying the soy. Clover formed a thick, green carpet over the vale of Tinghae. The drying floors and roofs of the island were tinged from a distance with pink, as slices of sweet potato dried in the cool air. As Great Snow dusted the peaks, the temperature fell and the canals froze over. The brushwood covering the hills was cut for fuel. The sight of the farmers trudging out to tend the ancestral tombs brought home an important truth about China: now that work was less pressing, the rotten coffins were being rethatched, the overgrown grass on the grave mounds cut back. The tombs might look to outsiders as though they had been forsaken, but on this island men were laid to rest in the company of their ancestors, on land they had cultivated with their own hands: 'Hence springs one powerful cause of the cherished fondness of a Chinese for the place of his birth,' observed Grant, 'and his unwillingness ever to forsake it.' Little wonder, then, that Chusan's gentry never gave up hopes of returning once the British were gone.

The ash of the burned brushwood was mixed with animal dung and human waste to provide fertiliser for the coming season. The British feasted on fish, on oysters, cockles and mussels, on the deer, duck, teal and pheasants which were so plentiful. With the crops gathered in and the fields frost-hardened, the Chinese prepared their houses for the coming year. The temples were filled with devotional offerings; in every home from the richest villa to the meanest hut a table was laid out with food. As attention turned away from the fields, this was a popular time to marry: wedding processions were commonplace, and their cacophonies filled the wintry streets with colour and noise.[37] All year, the islanders had been busy from first light to nightfall. Their villages had been kept cheerful and neat. No men had lounged about; no idle women had gossiped in the streets like they would back home.[38] Britain, Dr Grant felt, had plenty to learn from such careful husbandry, such tireless industry. There was much to be gained by adopting Chinese irrigation techniques and a system of fertilising the land where little was ever wasted.[39]

Dr Grant — he was not ashamed to admit it — felt admiration for the Chusanese. It was an admission that would have been scoffed at just a few years before. Gützlaff too, in one of his regular *Chinese Reports* to his sponsors, mused that:

> the moment, when the Chinese maintain the freedom of trade with other nations, and find themselves able to move to other countries with wife and family, will be an epoch-making time in world history, and America as well as Europe and the islands of Australia will soon have to consider the enormity of the event.[40]

Even Captain Pears, whose early impressions of the Chinese had been of detestable, filthy beasts, was later moved to confide in his journal that he could not look upon the Chinese coast without feeling a probability, a certainty even, that a fine and powerful nation would yet be established there.[41] He longed for a thousand of the fearless sailors he had watched outrun a British warship despite its firepower, to cut their pigtails off and to make of them the finest battalion in the world.[42] Even the Chinese themselves did not have this much faith in their global potential.

Others who passed through British Chusan were similarly fascinated by the minutiae of life there and recorded what they saw.
Far from staying forever unseen behind closed doors, as had been
the West's general impression of Chinese womanhood, Tinghae's
ladies could be seen in numbers on the city streets, teetering along
on their tiny bound feet.[43] Tinghae even had its fashionable *beau
monde*, who would promenade in their white stockings, brown
silk pantaloons and green jerkins woven upon the silk looms of
Suzhou, their heads shaved and pigtails braided with the utmost
care and tied with a silk ribbon.[44] On their feet would be a pair
of the upturned wooden pattens so beloved of Chinoiserie illus-
trators (how delightful, that one aspect of that willow-pattern
world turned out to be true!). In hands from which protruded
fingernails of several inches they might hold a light walking cane,
or a paper parasol if they feared becoming tanned like a common
peasant. The clothes of those farmers, by contrast, were rude, the
same for both sexes, woven from a fibrous, nettle-like hemp and
dyed blue with wild knot-grass.[45]

So much was clear to onlookers who sauntered about Tinghae,
visited the markets, or stood amongst the chattering crowds to
watch the rope-dancers, the jugglers, or the local version of Punch
and Judy,[46] for the conspicuous aspects of town life impinged
on all but the most disinterested of foreigners. Even inquisitive
observers like Alexander Grant and Edward Cree, unable to
understand Wu dialect, could go little deeper than record what
they could observe as bystanders. To these men — and to the rest
of the field force even more so — it seemed the Chinese celebrated
their New Year simply with the deafening reports of firecrackers
and the clanging of gongs. A fortnight later they traipsed through
the streets with lamps held out on sticks. Weddings were adver-
tised with the echoing rasp of reeded bamboo pipes. Funerals
were singular for the islanders' white mourning habits and the
sheer size of the coffins. The gods were comically clothed in
satins and, with undulating paper dragons leading the way, were
paraded about the town on sedan chairs. But nobody could say
why. When Robert Morrison, the first Protestant missionary to
China, tried once to give an account of Chinese religious practice

he found it so bound up with every aspect of life that, exasperated, he cut himself short and commented only that 'the details would be endless.'[47] So it had been since before the time of Christ, and so it remained until more than a century later and the coming of Communism.

Under the very noses of the British, the endless details of Chusanese life went on unseen behind the thin squares of oil-soaked paper that passed for windows.[48] On the last day of the twelfth month, families swept the old year from their homes on a cloud of dust, and when the fifth watch of the night was sounded they rose to set out incense and candles. Men and women donned ritual clothing to worship the gods of heaven and earth. They laid out fruit, wine and dainties for the ancestors. The eldest sons went out to pay respects to their clan, to in-laws and neighbours, and families entertained each other with food and wine. The ancestral portraits were hung and offerings presented to them. Every morning and evening until the fifth of the new moon, incense, tea, fruit and cakes would be set out and respects paid. Come the thirteenth, the portraits would be rehung and the ceremony performed again until, on the eighteenth day, the portraits were tidied away for another year.

At the year's first full moon, globes of many lamps were set up in the ancestral temples. Each neighbourhood set out in formation, banging gongs, hitting drums and generally making a clamour and din in the streets. As for the raucous music of Dr Grant's wintertime wedding processions, it marked the first time the bride herself had left for her new home, the public culmination of a long series of matchmaking, divination and mutual gift-giving behind closed doors. That morning at the fifth watch, after making offerings to the gods, the groom's family had despatched a colourful sedan chair to the bride's house. Her doorkeeper, after thrice refusing the money proffered by their envoy, had let it in. Her mother and sisters had wailed for her to stay, and her retinue of brothers had turned back halfway to her new home. Once the doors had closed behind her, she would ascend into the main hall for the formal ceremony of marriage before performing her first ritual tasks as a wife.

As for Edward Cree's hastily sketched funeral procession, the subject of so many endpapers in books of travellers' tales of the time, it had been just the culmination of unseen, solemn rituals. Weeks before, silk floss had been placed over the nostrils of a dying man to determine the exact moment of his death, and then incense and candles had been placed in a niche by the hearth. He had been washed, and his feet bound together. A wedge placed in his mouth had kept it open to receive a last meal of rice for the next world. His hair had been combed, his nails clipped. The next day, the body had been dressed for burial and moved to the hall. There, at the appointed time, it had been laid in a coffin bought years before and stored in anticipation of this sad day. Relatives had donned mourning clothes that declared their affinity, from the roughest sackcloth of white hemp to a simple cap. The lid had been nailed on as the relatives turned to look away and, at the correct moment, wailed as though their hearts would break. A crimson flag bearing the name of the dead and a long, pleated silk bearing the exact moments of his birth and death had been laid out. The prescribed seven times seven days of mourning had been observed with prayers and demonstrations of utter grief. On the morning of the funeral, the family had clung onto the coffin and begged for it not to be taken from the house. They had processed in the correct order through the main gate. Masked dancers had stilled the departing soul and thrust spears into the air to drive away malevolent spirits. The flag had been spread out, the pleated silk placed upon it in the grave, the grave-goods burned. The family had done everything they could for the departed — a carefully weighed expression of grief and a confirmation of cultural identity. Such choreographed rituals must have followed each and every death of an islander at the hands of British soldiers, yet it is doubtful that even one of them had ever been aware.

As one, the islanders reaffirmed their bonds in the festivals that punctuated the twenty-four *qi*. At Qingming, the tomb-sweeping festival, each family made graveside offerings of glutinous and black rice, of meats and sweet wine. Soil was added to the grave mound, bamboo was pushed into the earth, and ghost-money hung from above. Willow twigs were pushed into the doors of the tombs, and people wove slender sprigs into their hair. On the birthday of the sun, altars were erected in the island's temples and the scriptures chanted over for the benefit of souls in purgatory. A fortnight later, with the arrival of Summer Begins, beans and glutinous millet were boiled together. The concoction, with bitter cherries and tender spring bamboo shoots, was offered to the ancestors. When Dragon Boat Festival came, people picked posies of sweet-flag and artemesia to decorate the door lintels for good luck. Some bound sprigs with colourful cord to wear at their waists, or placed them in trunks to perfume their clothes. Sweet-flag and red cinnabar were mixed with wine and drunk to keep evil spirits at bay. Rice dumplings and cakes were offered to the ancestors. At dawn on the first day of the sixth month each family went out to draw water that did not spoil with age; it would be put aside and as the year advanced used to prepare pickles and sauces to last through the winter.

On the first day of autumn the children ate smartweed, leaven, goosefoot and turnip seeds, all of them bitter-tasting to cleanse the coming harvest. One week later came the night when all the magpies of the earth, those ancient symbols of conjugal bliss, flew up to bridge the Milky Way so that the Cowherd and his bride the Weaving Maid — the stars Altair and Vega — could meet. That morning, the women of Chusan washed their hair in hibiscus-leaf water, and at dusk they set out fruits. When the moon had gone down they tried to thread them onto a needle as a test of their skill. On the last day of the month, a small child from each family offered fruit to the selfless *bodhisattva* who comforted tortured souls in hell. For the Mid-Autumn Festival, the islanders made offerings to the moon in their courtyards. They prepared moon-cakes, put out wine, and enjoyed the moonlight. On the anniversary of the city being put to the sword when the Manchus defeated the Ming, the whole island would beat drums to drive away demons. Broth and rice were offered to the lost ghosts who still wandered the hills with no descendants to care for them.

The Winter solstice was a time for clans to gather, to prepare sacrificial meats and wines and play music. Each sacrificed to their clan founder and to the tablets in the ancestral temple. Throughout the last month of the year, the *duomin* could be seen going from house to house driving out evil spirits. They had red whiskers and swords, and on their heads they wore kerchiefs with the demon-eating deity Zhongkui on them. As the old year faded away, families cleaned the house, and come nightfall they set out dainties and fruits to bribe Zaojun the hearth god. On New Year's Eve, meat and wine-must were set out for the spirits. The peach-wood charms on the door lintel were changed, fresh spring couplets were written out, the portraits of the door-guardians renewed. Firecrackers were let off, and pills of herbal medicine burned to ward off pestilence. Old and young sat down to await the dawn of a new year. And in that coming year, never a moment would pass without some ritual, some observance, being required for the smooth working of this tiny corner of the Chinese world.

The populace struck observers as poor, yet it could not be denied that instances of utter destitution were rarer than back home. Marriage was undertaken at an earlier age than in England and was almost universal amongst men above twenty.[49] Daughters were taught skills such as sewing, while the sons of families who could afford $3 a year were sent to school aged six. There they learned to read the Confucian classics and to write with a legible hand. For the gentry, and for families who could spare a labouring son in the hope of future riches, there were studying and public examinations in one of Tinghae's colleges — the same foundations whose books had been looted for souvenirs in 1840.[50] Each year, several dozen of Chusan's young men would pass the first of the civil service examinations and be granted the title *xiucai* — 'man of talent'. A number of the elders who remained on the island under British rule had also passed the next level of examinations in Hangzhou to become much-admired provincial graduates, entitled to call themselves *juren* — 'recommended men'.[51] Imbued with Confucian learning and an unshakably China-centred worldview, as long as these immoveable pillars remained on Chusan the island could never fully accept the legitimacy of foreign rule. So much had been hinted at by their *Manifesto*.

A sportsman's paradise

FOR THE Chusanese, too, prolonged peace allowed for a more rounded impression of the British than had the war. One shameful aspect of that character, it was admitted, was the drunkenness of soldiers and sailors bent on spending their liberty days as quarrelsome as possible.[1] The sudden arrival of an army of men physically so different from themselves — they had pale skin, cropped hair with no pigtail, and habitually wore peaked caps — must have been as shocking as if a horde of Masai warriors had descended upon the Isle of Sheppey. Though the ruling Manchus were a soldierly race, Confucianism's instinctive wariness of military prowess ran deep and the capacity of the British for war was frightening and alien. While at an abstract level the occupation was a game of cultural one-upmanship which the foreigners would never win so long as an emperor sat upon the Dragon Throne (for what to the West were self-evident truths on individual liberty and on man's place in Creation were in Confucian ears just so much untutored babbling), the war would leave the unmistakeable impression in pockets of Western influence along the coast that these were a people whose world did not revolve around the Son of Heaven. It would be no coincidence that just seven momentous decades later the last Son of Heaven would be dethroned.

The islanders had plenty of time to observe the private lives of a cross-section of British society. The impartial administration of justice by a British civil magistrate, the patient hearing of complaints, and (eventually at least) fair payment for supplies had all, it was believed, left a positive impression upon the man on the street.[2] Living cheek-by-jowl with more than a thousand officers and men, not to mention their wives and children, along with the many foreign merchants and missionaries who passed through Tinghae, the islanders could not fail to observe the details of their lives and draw conclusions as to their worth.[3] Chinese cooks were hired, and factotums, of whom British standards of efficiency and hygiene were expected. Each evening, officers dressed for dinner and sat down in a wallpapered dining room to a meal eaten with a knife and fork from porcelain plates. They drank wine from crystal glasses by the light from silver candelabras, sipped mulled port, or coffee and tea with milk, and took ice with their water, a practice unthinkable to the Chinese. They hung oil paintings of their monarch, and landscapes in a style quite unknown to local artists. They changed into nightclothes to sleep rather than wear the same garments day in, day out, and they washed their skin with soap. And they had a symbol, a cross that looked like the Chinese character for 'ten', that appeared on the buildings where they prayed and sang to their ancestor Jesus. Men would soon arrive to tell the islanders more about Him.

But amongst the most conspicuous aspects of British cultural life were demonstrations of sporting skill, which was held in rather lower esteem than the displays of moral rectitude that Confucianism cherished. Since the majority of troops in the European regiments were Irish farmhands, an annual festival of sports was instituted for Saint Patrick's Day.[4] Stewards were appointed from amongst the officers, and a subscription entered into to provide a prize fund of £50. The day's events got underway at noon on Royal Marine Square with the Officers' Pony Sweep-stakes. Next came foot races over 100, 150 and 200 yards, a sack race, and wrestling contests. When the shot-putting, the pig races and the climbing of the greasy pole had all been contested, the jumping events could start. At the Sinkong barracks meanwhile,[5] the Royal Irish organised a Saint Patrick's Day celebration of their own. A marquee was pitched, and the regimental colours and a Union Jack raised alongside a Chinese flag that had been garnered from somewhere or other. Word spread, and farmers from the nearby village gathered to spectate. They watched with interest as competitors stripped to the waist for the sprints, the bullock racing, the sack jumping, weight-heaving and wrestling. The oddest moment came when one villager took part in the tradi-tional Cumberland gurning contest: putting his head through a horse collar, he pulled the ugliest face Edward Cree had ever seen and won himself first prize.

Come the warmer weather, recreational pastimes were organised for the men — quoits, football and sea bathing. The late Yuqian's broad rampart became a popular place for officers to take an evening promenade with their wives.[6] Just as at Shanghai, the curving waterfront became known by the Anglo-Indian name of 'the Bund'. And when the cold came around again the fires in the mess rooms were lit and wall hangings put up to keep the chill air out. The field force even amused itself with theatrical productions: for eighteen rupees a month a large temple in the city was hired, its *bodhisattvas* and *arhats* shifted to the back of the main hall to be hidden behind a painted backdrop.[7] Where they had stood a stage was erected, equipped with footlights and a trapdoor. Machinery was installed to raise a curtain, scenery was built, a band raised and rehearsed, playbills printed and tickets sold, and the grandly named Theatre Royal Chusan opened its doors for performances of such delights as J.R. Planché's *The Two Figaros* and John Maddison Morton's *The Sentinel*.[8]

But this remained an army of occupation, and when in 1844 the Westmorelands were relieved by the 98th Regiment of Foot the island's new governor, Lieutenant-Colonel Colin Campbell, instituted regular battle drills lest Chusan's tranquility blunt their fighting efficiency.[9] To the bemusement of the islanders, their valleys became a training ground for skirmishes and set-pieces. Attackers would storm villages and bamboo groves while defenders repulsed them, would charge through the mountain passes of the interior, practise crossing canals under fire or escalade the city walls.[10] The mandarins in Ningbo and Hangzhou duly reported the exercises to the throne but admitted themselves baffled as to the reason. They were equally baffled by the British officers' love of hunting, thinking it strange that men whose status afforded them the luxury of being carried in sedan chairs and growing fat chose instead to wade through muddy fields to shoot their own food.[11] The cultivation of martial virtues in men of rank under no threat of war was undesirable, positively uncouth, but it went a long way to explaining why all the generals who had tried to defend Chusan now lay cold in their tombs.[12]

As the lack of provisions had become acute the previous year, Edward Cree had proved himself a particular lover of hunting. He became now little short of a one-man environmental disaster, landing every few days to shoot game.[13] Swaddled in the warmest clothes he could find, he would set out into the snow-dusted hills with rifle, pistol and fowling-piece to bag partridges, pheasants and plovers, widgeons, woodcock and curlews, ducks, doves and snipe. Winter's cold brought great flocks of migrants for his stewpot. While the crew of the *Rattlesnake* organised snowball fights on deck, Commander James Brodie landed with Cree and together they made their way to Swan Lake, a shallow body of water and mudflats near Sinkong. There they shot a wild swan and some ducks. Passing on through some pretty countryside, they bought pork chops and sweet potatoes at a pork butcher's shop and attracted a crowd of young and old who watched them with amused curiosity as they fumbled with chopsticks. After a few such hunting expeditions to Swan Lake they considered themselves firm friends with the butcher and his wife. The same could not be said of those unfortunate Chinese who wished to keep a wary distance: Cree was quite prepared to fire his gun as a first resort to encourage boatmen to ferry him across canals or to argue his point with anybody who dared remonstrate. When an islander made off with a great swan which fell to his gun on the far shore, Cree fired after him in full view of a hostile crowd who egged the man on. Swan would have been a rare luxury for his family.

Men like William Tyrone Power, a travel-writer and later Britain's agent-general for New Zealand, similarly found Chusan 'a sportsman's paradise'.[14] On jaunts to the islands he could bag swan, goose, duck, widgeon, teal, rail, bittern, hare — and so the slaughter went on. Only in India, a posting with which many of the officers and gentlemen of Chusan were familiar, was labour so cheap as to provide such opportunities for refined sporting excursions:

A covered boat, about seventy feet long, was fitted up with draperies and hangings, and divided into a sleeping apartment and sitting room, the latter furnished with armchairs, tables, stove, and all the appurtenances of a bachelor's snuggery. A second boat was fitted up to accommodate the servants, and as a kitchen, following astern, except at mealtimes, when it was ranged alongside, and a small hatchway being opened, the hot dishes were handed out of the kitchen into the dining room. The meal done, the hatch was closed, the boat dropped astern leaving the sportsmen to enjoy their cigars as exclusively as if in a London coffee-room, the only attendant remaining being a bearded, turbaned Bengalee, who stood like a statue at the end of the room, and who moved noiselessly about the performance of his duties to replenish the fires or supply the sahib's wants.[15]

Other like-minded men enjoyed the freedom which British rule made possible. One in particular was most methodical, setting out before dawn to make the most of the day and arriving at his chosen hunting ground as the sun rose. His Indian attendants would be sent on to sweep and clean the local temple, to light a fire, and prepare a hot bath for sahib's arrival. A breakfast service would have been brought along, not forgetting a change of clothes, towels, sponges, and books, pens and paper in case the middle of the day proved too hot to shoot. Once our man had bathed behind a screen brought along to hide his modesty from the watching Buddhas, he might lunch on curried spatchcock fowl. He might stay overnight in a nearby house, paying its owner for the privilege and flirting with his daughter.[16]

In February of 1844, with trade continuing peacefully, a man named Sir John Francis Davis was appointed governor of Hong Kong and Britain's plenipotentiary and commander-in-chief in China. He brought years of experience to the posts: having arrived in Canton in 1813 as an enthusiastic young employee of the East India Company, he had sailed north with Lord Amherst on the ill-fated embassy of 1816 and had held the superintendency of the Company's Canton trade. A gifted linguist, he was one of that rare breed — a British government appointee who spoke Chinese and understood China. Soon after his appointment, Sir John embarked on a tour of the northern ports opened under the Treaty of Nanking — Amoy, Fuzhou, Ningbo and Shanghai. He quite naturally took the opportunity to visit Chusan, and arrived in Tinghae in late 1844 to find the city healthy and peaceful:

Nothing could exceed the good humour and contentedness of the native Chinese. It was impossible to traverse the suburb between the sea and the town without observing plain proofs of the good understanding existing between the military and the people…. In fact, the people of Tinghae enjoyed opportunities of enriching themselves by industry during our occupation which may not very soon recur; though Chusan is a point of such importance, political and military, if not commercial, that the course of time and events might again some day make us acquainted with it.[17]

It was to prove a curiously accurate prophesy on many levels. The only fault Davis could find after three years of British rule was that the permitted scale of punishments was if anything too lax.[18] Up before the beak time and again, malefactors had long since learned that Magistrate Bamfield had no authority delegated to him to exceed a tariff of three dozen lashes, a fine of $10 or 25 rupees, or a month in gaol.[19] Under the Chinese law still applicable across Kintang Sound on the mainland, punishment for common criminals often involved the cangue, a kind of portable wooden stocks weighing anything up to 200 lbs. It was a dehumanising affair, sometimes endured for six months at a stretch, the prisoner passing his nights in gaol and being led come daylight to the city gates for public viewing. His neck and both his hands confined, he relied on sympathetic passers-by to feed him.[20] But there was an aversion to such prolonged humiliation amongst the British, and on Chusan the cangue was curtailed in favour of the sharp swish of a cane. Compared to the cangue, though, a good thrashing was a blessing. True, criminals ran the risk of being handed over to the authorities in Ningbo if this proved no deterrent, but for recidivists that risk was worthwhile once their hide had been toughened up. Acting on a request from Bamfield, Davis straight away tripled the maximum penalties available to the court, but the fact remained that only relatively minor cases were being heard by the British — so much at least had been agreed with the mandarins on the mainland.[21]

In the immediate wake of the Treaty of Nanking the troublesome kidnappings on Chusan had ceased almost overnight, and from the perspective of Tinghae the island had become tranquil. Karl Gützlaff had soon written to Pottinger remarking that he had nothing to do, the magistracy unused and the gaol empty. Yet beyond the city walls the violent removal of Chinese governance the previous year had had a profound effect on life for the islanders. The British, unfamiliar with the lie of the land and with society and custom, only crudely filled that power vacuum. They were, for the most part, concerned for those living over the hills north of Tinghae only insofar as they posed a threat. Criminals (many of them indigent soldiers who had fled the rout on October 1st) were roaming the valleys unchallenged, the British unaware of the misery the villagers were enduring. Unless mandarins fully acquainted with the conditions on Chusan were sent to deal with them, a Chinese negotiator had explained to Pottinger as the implications of the treaty had begun to sink in, the islanders would get no respite. The north-coast fishing village of Kanlon, he suggested, was far enough from Tinghae for a mandarin not to inconvenience the British while he exercised authority over the native population.[22] Pottinger himself was in favour of such an arrangement — by allowing a low-ranking functionary to keep a tight rein on the natives order could easily be maintained. The decision though rested with Sir Hugh Gough as commander-in-chief of land forces, and to him the idea of a Ningbo mandarin residing on Chusan in an official capacity was objectionable: their constant undermining of British rule thus far made a clear division of jurisdictions essential if there was to be peace.[23] Arrangements were instead made for a Chinese official named Lin, a former gaoler from the town of Yuyao, to reside on the island of Tygoosan that sat halfway between Tinghae and Zhenhai.[24]

Pottinger told the islanders of the arrangements:[25] though living under British rule, they were at liberty to sail to Tygoosan and approach Magistrate Lin with civil suits and criminal cases. The British for their part undertook to secure, on application from Lin, the attendance of witnesses and defendants. Islanders were told they may, if they wished, bring civil cases before the British magistrate. In criminal cases of any import, suspects would be arrested by the British police but thereafter would face Lin. Only in minor criminal cases would the British pass sentence. Defendants, Lin was assured, could be sure of the impartiality of British law. But it was that very impartiality — to the British an objective proof of the superiority of their legal system — which in practice would alienate the upper stratum of Chusanese society. Christians, Hindus and Muslims cared little if anything for the distinctions of rank which underpinned Confucian China, while the Chinese of the native police force were little better than rogues — poachers turned gamekeepers who had been given a uniform, a royal commission, and authority over their superiors. Just as Peking would condemn as 'unequal' any treaty which placed the Son of Heaven on a par with a ruler such as Queen Victoria, treatment thought equitable by a British magistrate could be intensely shaming to a Chinese of standing. On one occasion, a man of some status found himself dragged through the streets of Tinghae, tied by the pigtail to a common man arrested at the same time, while the crowds stared in shocked disbelief. The case against him was dismissed but the damage had been done.[26] Where an Englishman wrongly accused could have left the magistracy with his head held high and a lawyer's business card in his hand, this Chusanese gentryman had been irremediably humiliated. The misunderstanding worked both ways: with excusable ignorance, wealthy islanders initially approached the British court with the same innate authority they had the Chinese before. Bribery was assumed still to be a legitimate means of buying off one's punishment. Tales of filial sons accepting a rich man's capital sentence to raise the money to bury their father in a fitting manner were repeated for their praiseworthiness, and there were plenty of stooges willing to accept another man's corporal punishment for a fee. A Chinese court for its part might be expected to give its blessing to such an arrangement. One day, though, a merchant appeared before the British magistrate charged with possessing stolen property. He produced a man who swore to having been the genuine thief, and witnesses to corroborate the story. But when sentenced to a lashing and the cutting-off of his queue the scapegoat quickly changed his tune, bleating that the merchant had paid him $100 to take his beating but had said nothing of the far more serious punishment of the loss of his pigtail![27]

Gentry families and wealthy merchants, it seems, slowly but surely expressed their disapproval of this new order by removing to Ningbo. The Ningbo authorities for their part agreed not to interfere with life on Chusan unless approached. Still, mandarins of the most junior grades would from time to time be discovered on the island, some apparently trying to squeeze taxes, some executing arrest warrants in contravention of the arrangements. One incident was so incompetently timed as to be discovered during Sir John Davis' tour of inspection.[28] Davis sent two of Magistrate Lin's men under arrest to Canton with a written remonstration addressed to his opposite number, Commissioner Qiying, the same man who with Yilibu had negotiated at Nanking. Qiying, afraid that the British would seize on the breach as an excuse to renege on his treaty and retain Chusan, angrily demanded his subordinates put an end to such infringements.

But despite British guardedness and Chinese fears, it might sometimes have helped Governor Sir James Schoedde if Magistrate Lin *had* had a direct hand in Chusan's affairs.[29] For the same cold waters that brought legions of fish to the islands by winter also enticed fishing junks from all the coastal provinces of the empire. Each was well armed against the pirates who circled the fleet, fully manned to raise the heavy matting sails and haul the nets from the depths. So until the warmth of spring drove the catch away, Chusan's territorial waters were home each year to tens of thousands of rootless boat-dwellers.[30] Before the arrival of the British, outsiders had been required to register with the island's mandarins. To distinguish her from an unregistered pirate vessel, each junk would be obliged to have her name and number painted in conspicuous characters on her sails and hull, and her master would be held to account for any untoward behaviour. Before Gützlaff left the island for Hong Kong in late 1843, he was sure always to lodge a body of soldiers to keep the peace at the fishing port of Sinkamoon on the southeast coast ('the very seat of iniquity,' he called it);[31] but neither he nor Magistrate Bamfield who succeeded him ever grappled with the enormous challenge of a full-scale registration of the wintertime junks. It was to this end, hearing stories of piracy, that Magistrate Lin that winter sent a pair of secretaries to Sinkamoon. They were asked civilly by Governor Schoedde to return to Tygoosan, whereupon Lin wrote to explain that he merely wished to ensure tranquillity. Only with Gützlaff now in Hong Kong the letter was imperfectly translated. Perhaps because he was not immediately at hand, Robert Thom, one-time interpreter on Chusan and now a resident of Ningbo, was not asked to cast an eye over it to confirm Magistrate Bamfield's impression that Lin's language was rude and domineering. Instead, the perceived slight was passed up the chain of command to Hong Kong and the then commander-in-chief of British forces in China, Lord Saltoun, who turned to the plenipotentiary, Sir Henry Pottinger, for instruction. Pottinger wrote to the Foreign Secretary Lord Aberdeen in London where, it might be assumed, the incident was mentioned to the Prime Minister Robert Peel. Gützlaff's expert opinion, when eventually shown Lin's note, was that it was quite as polite as would be hoped, but that Bamfield's reply was scarcely intelligible. A well-meaning oversight by a mandarin on Tygoosan had become a talking point in the highest circles in the British Empire, and all because Britain had no permanent, professional body of Mandarin translators.

18

In the hospital their hearts are soft

IT WOULD be the latter part of the nineteenth century before an English university appointed a chair in Chinese. The first holder of the post at Cambridge, Thomas Wade, had in fact set out to learn the language while a lieutenant in the 98th Foot during Sir Henry Pottinger's Yangtze campaign of 1842 (Wade had taken part in the bloody fall of Zhenjiang). Governor Davis of Hong Kong, as we have seen, had started out as a clerk at the East India Company factory in Canton. But most of the Britons who arrived in China in the 1840s with a knowledge of Mandarin and its dialects were perforce missionaries like James Legge, who in 1876 would become Oxford's first Professor of Chinese. A wave of these crusaders washed silently over Chusan in the weeks and months after its capture, following in the wake of a war that had done so much harm but wishing only to share the benefits of modern medicine and to apply the balm of Christian faith.[1]

By 1840, Christians from continental Europe had been living and working in China for centuries, advising the emperor and his court on the astronomy, mathematics and cartography at which Jesuits excelled. These Roman Catholic missionaries had quickly adapted to local custom, had changed their behaviour, their dress, even (so it was alleged by their jealous detractors) their articles of faith to gain acceptance and win souls. Protestant missionaries, by sharp contrast, with their dogmatic emphasis on Scripture and a refusal to accommodate native sensibilities, were long forbidden from evangelising in China and instead toiled with limited success amongst the Chinese diaspora in Indonesia and Malaysia where the Son of Heaven held no sway.[2] The two creeds differed radically in how they approached mission work, the Catholics stressing rites, rituals and spectacle and setting no great store by the written Word, the Protestants preferring intense Bible-study classes and pamphlets. (Such a blunt and wasteful instrument as pamphleteering the semi-literate was scoffed at by the Catholics, who wrote with undisguised glee at how Protestant tracts ended up as cigar papers, as wrappings in the bazaars, as free wallpaper in people's homes, even as toilet paper!)

Before the first capture of Chusan in 1840, very few Protestant missionaries indeed had ever entered China proper, and even these had only penetrated a few illicit miles inland from Macao to Canton. In the absence of a Damascene conversion in the heart of the Forbidden City, the only conceivable hope for the Protestant version of Christ's message being heard within the Celestial Empire was the annexation of some or other plot of Chinese soil as a spiritual antechamber. 'We earnestly hope and pray,' went just one of many similar editorials in the *Missionary Register*, 'that the [outcome] may be, by the over-ruling Hand of God, the suppression of Evil, and the opening of that vast Empire to the benevolent labours of true Christians.'[3] While most Protestants did not thirst for a war to open up China's gates, of what ultimate importance was the early arrival of a few heathen souls in the hereafter when the potential prize — a Protestant China — was so great?

News of Tinghae's fall, and the realisation that Protestant missionaries were free to preach there under the protection of the Crown, struck the London Missionary Society in Macao as nothing short of an act of God. The Almighty, it was clear, had engineered the opium crisis and its violent resolution as a sign of reproof to idolators, and now through men like themselves He would pour upon China 'the blessings of an enlightened faith, and erect for them the fabric of a liberal and beneficent government'. Such at least was the sincere hope of one Dr William Milne.[4]

Dr Milne more than most felt the burden of time wasted on the fringes of the idolatrous empire. His father, the Reverend William Milne, had first visited Macao and Canton in 1813 and had made a name working amongst the overseas Chinese in Malacca before a tragically early death. Born at sea during his father's travels, William Milne junior, still only twenty-five, was obsessed with the prospect of breaking into China to spread the Word. Scarcely had the Union Jack been raised upon Tinghae's south gate than John Morrison (he was an interpreter to the Chusan expedition and himself the son of a pioneering Protestant missionary) wrote to Dr Milne, urging him to establish a station for the London Missionary Society on the island.[5] A month later a meeting of the Society was commended to God, and by the time the meeting closed it had been resolved to send one of those present, one William Lockhart, to Tinghae.[6]

William Lockhart was no ordinary missionary: he was not even ordained.[7] Not yet out of his twenties, he struck people as a serious young man, a teetotal non-conformist who divided his time between chapel, study, and lengthy walks. His perambulations would prove good training for his time on Chusan. Having passed his medical exams at Guy's Hospital, he had looked set for a career as a surgeon. But his conscience had other plans for him, and after attending a fund-raising lecture for the London Missionary Society Lockhart decided that missionary work was to be his vocation. On applying, he was appointed to the newly formed Medical Missionary Society, its avowed aim to supply Protestant missions with doctors in the hope of imparting the practical benefits of Christendom to the benighted sick of China by curing them of disease and easing their pain.[8]

Having sailed from Gravesend in 1838 bound initially for mission work in Macao, Lockhart arrived in Tinghae in September of 1840 to find the city deserted and the garrison dying.[9] Without delay he called on Gützlaff and his wife, an acquaintance from England and a friendly face in a most alien country.[10] Heavy rains and Captain Anstruther's kidnap delayed the start of his work, but soon he found a house which would serve as a hospital while something better was found. It was small, full of 'every species of filth and rubbish,'[11] but here it was that Britain's first medical mission to China opened its doors.

An initial disinclination on the part of the locals to trust Lockhart can be excused: rumours abounded of how the secret ingredient in the barbarians' glass mirrors (the Chinese used polished metal) was actually human eyeballs, and everybody knew that Christians founded their churches upon the bodies of sacrificed children. More prosaically, the ruined wharves were a reminder of the foreigners' propensity for perfidy and violence, and islanders could expect punishment for fraternising with them. Lockhart began attending to those few sick he could induce to come to his surgery. After a fortnight he was delighted to move into a larger house, sharing it with the indolent servants of its absent owner, the Gützlaffs and their nieces Kate and Isabella, some blind girls they had adopted, and a large and affectionate portland dog named Boatswain.[12] It was commodious but dirty, though this was the case for even the richest residences in the city, which did not in the least degree answer British ideas of comfort.[13] There Lockhart began to practise on a permanent footing, tending to his patients in a range of outhouses. His mornings were spent treating cases, his free time devoted to learning Chinese under the guidance of his housemate the interpreter John Morrison and then spreading word of the hospital to passers-by on the street.[14] In scarcely more than a month he had had more than 550 patients apply to him with various ailments.[15] That his cures were successful and offered free of charge — a stark contrast to the local physicians' expensive quackery — soon swelled his waiting list.

When the troops struck camp and moved into the empty houses in Tinghae in the autumn of 1840, a degree of normality gradually returned to the city and Lockhart found his skills in even greater demand. He began to treat respectable citizens, and was pleased by how well he was received.[16] Trips to the more settled of the inland valleys became frequent, with Lockhart using the visits of military patrols to administer to the sick in their own homes and to hand out leaflets listing what ailments he could cure.[17] Governor Burrell was supportive, believing such excursions to be useful propaganda in showing the Chinese that their new rulers were mindful of their welfare and not just rampaging invaders;[18] and in attracting people back into the city they proved a great success. As word spread, the sick even travelled from other islands and from as far away as the mainland.[19] Some came involuntarily — more than once, Lockhart was called upon to patch up the victims of the ongoing clashes between troops and islanders.[20] Though moved by the suffering of those innocent casualties, the compassionate young doctor often found himself truly shocked at the callousness of a race that deigned to term the British 'barbarian' — a beggar he found lying in the street had to be treated for the gangrene that had eaten into both his feet with not a soul bothering to help him.[21]

Through a medic's eyes, the health of the native population was scarcely less compromised than the garrison's.[22] Opium addiction was widespread, and sapped body and spirit. Dysentery affected many of Lockhart's patients just as it did the soldiers, but there was little he could do to help. More common was the same malaria that was affecting the troops, for which he could at least prescribe quinine in place of the traditional remedy of powdered tiger bones and ginseng.[23] Chronic skin diseases were endemic, a problem Lockhart put down to the Chinese habit of wearing the same unwashed clothes day in, day out for months at a time. Foot-binding was universal amongst the island's women, and was a source of terrible pain and infection. Eye disease was common, and was seemingly the fault of the street-corner barbers who used ivory scoops to scrape clean the insides of their customers' eyelids after each haircut.[24] Unsurprisingly, eyes would end up red and irritated, a sign taken to indicate that the barber had not performed well enough. Rather than leave the mucus membranes to heal, the next washing would be done with extra vigour until in many cases the surface became granulated and the lids inverted. In great discomfort, the patient would now visit a Chinese doctor to have strips of bamboo tied onto the lid until the trapped fold of skin sloughed away. The method was agony, and left the sufferer with only partial sight. In one miserable building in Tinghae, close to a stagnant canal, were found living twenty-nine indigent souls, all suffering from ophthalmia and some already blind.[25] Lockhart wrote home to ask for a set of Tyrrell's best ophthalmic instruments — cataract knives, pointed forceps for the tear ducts, curved ones to treat inverted eyelashes, and syringes and scissors with ivory handles (for ebony quickly spoiled in Chusan's climate).[26] In the meantime, he urged barbers to leave people's eyes alone as God intended.

Over the coming months, Lockhart would record each of the conditions to walk through the door of his mission station — elephantiasis, jaundice and hepatitis, rheumatism, psoriasis, paraphymosis, lupus, syphilis and gonorrhoea, trichiosis and cataracts, hernias, fractures and dislocations, burns, vomiting of blood, haemorrhoids, dropsy, attempted suicides from overdoses of saltwater or opium, even a severe bite from a pig.[27] The list of suffering was almost endless, the island's native medicine men incapable of relieving it. A contemporary of Lockhart's in China, the American doctor Peter Parker who practised in Canton and Macao, despaired that the Chinese were 'more ignorant of medicine and surgery than of most other things which confer direct physical benefit on the race.'[28] Its doctors, he observed, never underwent any systematic training in dissection, and were obsessed with pulse-taking. The result, in his eyes, was 'knavery and quackery, of the most ingenious and yet of the most absurd character.' He provided the example of a man he had passed in the street, an infected finger inserted into the abdomen of a live frog, the frog tied fast to stop it hopping off. Perhaps, ruminated another physician, it was an unwholesome diet of vegetables, rice, putrid salt-fish, weak tea, tobacco and the occasional opium pipe, not to mention their cramped, damp and ill-ventilated housing which left the Chinese so unhealthy.[29]

But Lockhart had not made the long journey from Liverpool just to win friends for Queen Victoria with his medicine chest. Such work, he hoped, might provide an honourable counter-point to the injustices done by the British; but cures for what ailed the islanders physically were just a prelude to a deeper healing. Lockhart's first forays into evangelism were directed at a wide audience. At home in the hospital, he held a regular Sunday service in faltering Chinese for the benefit of his absentee landlord's doubtless bemused servants. On long walks into the interior he would hand out religious tracts to anybody who showed an interest,[30] though the curious recipients were almost certainly more interested in the intrinsic value of a printed book than in its potential to save their soul. In the streets of Tinghae and amongst the crowds waiting to board ferries to the outlying islands, the doctor with his pamphlets became a familiar sight. These busy travellers, though, were less receptive than the more focused sick. 'In the hospital,' as one missionary publication put it, 'their hearts are soft.' Quickly a more targeted approach evolved.

The literate would be given tracts to read and, on their discharge, a handful of short works, 'little messengers of grace' to take back to their village.[31] As with time the Medical Mission became more established, the spreading of the Christian message became ever more closely entwined with the dispensation of medical relief. New patients would be given a card bearing their patient number and disease, beside a Biblical verse for them to memorise and quote aloud when asked.

The handing back of Chusan to Chinese control in February of 1841 meant the closure of Lockhart's little hospital and an end to free medical care for the island's sick. He had treated 3,502 patients and handed out six thousand Christian tracts.[32] But just two years later, with the peace that followed the Treaty of Nanking, the doctor was back in Tinghae with his nineteen-year-old bride Kate — she was a cousin by marriage to none other than Karl Gützlaff — and their infant daughter Lizzie (Kate, then just fifteen, had sailed to Macao in 1838 upon the same vessel as Lockhart, had lived with him and the Gützlaffs in Tinghae, and they had married in May of 1841).[33] The Lockharts spent only five months in Chusan this time around: William was keen to leave Tinghae for the newly opened treaty port of Shanghai, which promised access to ever larger numbers of the physically and spiritually unwell. In the meantime he unbolted the old hospital doors and started to readmit patients. There was little he could do, though, for his own daughter. When he returned home each evening he found Lizzie withdrawn and listless. Plagued by mosquitoes and fleas, she would stretch her bitten hands out for her father to scratch, ignoring the toys and dolls her grandfather had sent from home. The debilitating effects of a long sea voyage from Hong Kong were evident. Kate wrote to her father-in-law soon after she had set up home in Tinghae: Lizzie was

> very beautiful in her mother's eyes in all respects of course… but she is not fat, large, rosy, bouncing etc etc as what are called fine china usually are, but thin and now pale, with clear dark blue eyes and a little wee body of her own, which contains I think a little intelligent spirit.[34]

But Lizzie never rallied. In August she passed away and was laid to rest aged just eighteen months. By November her grieving parents were in Shanghai. Though William made one brief visit to Tinghae, it was in the growing city a couple of days' sail from his daughter's grave that he chose to carry on his work. But it had been in Tinghae, the London Missionary Society acknowledged, that something had been attempted 'to break the fallow ground' for Protestantism. There 'some seed had been watered,' and Lockhart's time on Chusan might now 'hasten on that day of days when this "desert shall rejoice and blossom as the rose".[35]

When William Lockhart and his young family landed on Chusan in 1843, there had arrived with them a woman named Mary Ann Aldersey, a wealthy spinster described by Karl Gützlaff as 'one of the most zealous workers ever to sacrifice their life and their fortune in the service of the Lord.'[36] And that was praise indeed from such a zealous worker!

Born into a nonconformist Congregational family, Mary had grown up fascinated by stories told to her by her nanny, a missionary's wife who had travelled to India to teach girls. So it was not surprising that as an adult she would gravitate toward the Society for Promoting Female Education in the East, whose aim was 'to raise the oppressed daughters of the heathen to become estimable upon earth, and to attain the bliss of heaven.'[37] The Orient being as it was, that task of necessity fell to other women to accomplish: in the patriarchal societies of the East it was difficult enough for male missionaries to interact with potential male converts, near impossible for them to proselytise to females. 'Who but a woman can understand the heart of a woman?' asked the compiler of the Society's correspondence.[38] Others were more damningly judgmental of the Oriental male: 'Since monkeys and parrots have been taught,' it was claimed that one Chinese moralist had once asserted, 'women might no doubt be instructed, if their husbands are disposed to make the experiment.'[39] Gützlaff, too, was positively scornful of Confucian ideas of morality:

They are the slaves and concubines of their masters, live and die in ignorance, and every effort to raise themselves above the rank assigned them is regarded as impious arrogance.... As long as mothers are not the instructors of their children, and wives are not the companions of their husbands, the regeneration of this great empire will proceed very slowly.[40]

China, such men and women predicted, would soon be prepared for as many female teachers as Christendom could send.

When in 1824 the pioneering China missionary Robert Morrison (and father to John Morrison, besides, who was later the interpreter to Captain Elliot) visited London, Mary had jumped at the opportunity to attend his classes in Mandarin.[41] Such studies, she was warned, were not lightly to be undertaken by women: when the symptoms of hysterical insanity were remarked upon in one of two ladies training to work in the Far East, it was noted that the condition was a consequence of her application to the Chinese language, with its phonetic and graphic complexity. Mary, thankfully still sane despite acquiring a working knowledge of Chinese, invested in Morrison's new six-volume dictionary and set about teaching the language to other would-be lady missionaries. It was only when a clergyman whom she had approached to sponsor the Society for Promoting Female Education in the East asked her pointedly why she herself did not go that Mary considered herself for the role. Still, her father's disapproval of such a course of action meant that Mary for several years put all ideas of missionary work from her mind. Only when she had quite forgotten her plans did her father have a change of heart. Her passage to Malacca was booked and Mary ready to sail when her sister-in-law died suddenly leaving eight children, their claims upon her 'stronger even than that of the heathen,' she would write. Yet five years as mother to this new household, her free time spent studying Chinese from a gentleman wearing a silk robe and a pigtail, left Mary if anything better qualified for missionary schooling. Aged forty and no longer in the best of health, she finally bought a passage to the East.[42] In the long, dry summer of 1843, she stepped ashore at

Tinghae's wharf and passed through the Gate of Enduring Peace to begin a new life.

Despite her determination (and the authentic-sounding name of Ai Disui which she now adopted) Mary struggled to speak the local language, a variant of the Wu dialect of eastern China. To be fair, she did not hear a word of it until aged forty, and then made do with a single tutor. Her pupils, it was said, understood her even if strangers could not. Through her landlord Mr Kin (a man apparently of some status on the island and a friend of other Christian missionaries) she grew acquainted with the island's society.[43] Its menfolk did not impress her — they were addicted in the main to opium — but their wives she found superior in body and mind.[44] She was fascinated by the young women, and would watch them as they spun silk from silkworms they had themselves reared and with this wove beautiful summer dresses. Mary found herself drawn especially to widows. Chusan's women, she discovered, would rarely remarry after a husband's death, upon which they would lose to their in-laws any authority they had had over even their own children. Bereavement and isolation left many women alone and fearful, all the more ready to listen to Mary's words of Christian consolation and with nothing to lose by following her. She took on a cook, an assistant, and two nurses, all of them widowed, and with their help she opened a girls' school in Tinghae, its first pupil an orphaned child entrusted by her late mother to Dr Milne of the London Missionary Society. It was the first of its kind in China. From a surviving illustration of the school Mary would later found in Ningbo, we can picture a class:[45] the girls, some two dozen, sit on benches at long tables, reading from Christian primers. Their schoolroom, rented perhaps from Mary's landlord Mr Kin, is single-storied, built of wood, with walls of paper screens. At the head of the class sits a Chinese teacher, his desk and high-backed chair of better craftsmanship than the girls' tables and benches. Before him are a teapot and his writing paraphernalia. The pupils have been bound to the school for set terms, during which time Mary has promised their parents that she will pay for all their needs. They have risen early and their day has started with morning prayers in Chinese at 7am. When after a year she closed the school in Tinghae and sailed for Ningbo, Mary found herself suspected in the prefectural capital of some ulterior motive. What else could explain a woman travelling tens of thousands of *li* to teach mere girls? Rumours abounded that she had murdered some of her charges and eaten them, that she had plucked out their eyes to make her Western medicines and glass mirrors. This Witch of Ningbo as she came to be known was seen communing with ghosts on her wall-top walks each morning. The Ningbo Chinese, it was whispered, believed that just as the British were ruled by a queen so their trading community in the city was ruled over by this remarkable woman.

But even Mary Aldersey's little school in Tinghae was not the first attempt to introduce the benefits of a Western education to the island. In early November of 1840, as the political situation on the Zhejiang coast was improving, Karl Gützlaff had greeted the arrival from Macao of his second wife Mary ('neither young nor beautiful,' but a blue, scraggy woman in Edward Cree's opinion) and her young cousin Kate Parkes, who would later become Mrs William Lockhart. Since 1835, Mary Gützlaff had been running a school for Chinese children in the Portuguese colony, her boys and girls a mixture of the blind and the sighted, teaching English and Christianity with funding from the same Society for Promoting Female Education in the East which would in time sponsor Mary Aldersey's work. Settling in Chusan, Mrs Gützlaff had set about establishing a school offering a similar curriculum. Her husband began to teach a large class of men. Freed from the onerous duties of civil magistrate by Captain Caine's promotion to the role, Gützlaff spent his time riding out into the villages of the interior, distributing Christian tracts and performing minor cures. It was precisely the life which for a decade he had dreamed of leading.

A year even before the fall of Tinghae, English churchgoers had been made to feel a pang of guilt by the opening lines of Gützlaff's *Missionary Travels to China to Distribute Bibles*:

My dear readers, has the thought ever arisen in your hearts, when sitting down, with kind friends and companions, that the tea which contributed so much to your enjoyment and comforts, came from a land of idolaters; and that the hands which had prepared it for your use, had never handled the book of life? If this be the case, you surely have a vast debt of love to pay, and should no longer delay contributing your mite to assist the poor Chinese.

It was just the kind of well-intentioned emotional manipulation at which Gützlaff excelled.

With the Yangtze campaign at an end and the Treaty of Nanking signed, come October 1842 Gützlaff was thankful to set foot again on Chusan, now confirmed for some years to come at least as British soil. Soon his health was as strong as ever it had been in Asia. The Good Lord, he informed his sponsors in one of his regular *Chinese Reports*, had cured him of the agues that had threatened to finish him.[46] Reinvigorated, and for the time being acting as the island's civil magistrate once more, he lost no time in formulating plans to transform Chusan into a beacon of civilised values. 'Was it just simple chance that brought the English to Chusan,' he asked, 'or will it please the Lord to illuminate the dark parts of the earth from this point with His light?'[47] As ever, his rhetoric conveniently ignored his own role in sounding a passage for the Royal Navy directly into Tinghae harbour.

With his characteristic self-assurance and an unshakeable conviction that the islanders could not hear enough of the Word, Gützlaff straight away began the task of pamphleteering. House to house, street to street, he handed out Christian tracts. Before the month was out he had held his first open prayer meeting for a Chinese audience, a discussion of the Sermon on the Mount.[48] When not dealing with the duties of the magistracy, the task of translating the Old Testament into Chinese took up much of his time. How extraordinary, he mused in his *Reports*, that when the islanders badgered him about the continuing delay in publishing it he had no satisfactory answer. If only his backers could send him extra funds…. But if subscribers back home could be pressured into supporting Gützlaff's ambitious schemes, the same could not be said of the local Chinese. In February 1843 a letter arrived in Hong Kong. A coterie of Chusan's Confucian gentry had written in exasperation to mandarins on the mainland, who had passed their complaints on to the British.[49] 'On December 29th last year,' they wrote,

> Gützlaff issued orders to the scholastic gentry of Tinghae to take upon themselves the offices of the elders, to watch over and soothe the good, to seize and apprehend evil-doers. Day after day he handed out papers, calling upon the people to subscribe to the rebuilding of a college, of a foundling hospital, a poorhouse, a refuge for the old and destitute; for the burial of the dead, to engage teachers of both sexes for the instruction of the young, and to pay for a police force.[50]

Nor was this the first time that a mandarin had had to write to Hong Kong with tales of woe: just a fortnight earlier Sir Henry Pottinger had read that Chusan's gentry were fed up of harsh treatment. There was talk of people being unfairly fined or flogged, of animals being allowed to roam free to graze the crops, of soldiers forever frightening honest village folk. Such misbehaviour could quite easily be remedied by a strict reining in of the troops, but the matter of Gützlaff's social programme was more grave. Britain's civil jurisdiction had been clearly demarcated, and the Chusanese had understood themselves to be free from interference on matters not affecting public order, and on matters of cultural practice. Gützlaff, fluent in Chinese and feeling himself at liberty to do with the island as he — and God — saw fit, had exceeded those bounds with his master plan to improve their lives. By 1843 he had completed a census of Tinghae (he put the population of the island at 270,000,[51] of which one tenth lived in the city),[52] enumerating its men, women and children and dividing the last into boys and girls with a view perhaps to establishing schools. Every family had been visited, allotted a number, and the occupation of the head of the household noted. Gützlaff had divided the island into portions, had nominated a headman for each, and had made him answerable to the magistracy. Through these he had issued edicts dunning the gentry for social funding, and had promulgated a new system of price-fixing for a range of goods and of fines for civil offences. But Chusan, Pottinger was indignantly informed by its gentry, was not short of charity: the foundling hospital might only have been set up seventeen years earlier, supported by a nominal subscription from each household, but the paupers' refuge beside the north gate had been founded in 1103 under the Song dynasty![53] The emperor in his mercy had already made money available for the hungry and the homeless. Granted, the island's public buildings needed repair from time to time, but it was not Gützlaff's place to extort money from a populace impoverished by war to pay for his foreign institutions. Boys were by ancient practice educated at their parents' expense; girls were educated at home in embroidery, needlework and cookery. More objectionable than the efforts at female education being practised by Mary Aldersey (after all, who cared if a few widows and girls learned to read?) was Gützlaff's attempt to make the elders pay the wages of an island-wide police force — this had never been their role. Feelings of confidence were gradually growing up on the Zhejiang coast, where before there had been only rancour. Gützlaff's colonial zeal, it seemed, might prove enough to disturb this. A popular revolt against British rule might be excited by such policies, Pottinger was warned, and it might not be long before his precious commerce was affected. Pottinger asked for a court of enquiry to be set up. Chusan was held 'under such peculiar and unprecedented circumstances' that British rule ought to be 'even more scrupulous and forbearing (as well as more fostering) towards the people than if they were actually subjects of the Crown of England.' He bade his Chinese opposite number send agents to Tinghae to look into the islanders' complaints.

When four months later one Ambassador Wang reported his findings, it became apparent that at the root of the islanders' dissatisfaction was not so much Gützlaff's social reforms but Tommy Atkins' ignorance when it came to matters of culture. Heavy-handed soldiering had allowed the more pugnacious islanders to goad the troops into ill thought-out retaliation. Gützlaff had been endeavouring to adopt an air that hovered uneasily between Christian reformer, impartial magistrate and Confucian patriarch. So long as relations remained strained, and so long as he was the everyday face of British rule and answerable in Chinese eyes for everyday abuses of power, his dreams of moulding Chusan in his image must have seemed unattainable. Governor Schoedde's timely appreciation of the underlying problem, at least, had made the rules of behaviour clear to his men and led to a crackdown on the troublemakers. And from the Chinese side, the arrival of Ambassador Wang on Chusan had had many of those erstwhile troublemakers scurrying to leave. Back in London, the matter was considered important enough for a Foreign Office memo to be sent to Hong Kong: surprise was expressed that a man of Gützlaff's experience should interfere in affairs over which the Chinese were known to be peculiarly sensitive, and he was cautioned against forcing his social program down their throats.

Not all of Gützlaff's policies were unwelcome, though: it was hard even for Confucians to object to a ban on begging. Distinguishing in stark terms between the deserving and undeserving poor, Gützlaff collected together the island's paupers and distributed alms to just six dozen — the old, the blind and the maimed — who were in genuine need.[54] He had once commented how delighted he would have been to tell the emperor himself that Jesus loved him,[55] and it is hard to envisage him missing the opportunity to explain to these wretched souls the concept of Christian charity. His plans seem to have borne fruit — by the middle of 1843 there were reportedly only two or three beggars to be seen in the city, which, if it is not an exaggeration, was a remarkable achievement for the time.[56] Everything Gützlaff undertook was coloured by his ultimate goal of baptising Chinese. Even when studying the latest works on irrigation and flood control his mind was ever on how that knowledge might be applied to the struggle for converts.[57] His distribution of basic medical care in the villages continued, given ungrudgingly but always with a Christian tract following close behind the mercurial ointment. He called his island the Lord's Vineyard,[58] and when in March of 1843 a spectacular comet appeared in the night sky above it he was spurred on. 'We await the coming of the Lord,' he said of the celestial sign, 'while the Chinese await nervously great events in the future. It is a beautiful star, so marvellous and comforting, so majestic.'[59]

A small building in Tinghae served as a chapel for a growing congregation.[60] Still struggling against the pressure of work and a lack of funds to complete a revision of the Chinese New Testament, Gützlaff had his flock read aloud from short works in Mandarin with titles such as *God the Creator*, *God's Love for Mankind* and *Who is Jesus?*[61] When time allowed he would visit chapel-going families in their homes. One old man in particular would always follow him on his house-calls, elucidating his arguments and railing against the native deities who, taught Gützlaff, had so clearly abandoned the islanders.[62] Gützlaff persisted in taking long treks into the interior to preach, riding out sometimes with the Duke of Wellington's pious nephew, the same Lieutenant George Wellesley who had narrowly escaped kidnap on those same paths.[63] Still, though the number of islanders who had any real understanding of Christ was tiny, Gützlaff remained incorrigibly optimistic: 'I have not the least doubt that with perseverance, earnest prayer and constant work, many souls might be saved on this island for the Lord.'[64]

Yet three months later the strain of toiling for scant reward was showing, and Gützlaff's writings gradually took on an air of resignation at opposition to his plans. He admitted that his talks on the Nativity and the Passion were arousing little interest; that his house visits were uncovering a deep seam of ignorance and worldliness — what the Chinese might have called disbelief.[65] Not surprisingly, the greatest attention was paid to what he had to say when, in June of 1843, the drought which Dr Alexander Grant noted in his agricultural almanac grasped the island. There was every prospect of real famine.[66] Now, as Gützlaff passed through the parched valleys with their cracked soil, the farmers begged him to pray to his God for rain. 'The lamentations were truly heart-rending,' he recounted, 'the children wailing, the peasant stood grieving at how all his toil looked as though it would be in vain.'[67] A short distance from Tinghae's north gate, a widow kept a landscaped flower garden. Gützlaff made of one of its pavilions a prayer-room where during that long dry spell he would pray for rain. It came at last, torrential downpours turning the island overnight into a paradise of blossoms.[68] Alas, the farmers, Gützlaff observed with a heavy heart, attributed God's miracle to the processions of Buddhist priests and carved idols that had not long since wound their way through the valleys. Theirs was a well-trodden road; the path Gützlaff taught was long and challenging, baptism exceedingly rare, and apostasy common. For all the time spent toiling in Tinghae just one single member of Gützlaff's congregation, a zealous man who had persuaded many others to attend chapel, would ask to be baptised. Even then, Gützlaff thought him still far from the Kingdom and in the end turned him down.[69]

It might have been a case of sour grapes, but Gützlaff at least was sure that he had never intended to spend forever on Chusan. Even before his social program ran into difficulties, thoughts of other places — Fuzhou, Japan, Korea, even Samarkand — had entered his mind. When, late in 1843, he heard from Hong Kong that he was to be offered the post of Chinese secretary to the colony, he accepted. The Foreign Office had refused to grant him the post he had hoped for — that of British consul in the treaty port of Fuzhou — as despite his marriages to two Englishwomen he had never adopted British citizenship. Then, shortly before his departure from Tinghae that autumn, he thought he glimpsed what under different circumstances might have become of his mission: 'Yesterday I had a crowd of my women for an audience, and what most astonished me was that they understood almost every word and took on board some concepts regarding the Saviour of sinners. The common insensitivity with regard to religious ideas and the natural difficulty of communication make this all the more astounding.'[70] But depart Gützlaff did, leaving British-administered Chusan without a single ordained Protestant minister.

If Protestantism could be accused of underestimating Chusan as a field for mission work, the same could not be said of its rival

Rome. At almost the precise moment in 1842 that Karl Gützlaff was readying to set out for the Yangtze campaign, an intelligent young French Catholic had stepped onto the wharf below Josshouse Hill.[71] With Gützlaff's victorious return to Chusan, Father Francois-Xavier-Timothée Danicourt of the Congrégation de la Mission — the 'Lazarists' — would for a time live in Tinghae alongside him. On occasions he would even visit Gützlaff's home to talk — they remained always on amicable terms — but the two competed all the while in earnest for souls.[72] It was a game at which Catholicism was proving by far the more adept: the three dozen European Catholics working within the empire could already realistically claim some 200,000 converts, a figure that stood in stark comparison with Protestantism's mere pewful, with plenty of room left to shuffle along.[73]

Father Danicourt's calling had been foretold even as he lay in his crib, when the angel Gabriel (if we are to believe his biography) had appeared in the room. He certainly had an ear for languages, that most welcome of gifts in a missionary, and spoke English and Italian besides reading Latin and Greek. Just like Mary Aldersey and the gentlewomen of the Society for the Promotion of Female Education, Danicourt had learned elementary Chinese before leaving France for Macao. The peninsula dangled like a tiny polyp from China's belly, absorbing a steady stream of priests from Europe's seminaries and pious Chinese from across the empire and secreting them into the interior as fully formed missionaries. There he stayed for seven years, tutoring novices and perfecting his Mandarin, before news of the death of his father spurred him toward the more perilous task of frontline missionary work. A few months later he received the news that his mother too had passed on, and thus was cut the last emotional thread keeping him from devoting his life to China. News of the peace was not long in coming, and Rome, no less than Canterbury, saw in Pottinger's successes the hand of God shaking the throne of Satan. With new ports now opened to missionary work, Danicourt was sent north to Tinghae.

While Chusan's mild climate reinvigorated him, he could scarcely express the degree to which its people had fallen from grace. Even the presence at one time of a fellow French Jesuit on the island — a certain Father Jean de Fontaney had been around when Allen Catchpoole had occupied the Red Hair Hall[74] — had left no discernible mark. And for all Gützlaff's fine words and pamphleteering there was not yet one single indigenous Christian. Danicourt explained the situation to a confidante:

> To give you an idea of the empire which the devil rules here, consider that there is not a mountain, nor a hill, a valley, a thicket or a house where there are not one or more pagodas of whatever size…. The people are infatuated with idols; they do nothing without intermixing in some superstition or other, so that this beautiful island, whose fertility all strangers admire, has since time immemorial been stained by the superstitions and abominations of paganism. This is what we must fight to overturn.

How could Danicourt set about such an uneven struggle? For a start, he set up a Catholic chapel and consecrated the entirety of the archipelago to Mary Immaculate.[75] Before the year was out, a Buddhist monk of some standing on the holy island of Putuoshan had been persuaded to convert, and by the start of 1843 was in Macao where his knowledge of canonical literature promised to be of great help to the seminarians' endeavours.[76] Little wonder, that Gützlaff's distaste at the ease with which men like that pledged themselves to Pope Gregory XVI was tinged with envy: his conversion was suspected of being little more than a superficial acceptance of the sacraments and a swapping of his Buddhist paraphernalia for the Catholic rosary, a far less demanding change than the heartfelt transformation Protestantism required.

While Mary Aldersey was busy educating young girls, Danicourt expanded his little chapel into an adjoining building which became a school training abandoned boys for the priesthood. Raising a generation of native Catholics from early childhood, the Jesuits knew from experience, was the best way to guarantee the spreading of the faith. Even if no Jesuit ever spoke the words often attributed to them — 'Give me a child for the first seven years, and you may do what you like with him after-wards' — this was precisely how Danicourt began work. He cared for the spiritual needs of Irish Catholic soldiers in the newly built Chusan Hospital for Europeans (it was a two-storey edifice beside the parade ground, built it seems at a cost of $10,000 with granite blocks robbed out from the city walls,[77] whitewashed in the Anglo-Indian style with a shaded veranda and Venetian shutters on its glazed windows, the first such use of glass on the island). Attendance at daily prayers, mass and confession grew. Monsieur Tcheou, Danicourt's old Mandarin tutor in Macao, was placed in charge of a second North Chapel, and one by one he diverted islanders from the cult of Guanyin the goddess of mercy to the not-dissimilar cult of the Virgin Mary.[78] In little more than a year Tcheou alone had baptised twenty Chusanese[79] — not a great number, but still twenty more than all of the island's Protestants had managed since 1840.

On Easter Monday of 1845, exhausted from overseeing a hectic Holy Week for his growing congregation, Danicourt set out on a restorative trip around Mary Immaculate's fiefdom.[80] At one point, hearing a distant bell he scrambled to the top of a hill from where he spied a crowd flocking toward a temple. Dropping down into the vale in his distinctive cassock and tricorn hat, Old Gu (he had taken the Chinese name Gu Fangji) was immediately recognised. As the Buddhist priests processed in their saffron ranks, he began to address the faces that now turned in curiosity toward him. But what had brought them here, to a temple in a remote valley? The grave-sweeping of Qingming was a week away. Were the idols he now so vehemently cursed the same gods from whom a bereaved family hoped to gain some earthly comfort? It is not hard to imagine the effect on a congregation in Danicourt's native hamlet of Authie of a Buddhist mounting the pulpit to declaim against the vain worship of Jesus. Only that was not the Buddhist way. The islanders were content in their worldview without needing to confirm it through the proof of evangelistic success. They were happy to leave their tombs in desolation for most of the year, so long as they could pay their respects on the correct day. Danicourt, like his Protestant rivals, never really understood the people he sought to reach. For all the earnest desire to save the immortal souls of its people, it is easy to believe that Danicourt and the rest were revolted by China. After a decade in the country he summed up his emotions in a long letter to Paris.[81] The Chinese were morally and spiritually bankrupt, he declared, a fact evinced by the way they treated their dead:

> Most anywhere one goes, the tombs present a hideous spectacle. I have seen in the larger districts vast cemeteries covered with ruined sepulchres, with rotten coffins. There is nothing so ghastly as the scattered bones, the bleached skulls, those pigtails and human scalps lying abandoned amongst the grass and scrub. Here is the respect, so highly spoken of, of this people for their dead. China might look beautiful from afar, but how repulsive it is up close.

China's pantheon, Danicourt grimaced, was full of 'masters of iniquity'. Buddha had frittered away his inheritance living the life of a tramp and had died in penury; Guanyin had been burned alive by her father; Laozi had strangled himself to death after a life wasted searching for the elixir of immortality. Even the humble Hearth God had hanged himself when subjected to scorn. 'What should one expect from a people who adore such divinities?' he railed. 'What is China if not a great den of thieves, a vast breeding ground of disease?' His examples, intentionally grotesque misunderstandings of folklore, were shocking to Christians back home but of no use in converting the canny Chinese.

And so that Easter Monday of 1845 he rounded in frustration upon the gods in the courtyard of that village temple. The British had twice taken Chusan, had killed and plundered, had burned their pagodas. If Guanyin heard the world's cries, why had she done nothing to protect the islanders? Danicourt had better things planned for them. From Tinghae he begged for nuns to be sent out to manage his schools and hospitals. In the meantime, native Chinese priests worked to awe the islanders with all the lively ceremonial they could muster, with all the noise, colour and incense that Buddhists enjoyed but which starchy Protestantism did not offer. Slowly, through preaching and exhortation, Danicourt's converts started to observe the Sabbath, a most alien concept to a culture whose ten-day week encompassed no day of rest. Asking already poor families to down tools for one seventh of the year proved a terrible imposition: some were reduced to such misery that men sold their wives so they might have a handful of rice to eat. 'Luckily,' Danicourt thanked God, 'we were able to buy back almost all of them.'[82]

The most elderly member of the North Chapel congregation died under British rule, and Danicourt decided that the funeral of 85-year-old Maria Ou should be a sight to convince her neighbours of the true faith.[83] 'Our biggest difficulty was to bury her with all the ceremonies of the church,' he informed his superiors. 'I much regretted having only a couple of dozen Christians, otherwise I would have electrified the whole town.' Still, Maria's cortège raised exclamations of wonder as it passed through the city to the foreign cemetery. And when Maria reached her final resting place, Danicourt took down the cross and nailed it to her coffin. It was the first Christian symbol to adorn a Chinese tomb on Chusan. As his clock ticked away the last days and weeks of 1845, Danicourt grew convinced that his mission would soon be flourishing under permanent British rule. 'It is more or less certain,' he wrote, 'that the English will keep Chusan, the healthiest and most secure of the Chinese islands.' And as December 31st drew closer, he was not the only person on Chusan and farther afield to have come to that conclusion.

19

Apples of Sodom

ONE OF those who felt sure that Britain would keep hold of Chusan was an Englishman named George Smith, a missionary who in the spring of 1844 had opened his instructions for an impending move to China.[1] His backer, the Church Missionary Society, thought it heard half of humanity straining to hear the Church of England's particular version of the Word.[2] This was to be the first time in history that the Anglican Church itself—rather than the instinctively evangelistic nonconformists—had sponsored a mission to the Celestial Empire. The names Canton, Amoy, Fuzhou, Ningbo and Shanghai hung on the lips of Anglicans, yet precious little was understood of what reality lay behind them. Smith was charged with visiting each of those five ports opened under the Treaty of Nanking to appraise their potential. The Church of England, ever cautious in the face of change, gave Smith no inflexible orders. Beyond the testing requirement that he learn Chinese while in the country, all rested with his ability to read into events the handiwork of the Lord. The Society could only urge him to follow 'the glorious footsteps of Divine Providence', reminding him to bear in mind Jesus' injunction to his disciples to be as wise as serpents and as harmless as doves. An anonymous donation of £6,000 from somebody calling himself 'Less than the least' had stipulated the funding of a China mission, and great things were expected.[3]

It was June of 1845 before George Smith glimpsed the peaks of Chusan, which by then had been under British rule for four years. At first he sailed on to Shanghai, where he was welcomed into the home of William and Kate Lockhart. Though the island was not strictly within his remit, Smith's perambulations on the Zhejiang coast would take him to Chusan four times in all. As it did to many of Ningbo's foreign residents, the island first called to him when Ningbo was visited by a 'sickly', as its deadly summertime epidemics were known with black euphemism. Smith, already weak from the climate, fled the heat of mid-August. At Ningbo's Chusan Wharf, he and a missionary friend and his wife bought their passage on a native junk plying the route to Tinghae.

After tacking for hours through the islands in a churlish wind, the party landed beneath Josshouse Hill. 'There was, however,' he noticed straight away after weeks in the thoroughly Chinese surroundings of Ningbo, 'something very unnatural in the appearance of European barracks and sentries — of the red coats and muskets of British soldiers.' The sepoys' black faces and the splendid uniforms of the officers stood starkly out from what was still, despite years of British rule, a Chinese town. In the battle-scarred temple upon Josshouse Hill, Smith held services for the troops.[4] Just as Gützlaff had, back in that freezing winter of 1833, he took a passage to the sacred island of Putuoshan, and like him he lectured the Buddhists on their folly. As always they listened politely, smilingly admitted the failings of their religion, and then, when Smith had gone, no doubt drew a sigh at his ignorance and went on with their lives. In Tinghae he lived with an American missionary named Augustus Ward Loomis and his wife Mary Ann. Their house was small, a two-roomed affair with a kitchen that rather resembled a blacksmith's forge. When Smith last saw British Chusan it was December, the sickly heat of the summer was a memory, and there were barely three weeks to go before the final instalment of the $21,000,000 opium indemnity was due to be handed over. He touched at Tinghae in a Shanghai vessel bound for Fuzhou. Though his longest sojourn on Chusan had been less than one month, far shorter than most, he had seen enough to give a most incisive and empathetic account of the nature of British rule there:

> It would have argued no very sanguine temperament, to have hailed the temporary annexation of Chusan to the empire of Britain as a rare and precious opportunity for an exhibition of the arts and civilisation of the West — of the mild but incorruptible majesty of British law — of the sublime morality and benevolence of the Christian character — and of the fostering influence diffused by British government on the commerce, the liberties and the happiness of the governed.[5]

No taxes had been asked of the islanders, whether farmers or businessmen,[6] the pirates who had once terrorised the islands had been mercilessly dealt with by the Royal Navy,[7] and a system of justice blind to a man's social position had attached considerable numbers of common people to the British. But then Smith punctured the vanity of the colonialist by holding a mirror to the dark side of his presence:

> Frequent deeds of violence on the part of the soldiery, numerous scenes of intoxication from the maddening draughts of *samshoo*, a general disregard of the feelings of the Chinese, and continual outbreaks of a proud overbearing spirit on the vanquished race, required something more of an opposite character, to counteract their natural effect on the native mind, than the mere spectacle of the power, the arts, and the wealth of the new-comers.[8]

This, then, was why the popularity of the British was in general limited to those — boatmen, coolies, servants, shopkeepers, laundrymen, cooks — on whom self-interest and lucre had operated, those for whom a handover would put an end to a good income. It behoved Britain to consider why a rule it considered superior to any other could so easily — so ungratefully — be shrugged off:

> The absence of any marked feelings of regret on the part of the inhabitants generally at their return to Chinese rule, and the positive joy at the prospect cherished by large numbers, are facts of interest at the present juncture, and give birth to many reflections on the real nature of their own Government. Although relieved from all taxation, and possessing opportunities of gain without fear of extortion under the British, they prefer their own Mandarins with all their faults.[9]

Such is the story of so many of Britain's colonial adventures.

During 1845 it became clear that, once a Chinese mandarin was again residing in the magistracy, even peaceful foreign missionaries like Smith would not be allowed to stay. They were given notice to leave, with the incentive of having premises provided free of charge for a period in Ningbo if they departed swiftly.[10] Smith, for one, guessed that things would not remain so forever. God forbid that it should come to pass, but if war were

239

ever to break out again Chusan would once more be the first target for British troops. And once occupied, Smith assumed, 'it requires no prophetic wisdom to predict its permanent retention, and its substitution for Hong Kong as a base for British power.'[11] He would be at least partly right in his assumption.

The people of Tinghae in particular, accustomed by now to the fact of British rule, were on the whole not anticipating a peaceful restoration to the Qing. Like A-Tin the farmer on Trumball Island, they had all heard that Hong Kong was no longer ruled by China, even if they did not know where Hong Kong was.

'A very general impression had prevailed among them that [Chusan] was to be permanently retained by us,' Governor Sir John Davis would recall. 'They could not understand how, having the power to secure so valuable a possession, we had not also the intention to keep it.'[12] Some played it safe: parents withdrew children enrolled in the mission schools, fearing reprisals if the rumours of a handover did turn out to be true, and merchants prepared to shut up shop and hide out in Shanghai or Ningbo until the first wave of official displeasure and extortions had blown over.[13] Whispers reached American residents' ears of some anticipated act of perfidy, some excuse to be engineered by the British as a way of keeping hold of the island. Down in Hong Kong, Governor Davis was sensitive to the delicate situation unfolding in Zhejiang. In late 1844 he wrote to the Foreign Secretary Lord Aberdeen, warning him that many Chusanese could not believe that their island would be handed back. Gützlaff, by now Chinese secretary in Hong Kong, had sensed much the same: 'The natives cannot persuade themselves that they are to revert to their old masters, and so lively are their hopes that they are still building in the expectation of seeing more English on their shores.'

Better-informed of Whitehall's policy concerns than the Chinese, the mood amongst the field force and the small merchant community tended toward a disappointment that the island had not been secured at Nanking rather than a belief that the treaty would be dishonoured. Yet from the outset the British had done little to dispel the general impression that Chusan might become a permanent addition to their Empire. Almost as soon as the cannon-fire had died away in July of 1840, attention had been turned to assessing its potential, with a Lieutenant John Ouchterlony of the Madras Engineers being asked to carry out a detailed survey that was published the following spring as *A Statistical Sketch of the Island of Chusan*.

Though English sailors had known about Tinghae's harbour since the seventeenth century, Ouchterlony now drew attention to Sinkong Passage on the west coast. Several hundred yards wide and six miles in length, it was sheltered by high islands and could provide eight fathoms of anchorage. The tides in this 'young Bosphorus'[14] were moderate, more predictable than Tinghae's baffling races (almost every British warship which anchored there would run aground during the occupation, some of them time and again),[15] and docks and slipways could easily be built on land reclaimed from the sea. Nearer as it was than Tinghae to the trading ports of the mainland, Ouchterlony thought it on the whole a more favourable site to found a city. Chusan in general he found to be perfect for growing Western staples. There was pasturage enough for sheep and cattle to feed a garrison. Horses might easily be raised on legumes, mangle-wurzels and clover. Every article of luxury or necessity for the table was readily procurable, the climate was temperate yet winter was cold enough to kill off the tropical diseases common further south. For now, Chusan's only roads were the wheelbarrow tracks between her fields, but these could easily be widened and metalled. The water in her canals was bad, but with a little effort fresh streams could be channelled from the hills to the town. Even the scenery was lovely. In all, Ouchterlony produced a glowing summary: there was no more agreeable spot for European troops amongst Britain's possessions in the East. Chusan, he assumed, was destined to become as important as any colony that of recent years had been added to the Crown. Ouchterlony, just as Gützlaff had when he urged James Matheson to press the government for Chusan's retention, saw a second Singapore in the offing.

Karl Gützlaff himself (who in some ways looked upon Chusan as his personal fiefdom to the greater glory of God) thought it worthwhile to spell out in a long letter to the Foreign Office the island's many advantages.[16] Its Chinese population was industrious and, though ten times that of Hong Kong, would require just a fifth of the policing. Its green tea and silk industries, though crude, could be nurtured. As for fishing, the island was home to an extensive and lucrative trade that could be turned to Britain's advantage and extended out to Japan and Korea. For European troops its climate was congenial; familiar fruits and vegetables would thrive in its soil, and even grapevines could be planted on its mountain slopes. Tidal docks could be excavated on Tea Island in Tinghae harbour, and excellent shipbuilding woods procured from Korea. 'We would look upon Chusan as another Malta,' he was sure, from which the British could protect their commercial interests across the East China Sea as far north as Manchuria. 'If we willingly abandon this spot,' Gützlaff had counselled his friend and confidante James Matheson as early as October of 1840, 'we deserve to suffer for our folly.' [17]

Many other military men agreed with Gützlaff's glowing portrait: 'This is a most beautiful island,' Colonel Wyndham Baker of the Madras Artillery wrote in a letter home soon after Captain Elliot's negotiations at Canton, 'and it is very likely after all that it will be kept in preference to Hong Kong, notwithstanding the large outlay which has been made on that barren place.' [18] 'Chusan is very much improved,' wrote Major Armine Mountain of the Cameronian Regiment, 'and if we retain the island permanently, I think it will become a very pretty place, and by no means unhealthy.' [19] Lieutenant Shadwell of the 98th, badly beaten three years earlier during the failed Wellesley kidnapping and so with more reason than most to disdain Chusan, thought Pottinger's preference for Hong Kong at the Nanking talks had been 'a fatal error'. Pottinger had since let it be known that he had disregarded Chusan because it would have been difficult to defend against the perpetual jealousies arising between the British and the mandarins on the nearby islands — 'poppycock,' in Shadwell's view. Pottinger, he confided to a friend, did not deserve the name attached to him back home.[20]

Neither did Dr Alexander Grant, who had spent the whole of 1843 investigating Chinese farming methods, see any reason come 1845 to restore Chusan to Chinese rule. His contributions to the *India Journal of Medical & Physical Science* read at times like an estate agent's window:

> Chusan, from its insular situation, the physical aspects of the country, and its position on the globe, ought to be a healthy locality. For a European settlement it combines many advantages, some of which are its noble harbour, and its proximity to the mainland, and were the system of dry cultivation introduced there is every reason to believe that the island would be more healthy than most of our possessions in Asia. In the hottest months of summer a very moderate temperature might be enjoyed among the hills in the vicinity, some of which are above 1,800' in height, and the long cold winter of this latitude enables the European constitution to recover completely from the relaxing effects of the preceding heat. Among the beautiful islands in the immediate neighbourhood, residents would have ample scope for locating themselves in situations which combine all the advantages of a country residence and an insular climate within a short distance of the seat of their business.[21]

In fact, by 1845 Chusan had more than simply shaken off its early reputation for sickness — it was the healthiest British possession in the East.[22] 'There are few islands in the world more picturesque and containing more varied features in a small space than Chusan,' thought the travel-writer and sportsman William Tyrone Power, who had arrived in May of that year.[23] For months he had been confined to the hellish island of Gulangyu, a mile-long rock in Amoy harbour which like Chusan was to be kept until the opium indemnity had been paid. Gulangyu had made the pestilential Hong Kong look like Lourdes, so fatal was the fever there. One detachment of Madras Native Infantry had been there just a few months yet had lost over half its 240 men, the rest reduced to walking ghosts. Chusan by any comparison was bewitching, Arcadian even: 'Numerous villages and a comfortable, cheerful-looking peasantry attest the excellence of the soil and the lightness of the foreign yoke,' Power observed, 'which, for a time, protects, without coercing them or meddling in their patriarchal mode of government.' No taxes, he noted, had been levied by the British, 'who, except in occupying two points on the island, and compelling a certain regard to cleanliness in Tinghae, and order in the bazaars, have not interfered in the slightest degree in the internal arrangements.' [24]

Nobody had imagined that the sun setting over Chusan would have cast the island in such a beautiful light. Every commentator had an opinion on what should become of it, the plant-hunter Robert Fortune amongst them:

> Everyone now seemed to regret that we had not secured Chusan as a part of the British dominions for the protection of our trade in China, instead of the barren and unhealthy island of Hong Kong; and some even went so far as to recommend that means should still be taken by our government to accomplish this desirable end. The time, however, for doing this had gone by, and I believe that every right-thinking person would have seen with regret any power exercised by a great and exalted nation like England to infringe a solemn treaty which had been entered into with a nation so utterly powerless as the Chinese. That we committed a blunder and made a bad bargain is quite certain, but having done so, we must abide by the consequences. Had we retained Chusan, it would not only have been a healthy place for our troops and merchants, but it would also have proved a safeguard to our trade in the north, which must ultimately become of greater importance than that at Canton. [25]

Fortune had encapsulated the dilemma: Britain had entered into a solemn treaty while holding a gun to China's head. If Queen Victoria now informed the Daoguang Emperor that she intended to retain Chusan even after the indemnity had been paid, the outcome could only be, in the opinion of the *China Mail* in Hong Kong, 'the certain and deserved imputation of bad faith' by the Chinese, who were 'a great but jealous people in the beginning of their intercourse with the civilised world.' [26] It was a choice between 'inglorious retention' and 'national honour'. [27] Chusan was being lauded in certain quarters as a paradise, yet 'the fruits we should gather there would probably turn out nothing but apples of Sodom, fair outside, but rotten within.' [28]

There remained however a serious sticking point to any handover — Canton. One provision agreed at Nanking had been that British subjects, along with their families and retainers, must be allowed to reside without restraint at all of the treaty ports. By late 1845 the southernmost of the five, Canton, was still not fully opened, and foreign merchants were prevented from living inside the walled city. But as the Chinese maintained, the treaty's wording linked the restoration of Chusan to full payment of the $21,000,000 opium indemnity, not to access to the ports, and certainly not to any right to reside within the walls of Canton. The British, after all, were trading as they always had in factories on the riverfront. Anyway, it was not that Governor Huang was refusing to admit foreigners — the problem was the Cantonese themselves, a rabidly xenophobic lot whom not even the emperor himself could compel to accept foreigners living amongst them (though their hatred is not really to be wondered at, given that just a few years back the Royal Navy had massacred the defenders of the Bogue forts while British soldiers had shot dead men of the local militia in the alleyways surrounding the English factory). Governor Davis sought guidance from London, and was told that Britons had as much right to enter Canton as China had to take back Chusan. China's failure to observe the Nanking treaty in full gave him a point of leverage: could he demand safe access to Canton and meanwhile hold Chusan forfeit? The *Chinese Repository*, that serious-minded publication serving Canton's missionary and merchant community, fell short of asking for Chusan's permanent retention, satisfied that an extra few months' occupation would demonstrate to China that its treaty obligations must be honoured. Queen Victoria, it felt sure, ought not to renege on her promises. [29]

But others of the newspapers that had sprung up to serve the burgeoning foreign community on the China coast dared to consider a breach of faith. [30] The *Friend of China & Hong Kong Gazette* published an editorial in the autumn of 1845 noting that the ongoing grievances all related to Canton. There the cramped factories, the insulting locals and the grasping attitude of the mandarins had changed not one iota since the war, and it was precisely such problems which had lain at the root of the conflict. It was an absurd situation. Governor Davis, the *Friend of China* hoped, had been instructed to tell the Chinese that unless they honour the treaty to the letter then Chusan would be retained. China seemed to place great store by the island, and such a threat would not be unavailing.

One newspaper positively advocated retention, regardless of the Canton question. Earlier in the year, the Calcutta missionary newspaper the *Friend of India* had trumpeted the opinion that a British Chusan 'would soon become one of the largest commercial marts in the world.'[31] 'Even as a matter of economy,' it thought, 'it would in the long run be judicious to sacrifice the money which has been sunk upon [Hong Kong]. It would be cheap to indemnify the merchants… to secure the removal of our commercial establishments to a spot where they will enjoy such pre-eminent advantages.' Other corners of the English-language press in the East smelled a rat. The *Friend of India*, so the editor of the *China Mail* guessed, had been persuaded of Chusan's importance by a gentleman who had not long before arrived in India from Hong Kong, 'a gentleman better known as an author than as an authority.'[32] That gentleman's name was Robert Montgomery Martin.

One August night in 1844 a ship had beaten up the Sarah Galley Passage and dropped anchor in Tinghae harbour. The next morning, a frail-looking man had been rowed across to the wharves. Robert Montgomery Martin had the previous month left Hong Kong, of which he was Colonial Treasurer, to convalesce after a near-fatal attack of fever. Within weeks he had become the most vociferous evangelist for the retention of Chusan and of the immediate abandonment of Pottinger's worthless prize. He considered the latter, as initially had Lord Palmerston, 'a barren rock' exhaling malarial gases that caused Europeans to die like flies. Chusan, on the other hand, was China's Montpellier, a veritable health resort, and Martin gushed with unconcealed enthusiasm for the place where he had recovered his strength:

> At early morn, the singing of the birds in the groves, the murmuring rivulets through the valleys and the fresh breeze from the mountains enhance the charms of the landscape and renovate the health of the debilitated resident of a tropical climate.

Though little different from many of the eulogies which on the eve of a possible handover were being written about Chusan, Martin's opinions were to be taken more seriously, and considered in fact at the very highest levels of British government.

Robert Montgomery Martin had been born an Ulster Protestant in 1801, and he was proud of his loyalty to the Crown.[33] He had first travelled to the East while a teenager, putting five years of surgical training into practice as a medical assistant in Sri Lanka. But a further eighteen months as a naval surgeon had left Martin's health broken and he had headed for the colony of New South Wales. There he had recovered his strength (and, while he was at it, introduced the smallpox vaccine to Australia) before sailing for Calcutta. For two years he had worked as a journalist, jointly publishing the *Bengal Herald* until in 1830 he had returned to England. It was then that Martin had begun in earnest to make a name as a polemicist. Part activist and agitator, part political dilettante, with a sharp eye for statistical detail but a tendency to ignore the broader canvas, he would write on topics from colonial agriculture and economics to Irish Unionism. Yet despite a recommendation from King William, Martin failed time and again to gain official employment in the civil service. Until, that is, in 1844 the colonial secretary Lord Stanley made him treasurer of a rapidly expanding Hong Kong. Martin stepped ashore in Victoria in May in company with the new governor, Sir John Davis. By June he had made up his mind: Hong Kong was no good for a colony, and abandonment ought not to be ruled out. By July he had fallen seriously ill with fever. Practically a skeleton, after a short sojourn in Macao he was in Tinghae to recuperate.

With Hong Kong's bare crags fresh in his mind's eye, it required no feverish imagination for Martin to envisage a bright future for his new home. He set out his thoughts soon after his arrival:

> Were Chusan a British colony, its hills and vales would be adorned by charming villas, rich orchards, and luxuriant pasturages. An English town, with all the advantages of modern civilisation, would become an example to the Chinese, and in the improvement of our position we should materially aid in the social advancement of the imitative nation contiguous to our shores.

A healthy military station, he argued, was vital for a British presence on the China coast. Should force again be demanded on the Yangtze, a Chusan regiment would be as fresh as any marching straight out of its English depot. And commercially, Martin calculated, Chusan was excelling most of the treaty ports. To a degree he was right: Amoy, Fuzhou and Ningbo had thus far proved disappointing, but Shanghai was faring much better.[34] There, Chinese tea-and-silk merchants preferred to barter than to hand over precious silver dollars, the result being a glut of bartered Western goods appearing for resale in the surrounding towns at well below the lowest asking price on Chusan.[35] For Western merchants, it made more sense to follow the crowds to Shanghai or even tiny Wenzhou[36] to barter one's own stock than to sit in Tinghae waiting for silver dollars that never came. Sir Henry Pottinger might have written to Lord Aberdeen in August of 1843 with news that Britain's trade on Chusan was worth an estimated $600,000 each month, but a year later the most profitable articles in Tinghae were not the cottons or woollens which the British were most interested in finding new markets for, but instead chests of Bengali opium: soon one tenth of the entire China market was passing through the archipelago, some 230 chests being sold in the harbour each month.[37] One had only to sniff the air or stand on Josshouse Hill overlooking the clippers' anchorages for proof. True, people had been buying other foreign merchandise duty free to slip into China under the noses of the Ningbo customs, but underwriting drug smuggling and tax evasion were no way to endear a British colony to Peking!

Martin spent just a few weeks on Chusan, casting an eye over its landscape and economy. His conclusions were as idiosyncratic as the man: the island's home-grown tobacco, which most thought coarse, he considered 'much prized'; the local cotton, which even the islanders thought rough, was 'excellent'; as to the islanders themselves, whom most considered incorrigible petty thieves, he praised them for their honesty and orderliness. Mistakenly believing he had been sent east on the strength of his colonial expertise[38] (the lack of others willing to die of malaria seems to have held greater weight with Lord Stanley), Martin had quickly come to see himself as a disinterested arbiter reporting his findings to a Whitehall that avidly awaited his opinion. In late summer of 1844 he had recovered his health and was back in Hong Kong, and by October he had forwarded an unsolicited *Report on the Island of Chusan* to London.[39] Next, he despatched a letter to Prime Minister Robert Peel, thoroughly denigrating the hopes placed on Hong Kong.[40] If a commission were assembled in the colony, he suggested, consisting of Governor Davis, Karl Gützlaff, and others (including the commander of HM land forces who, unbeknown to Martin, thought him 'quite mad'),[41] then a similar consensus might be reached. Gützlaff for one was known to have a decided preference for Chusan: 'With a fourth of the money spent on the ungrateful soil of Hong-Kong,' he had written (never dreaming that Victoria would a century later be one of the modern wonders of the world), 'Chusan would have exhibited a larger and a more beautiful city than we shall ever behold on the straggling hills of that colony.' But even the jingoistic Gützlaff was decidedly opposed to the idea of reneging on Nanking: Britain's political engagements 'must sacredly be preserved,' he wrote in a letter to the Foreign Office, 'and under no circumstances be violated whatever may be the advantages.'[42] Ignorant of the weakness of his arguments when viewed from a wider perspective, Martin closed his letter to Peel by saying that he was rushing back to England to put his case before it was too late.

The prime minister was unimpressed by Martin's opinions of Hong Kong, but admitted that the idea of a commission was worth considering and sought the views of Whitehall.[43] It was suggested that Sir Thomas Herbert and Sir Thomas Bourchier, who had both commanded warships at Chusan, along with Sir William Parker and Lord Saltoun, who had been commanders-in-chief during the war, could be consulted informally over the general accuracy of Martin's *Report*.[44] The suggestion found favour with the Home Secretary Sir James Graham, who told Peel that the unanimous agreement of those four men was entitled to the utmost weight.[45] Their private opinions, though, were known to be divided, with Bourchier and Herbert preferring Chusan and its strategic position close to the Yangtze. Sir Henry Pottinger could hardly be excluded from any commission, and he was famous for his trenchant views on the value of Hong Kong, his personal acquisition for the Crown. Then again, even Pottinger was on record as having respectfully suggested to the former foreign secretary Lord Palmerston that Chusan be retained. In November of 1841 he had written to Palmerston with high hopes for the island:

> I doubt not, but in our hands it would, in a very short time, become a vast mart of commerce.... [I]t seems to me, to become a question for the grave deliberation of Her Majesty's Government, whether it ought, under any circumstances, to be again restored to the Chinese government, who could not prevent the Merchants, and the Capitalists of the Empire, flocking to it, were it once declared to be a British settlement and a free port for a series of years.[46]

An open disagreement over Chusan's status would not settle the matter, but only add more uncertainty to the considerable misgivings with which Hong Kong was being occupied. 'Hong Kong is ours,' continued the Home Secretary,

> for better, for worse: Chusan must be evacuated on the payment of the last instalment from China in the course of the present year. There are grave objections to reopening our Treaty with China. Unless we do so, we must keep Hong Kong, or have no

settlement and no anchorage in those seas. Surely Hong Kong is better than none.[47]

Any approach to the Chinese aimed at reopening negotiations would, Sir James knew, be ill met. The next day, Sir Robert Peel received a note from the judge advocate general John Nicholl MP, the highest judicial figure in the British army. There was clearly a hornets' nest waiting to be stirred up over the Chusan question, but nobody was prepared to take up a cudgel and go about beating it: 'We cannot obtain Chusan if we desired it, and I agree with Sir James Graham, that being the case, that it would be unwise to disparage Hong Kong.'[48] Highly desirable real-estate Chusan may be, preferable even to Hong Kong, yet once Queen Victoria's signature had dried it lay beyond reach and any arguments for its retention were just an unpleasant reminder of a trick missed. Martin's arguments were not wrong (for many at the highest levels of government agreed Chusan to be the superior of Hong Kong); they were just irrelevant in a changed diplomatic climate. His *Report* had ended with the blithe statement that there were 'many cogent arguments of the highest state policy for our continued and permanent occupation of Chusan, and but one reason assigned for its evacuation in December 1845, namely, that we have promised to do so on the fulfilment of the terms of the treaty of Nankin.'

In sheer exasperation, an unknown Whitehall hand pencilled a note alongside: 'How can we help it without breaking our *faith* which is of more value than fifty Chusans?'

But others besides Robert Montgomery Martin were agitating for Chusan's retention during that final year of its legal occupation. In March of 1845, Sir Robert Peel was handed a note excusing an attached document for troubling him. *Remarks on the Advantages of Retaining Possession of the Island of Chusan* had been written by Benjamin Waterhouse, an agent for the trading house of Jardine, Matheson & Co. who had lived on Chusan ever since the 1841 invasion.[49] It was his opinion that, 'if permanently retained by Britain as a free port, nothing could prevent Chusan becoming an emporium of the first magnitude.' In the course of the year 1844, he admitted, the island had been neglected by British merchants, who considered it not worthwhile cultivating connections in a market soon to be closed. Certain Chinese merchants were bringing silver dollars to pay for British cottons in Tinghae, even though the authorities on the mainland seemed anxious to shoehorn foreign trade into as few ports as possible, but most foreigners were bypassing Chusan for the bounteous bazaars of Shanghai. Just as Governor Burrell had suspected pressure from Ningbo to be behind the departure of Tinghae's shopkeepers in 1840, so in 1845 it seemed that spies paid to counsel the islanders against trading with the British were the reason why so little tea, silk or crockery were arriving for sale. Few foreigners who had been long in China, Waterhouse reasoned, would question the possibility that its government, despite the Treaty of Nanking, still took a regulatory interest in those of its citizens who traded with the West. His suspicions were justified — the governor of Zhejiang boasted to the emperor of having infiltrators working undercover in Tinghae.[50] By diminishing Chusan's value as a marketplace, of course, they rendered it less attractive to the British as the handover approached. Yet to Waterhouse, by now one of Chusan's longest-standing residents, its advantages as a colony were nevertheless 'so obvious as hardly to require dwelling upon.' Its future as a place of trade rested on its remaining a free port, an untaxed fallback should the Chinese in Ningbo and Shanghai revert to the old 'chicanery and extortion' and so throttle Britain's trade there.

There was an equally vital political matter to consider. The French, Waterhouse added in a covering letter, had long had a warship in Tinghae harbour, and it was widely supposed that they might find some quarrel with the Chinese to allow them to take the island if the British left.[51] (The French ambassador to China, M. de Lagrené, had laughed at the idea of Britain handing Chusan back and joked that France would like it for herself,[52] but when he was speaking in earnest utterly disavowed any such wish.)[53] This was the one argument which sent cold shivers down Whitehall spines. Martin too was using it. In late April the home secretary Sir James Graham confided his misgivings to the foreign secretary Lord Aberdeen. The allegations were most serious, yet Martin was a most unreliable witness on whose testimony to accuse the French, now a friendly nation, of blackguardly bad faith. By September of 1845, with Martin still stirring up indignation, the *Friend of India* was fulminating over rumours that France was interested in acquiring Chusan, if not by arms (and it was clear that the French did not have enough men in the theatre to launch an invasion) then by stealth. France might thus 'quietly take that prominent position in China for which we have fought.' The *Times* of London disagreed — it was inconceivable that a jealous China would cede land to France, an absolute stranger whom she neither loved nor feared.[54] In Hong Kong the *China Mail* too brushed aside such rumours: 'We have no earthly fear of the bugbear held out in the Indian papers, that the tri-colored flag or the star-spangled banner will float upon the walls of Tinghai as soon as the ensign of England is removed.' As for Uncle Sam, Governor Davis was sure that 'the occupation of distant, foreign colonies forms no part of the policy of the United States.'[55]

Yet with just two months to go before any handover became due there was still deep unease. On October 18th, Sir James Graham asked the prime minister what was to be done. The prospect of a French Chusan was haunting him, and Martin's arguments had begun to rub off. 'We must religiously observe our engagements with China,' he admitted, 'but I fear that Hong Kong is a sorry possession and Chusan is a magnificent island admirably placed for our purposes.'[56] Peel in turn wrote to Lord Aberdeen, reminding him that if France obtained Chusan it would make their *entente cordiale* 'the laughing stock of Europe.'[57] The foreign secretary attached not the slightest credence to the reports. Still, 'ridicule so overwhelming' justified watchfulness; a French occupation would mean not just an end to the *entente* — it would mean war.[58] That was why he had had such difficulty in broaching the subject tactfully to the French ambassador. But broach it he had, and France was now aware that Governor Davis in Hong Kong was authorised to attack any foreign power who tried to occupy Chusan; the British forces in India were at his disposal.[59]

If there were proof positive of a Chinese plot to cede Chusan to a third party, he was authorised — nay, *required* — to retake and retain it permanently.[60] King Louis-Philippe's diplomats assured Britain that France had no plans to take her place.[61] This satisfied Graham, who thought Aberdeen's instructions most judicious, balancing perfect good faith over Nanking with prudent precaution toward Britain's rivals.[62] The foreign secretary himself saw in his instructions to Davis a glimpse of the new order which would come to bind the Qing:

> It is a very strong measure, to say that our own interests forbid us to acquiesce in the cession of the island by the Emperor of China to any other power.... This interference with an independent state, although in our case quite necessary, is so difficult of explanation that I have thought it desirable to obtain from the Chinese government some assurance or pledge which would give us a better right to act.[63]

In other words, Britain needed something in writing from China, a piece of paper which it might run up to the masthead if ever it had to justify invading Chusan for a third time.[64]

With time running out, Lord Aberdeen familiarised Governor Davis with his government's position:[65] it had, he said, been urged on no account to give up possession of Chusan. But regardless of the arguments put forward by Martin and others, the Treaty of Nanking was imperative, and good faith required that Britain give up Chusan as agreed, provided the Chinese for their part had fulfilled their treaty obligations. 'Such therefore must be our course,' was the foreign secretary's simple conclusion.

So, although Martin did not yet know it, his lobbying had already failed. Still, by October he was in England to lobby in person. (Before leaving Canton he had been attacked and robbed by a mob shouting 'Kill! Kill!', an experience which had, unsurprisingly, turned him even farther against that city and the pestilential Hong Kong at its river mouth.) Meetings with the colonial secretary, the foreign secretary and Viscount Palmerston followed, but by the time Martin had had the chance to put his arguments face-to-face the deadline for the final payment of the $21,000,000 had already passed.

20

No news could have given us such joy

THAT LAST payment had been accompanied by much controversy. The beginning of a great but jealous people's intercourse with the civilised world was, it seemed, to be conducted in tentative, untrusting steps. A flurry of official letters had passed between Governor Davis in Hong Kong and Commissioner Qiying in Canton.[1] The English version of the Treaty of Nanking, it transpired, had specified the end of 1845 as the deadline for the last payment, but the Chinese version had mistakenly translated this as the end of the corresponding *Chinese* year, which in fact concluded in late January of 1846. Qiying, understandably reluctant to deviate a hair's breadth from the agreement for fear of perfidy, informed Davis that China would hand over the silver by January 26th as specified in the Chinese text. Besides, Davis' offer to return the islet of Gulangyu in Amoy harbour a full year early, both a gesture of goodwill and a practical response to the death toll there, had unnerved Kiying: was this a ploy to hand back the smaller island but hold on correspondingly longer to the bigger? He had rejected the offer, explaining that for the sake of ten thousand years of harmony between the two nations he was willing to wait a little longer for both islands' joint return. (Even then, while pointing out the oversight in the drafting, Qiying asserted that the last day of 1845 corresponded to the 17th of the 10th month of that Chinese year. In fact it was the 3rd day of the 12th month, making his calculations inexplicably a month and a half out. His assumption that December, like all Chinese months, had thirty days, only added to the diplomatic confusion.)

The year 1846 was rung in across the harbour to the chimes of Big Ben, the striking mechanism having been installed on one of HM warships, and dawn revealed the Union Jack still flying on Chusan.[2] Everything had been on track, with Governor Davis informing Qiying on December 8th that the island was ready to be handed back. But that same letter mentioned that there was no point in Qiying's men crossing Kintang Sound until a date had been set, adding with a degree of menace that entry into Canton

CHUSAN

could no longer be postponed. His implication was clear. Qiying again insisted that the treaty specified full payment and access to five ports, *not* entry into the defiant walled city of Canton: 'Chusan might be just a small piece of land in a corner of China, yet in its relevance to the good faith continuing between our two nations it is the largest.' Davis in turn clarified his position: he would not have been liaising so closely with Qiying if he did not intend to hand back Chusan, but he had been clearly instructed by his political masters to obtain access to Canton just as to the other treaty ports. Even Davis himself, Queen Victoria's pleni-potentiary, could not enter Canton, a situation he described as 'a disgrace and a slight'.[3] Lord Aberdeen, his opinion of Chusan coloured if not swayed, it seems, by both Martin and Gützlaff's glowing reports, had at the eleventh hour entrusted to Davis the latitude to win as much as possible from the Chinese — and that explicitly included the retention, if practicable, of an island which was innately more desirable than Hong Kong.

'Although it is possible that the Chinese government are looking forward eagerly to the time which shall restore Chusan to their sole authority,' Lord Aberdeen had written,

and that it would be difficult to offer to them any consider-ation sufficiently valuable to induce them to cede that island to us in perpetuity, I do not think it right to leave you without such authority as would enable you to take advantage of any willingness which they might possibly show to entertain the question of our retention of Chusan as a British possession. You will understand, therefore, that seeing how many and how great are the commercial advantages of Chusan, and how much superior, so far as our experience has gone, to those of Hong Kong, or of any of the ports to which we have access, Her Majesty's Government would consider favourably any arrangement which you might propose, and which might lead to a cession of the former island.[4]

Aberdeen doubted that the Chinese government would be disposed to listen to such a proposition; rather than give Davis detailed instructions, it was enough that he felt himself authorised to negotiate if he perceived an opportunity to keep Chusan. Yet Davis, from months of dealing with Qiying, knew though that the Chinese were desperate to reassert control over the island. Rather than complicate negotiations by putting forward a request he knew to be unacceptable, he chose to use his position of power to lever what concessions he could on the subject of entry to Canton.[5]

On New Year's Eve 1845, Governor Davis received a letter, a long strip of paper folded like a concertina into sixteen pleats. Qiying's hefty seal was imprinted in red ink no less than four times upon it. The commissioner expressed himself forcefully, praising the high esteem in which Davis clearly held the virtues of sincerity and righteousness, but then asking in feigned incomprehension how the insertion of new articles into a solemn treaty could possibly be anything but an obstacle to their relationship. The final $2,000,000 of the indemnity would soon be ready to collect, and if the British chose not to accept it then China would not meet the 5% interest due for late payment. He once more insisted that entry to Canton had not explicitly been linked to the return of Chusan and, seemingly aware that he had no way of forcing a withdrawal if Britain refused, made one final observation; it struck Governor Davis' Achilles' heel — the 'certain and deserved imputation of bad faith' which the *China Mail* had predicted:

> If on account of the piffling matter of access to a city Britain breaks its word on the greater point of returning Chusan in good faith, I think it likely that your Excellency will have to weigh up the effect on opinion in the other nations of the West.[6]

His ploy worked. Davis reiterated his anxiety that other powers might take control of Chusan after the withdrawal — he had mentioned as much in passing a few months before — and suggested that a formal agreement might be desirable, a document without the publicity of a conventional international treaty but with all of its binding force.[7] When next Qiying wrote, it was to confirm that it was unthinkable that Chusan could ever be ceded to any other nation. Still, he was willing to enter into an agreement, and if a public document was inconvenient then something might be arranged in secret. With a week still to run before the deadline according to the Chinese calendar, the last of the opium indemnity was loaded onto a British steamer. Now, Qiying demanded, Chusan *must* be restored!

And yet the first rays of the Year of the Horse fell upon on a Union Jack. The stalemate dragged on into early February, with Qiying unable, despite his promises that the matter would in time be settled, to guarantee entry into a ferociously antagonistic Canton but Davis under orders to obtain just that. Qiying had talked himself into a 'rather false position', thought Davis, who suspected that any promises over entry to Canton would vanish as soon as Chusan were safely in Chinese hands.[8]

'What if your Excellency were to issue a proclamation to the citizens of Canton, telling them that their obstinacy was the cause of Britain's continued occupation of Chusan?'[9] Davis suggested usefully. Qiying was at his wit's end: 'I have written to you over and again on the subject! I have exhausted the ways of saying it, yet still you maintain your position!'[10] It was all very well for Davis to say that he had been instructed to gain entry to Canton, but how could his sovereign, 80,000 *li* from Canton, possibly appreciate the situation? Davis suggested that the use of force might bring the Cantonese to their senses, but with a population of several million to contend with it was more likely, observed Qiying, to rouse them into a rebellion which could only harm what Western trade they currently suffered to continue. The commissioner, tired of playing games, began to use decidedly undiplomatic language: Davis' behaviour was 'a charade of broken faith'.[11]

Only on March 1st was the stalemate broken. The emperor himself issued an edict, decreeing that entry to Canton was not part of the treaty and that Chusan's return hung solely on the payment of the indemnity. To have argued further would have been to accuse the Son of Heaven of ignorance. Davis was versed enough in the ways of China to know when to back down. The Canton question would need to be shelved. Still, Britain had *de facto* control of Chusan, and this at least held open the possibility of wresting a guarantee over its future fate. On March 14th, Davis wrote to assure Qiying of the sincere friendship which existed between their two nations, and suggested that this be celebrated in a special treaty which would lead to a swift handover.[12] On April 3rd the two men met halfway between Canton and Hong Kong. Qiying showed himself to be anxious for a settlement, and Davis for his part made it clear that until an agreement was reached the affair would remain unsettled and Chusan occupied. The next day they met again aboard the steam frigate *Vulture*, and Davis produced two slim volumes bound in rich yellow silk. By signing this, the Davis Convention, the two sides agreed that Britain had not abandoned its claim to full access to Canton, but that it was better to wait until the population was more peacefully disposed before British merchants pressed their claim home. As to Chusan, China agreed that once the British had evacuated the island it would never be ceded to any other foreign power. The British, in return, promised that if any power invaded Chusan they would come to China's aid and restore the island to China with no expectation of reward. On the final page of the Convention the Daoguang Emperor himself added, three weeks later and in neat vermilion brushstrokes, the words 'Let all agreed herein be implemented forthwith!' Imperial riders rushed it from Peking to Canton at top speed and (although Qiying at the last minute rather naively tried to fool Davis into evacuating Chusan without sending him a signed copy of the Convention)[13] early on the morning of May 16th the SV *Pluto* dropped anchor in Hong Kong harbour with copies aboard. So long as the Chinese denied Chusan to any other power, Great Britain would forcefully reoccupy and restore the island to the emperor if it were invaded. But if God forbid the island were ever ceded, or if even China *intended* to cede it, the friendly alliance would end and the forcible reoccupation would be followed by no such restoration. Either way, the Son of Heaven had accepted that there was a portion of his vast empire which he could no longer dispose of as he wished. Unnoticed by the rest of the world, China had set another small precedent for the treaties which through into the twentieth century would see her territories divided between foreign powers like so many slices of a watermelon.

The British copy of the Davis Convention reached London to find a new prime minister, Lord Russell, in Downing Street and Palmerston once more at the Foreign Office. With it was a letter from Davis. 'A new era has commenced,' he wrote in a mood of optimism,

> in which the chances of irritation are greatly lessened by the mutual fulfilment of engagements. We set out, moreover, in the novel relation of admitted allies of China, and an identity of interests and engagements in respect to Chusan, which is calculated to remove fears and jealousies regarding that territory. One means of positive coercion may perhaps have quitted us with the restoration of the island; but it may be hoped that at least an equivalent advantage has accrued to us, in the increase of mutual confidence, and in the contraction of more intimate ties.[14]

The Chinese, as ever, saw things in a wholly different light. It was as though the two sides were describing a different event. Qiying boasted to the emperor of how he had managed the barbarian chief Davis: 'I commanded him no longer to raise complications which were outside the scope of the treaty,' he assured Daoguang, 'but to go about his trading in a law-abiding manner.' The entry into Canton, Qiying had apparently told Davis, could not be allowed, since Britain had already been graciously permitted to trade at other ports. 'He accepted this promptly and respectfully, and was most tame and obedient.'

When the ratified Davis Convention reached Whitehall, a perceptive official at the Foreign Office appended a short note and passed it to his superior:

> What shall be done with respect to laying this Convention before Parliament and publishing it? Such is the usual practice, but might there not be some inconvenience in giving to the world (the French and American world especially) the 3rd and 4th articles of this instrument, which, in truth, ought to have been separate, or secret, articles?

These were the articles which in effect blocked France and America from ever gaining possession of Chusan. It would be most embarrassing if Britain were ever required to look its allies in the eye and explain to them that a British convention had bound the Tuileries and the White House without their even knowing it. The next day, Palmerston added his instruction: 'This should not be laid before Parliament nor be published.' The Davis Convention was filed away and not mentioned again. It survives, bound now between red leather covers in a cardboard box in the vast underground vaults of the National Archives in the leafy London suburb of Kew.[15]

Friday, June 5th, 1846, the day set for the handover of Chusan, turned out to be so blustery that the Chinese delegation found itself trapped in Ningbo, unable to make the crossing by sail.[16] The indomitable steamer *Nemesis* was sent for, and it was aboard her that a diplomat named Xian Ling (he was a familiar face, having been amongst Commissioner Qiying's underlings at the treaty negotiations in 1842) entered harbour with an entourage of local mandarins who were to take up the reins of power. Xian Ling's party was received with as much pomp as could be mustered, the Madras Artillery firing a salute as the Chinese stepped ashore to the sound of the regimental band. Governor Campbell was present with a guard of honour, and at 2pm without further ado he gave a short speech, informing the islanders that they were once more under Qing rule. When Xian Ling read aloud a proclamation avowing the imperial favour and enjoining the people to 'await soothing', 'there were none,' he later reported to Peking with pride (and possibly a little exaggeration), 'who were not moved to dance with joy and sing out in praise.'[17]

The former governor accompanied the delegation to his residence, where Xian Ling publicly thanked Campbell for his mild and equitable rule and praised the discipline of the troops who had lived alongside the Chinese in perfect harmony. Under Campbell, he said, there had been no instances of insult or violence between the British troops and the islanders.[18] A meal was laid on at the officers' mess, and in the evening the Chinese were treated to a guard of honour and a salute. When three weeks later Qiying learned of the smooth handover, he commented that 'no news could have given us such joy.' After almost four years as an imperial commissioner, he had finally achieved his aim of pacifying the British. 'For several years now,' he informed the emperor,

> we have been managing the ten thousand entangled strands of barbarian affairs, tortuous like branches and knots thrown forth in all directions. These barbarians are by nature cunning, and so frequently tried to break the treaty that there remained almost no solution. But, trusting in Your Majesty's farsighted abilities, we received your instructions attending to the minutest detail.[19]

As always, the emperor was kept in the dark over quite how impotent he truly had been.

Sir John Davis arrived on Chusan one month later, to be welcomed this time not by a British governor but by a Chinese sub-prefectural magistrate. By now, sufficient Chinese soldiers had been ferried to the island to allow an official handover of the city gates. The two hundred Indian troops still billeted within the walls began to board steamers in the harbour. There were several points which Campbell needed to draw to Davis' attention, not least the fate of the cemetery. Since July 1840, many hundreds of foreign graves had been dug there at the foot of Josshouse Hill, albeit promiscuously intermixed with Chinese burials. It was pitiable, thought Xian Ling, that the bones could not be exhumed and taken back to their ancestral homes, little appreciating that neither Christian, Hindu or Muslim felt the need to sacrifice to the spirits of the dead. Still, he did his best, ordering an inventory of the graveyard and the erection of boundary stones to warn against encroachment.[20]

The living, too, needed protection. Though a clause in the Treaty of Nanking technically prevented the emperor from punishing Chinese who had had dealings with the British, the legality of punishing suspected 'traitors' on other trumped-up charges was debatable. It was understood that at least two men handed over in good faith by Captain Bamfield to the Chinese authorities after the treaty had nevertheless been tortured and beaten to death, while British enquiries into the well-being of other marked men had gone unanswered.[21] Simply as a matter of self-interest, it would not do for people to fear associating with the British.

'It is a matter of apprehension to myself,' admitted Davis, 'that on the evacuation of Chusan there will be many innocent persons in the town of Tinghae who will become the victims of rapacity and persecution because they acquired property by dealing with us, or adhered to our rule.' It was, he felt, a point which materially affected Britain's credit amongst the common Chinese.[22] The Foreign Office advised Davis to impress upon the Chinese in a friendly manner 'the extreme improbity and injustice' of any mandarin pursuing any legal charges against people who had dealt with the British. Short of painting Britain into a diplomatic corner which might oblige them to declare the Chinese in breach of the Treaty of Nanking (a few persecuted collaborators, it seems, were not worth risking a resumption of hostilities), Davis ought to do everything he could to guarantee the safety of the islanders. Consequently, in the run-up to the handover a proclamation jointly agreed upon by Qiying and Davis had begun to appear across the island. Anybody who had lived amongst the British, it said, or who had dealt with or worked for them, had been granted immunity from prosecution by the emperor himself. A few people had since made their way to the magistracy, and Davis now provided each of them with a document that would guarantee them asylum from Her Majesty's consuls in Shanghai and Ningbo.[23] Ordinary individuals whose names would otherwise have been lost to history were granted freedom from persecution and petty revenge — Wang Keayung who had headed Tinghae's native police force; constables Choo Tihping, Sew Haepaou and Ke Sungliu; Yaow Syeching who had spied for Gützlaff in Ningbo; Mrs Changchow who had informed on two mandarins sent illegally to arrest her....[24] And so the emperor took yet another small step on the road to relinquishing his absolute control over every last one of his subjects.

Mr Waterhouse and Mr Davidson, the only two merchants ashore in Tinghae[25] endeavouring to sell anything other than opium, began to remove their stock. The Treaty of Nanking threatened heavy penalties for foreigners who stayed after the handover, and Davis was both powerless and unwilling to come to their aid once they discovered what that might entail. Waterhouse especially must have been disappointed: his long letter the previous year in praise of Chusan had had no practical effect on Whitehall policy beyond pushing Davis for guarantees that the island would never become part of France. As for the military, the final departure of the 98th Regiment was set for July 22nd. In the meantime, work went on to disentangle the British presence.[26]

On an island basking for days on end under a bright-blue summer sky, in Tinghae, Sinkong and Sinkamoon the public buildings were handed back — the handsome stone hospital on Royal Marine Square, the barracks and regimental messes, the official residences and the storehouses of the newly built suburb to the east of Josshouse Hill — all apparently in good condition and without the Chinese being pressed for payment.[27] The United Service Club and the Theatre Royal reverted to house and temple. By July 23rd the last of the men had embarked, though it was not until the 25th that one grounded transport floated free and the Chinese at last fired a friendly salute to speed them on their way.

Father Danicourt had only the day before finished stripping out the interior of his European chapel, had loaded the last of it onto a hired junk, and left for Ningbo to carry on his work. A Chinese priest stayed behind in Tinghae to run the North Chapel and the boys' school. Acting as translator for Sir John Davis, meanwhile, Karl Gützlaff had been delighted by his first trip to Chusan in three years, busying himself as always with handing out his Christian tracts to villagers who seemed to recognise and welcome him.[28] (Quite unexpectedly, he stumbled across a large chest of New Testaments in Chinese and Manchu — they had been sent years before to a fellow missionary but never opened — and began to hand them out to the islanders.) By the time it came to hand the island back just two Protestant missionaries remained, the Americans Augustus Ward Loomis and his wife Mary Ann, though more were holidaying in houses on the wharves, enjoying the cool sea breezes during what was proving to be a particularly bad 'sickly' in Ningbo.

Despite the optimistic insistence in Gützlaff's fund-raising pamphlets that Buddhism was crumbling in these islands, he could only look on powerless as monks performed ceremonies to end the annual drought. For weeks, temperatures had hovered in the high eighties. Anxious processions wound through the streets to stir the spirit-dragons into sending down rain. There had been prostrations and oblations, fasting, a ban on slaughtering animals.[29] In the heat of August, Xian Ling sent for priests from Putuoshan to bring the wooden deities of heaven and earth.[30] They arrived to the sound of guns, gongs and cymbals to be met by nine mandarins kneeling and bowing in the midst of a rainstorm. The next evening at the dog hour, so the local annals meticulously recorded, 'the ground shook.'[31] Earthquakes, as every Chinese knew, were Heaven's way of ushering in political change. It rained on and off for five days. On August 8th the English trading schooner *Lapwing* left harbour, and, two days later, after hurriedly burying caulker Henry Avery in the British cemetery, HMS *Wolf* sailed for Shanghai. The last of the barbarians were gone. At the foot of the final page of that month's *Chinese Repository* came a simple announcement: 'Chusan has been restored to the Emperor, and the British troops withdrawn.'[32]

A statue to the three generals who died during the 1841 invasion now stands at the top of 49th Hill, in Dinghai's Opium War Relics Park (© L. D'Arcy-Brown)

21

Famous for their construction of guns

THOUGH HE avoided giving offence by saying as much to the British, the new governor of Zhejiang province was shocked by the sorry state of Tinghae. Where Governor Davis on the eve of the handover had seen an orderly and well-defended city where idolatry was giving way to Christ and hygiene, Governor Liang Baochang saw devastation.[1] Parts of the city wall had been torn down. Everywhere there were open patches of earth and weeds, gaping holes in the townscape like bomb-sites in post-war London. Dozens of public buildings and places of worship, and numberless private houses, had been pulled down or burned. Some had vanished in accidental fires, some had been razed in retaliation for kidnappings, others the British had looked at through Western eyes and seen not a vital focus of ritual but instead just a dilapidated room or an overgrown courtyard. As the offices of absent mandarins languished, they had attracted the attention of the commissariat. Many had turned to ash on braziers or had found their way into the fabric of new warehouses. The numerous altars to the gods of soil and grain scattered across the city had been vandalised, as had so many of the intimate neighbourhood shrines. The prayer halls, side-chapels and dormitories of Tinghae's great temples had been gutted and remodelled as barracks, mess rooms, wards or stores. Statues of saints and sages had attracted attention in proportion to the grotesqueness of their features — a prominent nose broken off here, a pair of horns smashed away there, the teeth pulled from the mouth of a grinning Buddha.[2] The twice-monthly convocations to invoke the city's tutelary god needed to be resurrected, and a sufficient apology to him needed to be made. Colleges stripped of their fine book collections needed restocking. But the needs of the islanders were even more pressing. Ever since peace had broken out in 1842, refugees had been making their way back to Chusan in dribs and drabs, but now many more, ordered to leave the overburdened cities of the mainland, were finding they had no home to move back into. Rice was distributed to the poorest families, and cash handed out to help rebuild their demolished houses. Taxes that had gone uncollected during the occupation were written off — Pottinger's ban on growing rice seems to have been relaxed by the summer of 1843,[3] but it had no doubt harmed the landowners and farmers in the Vale of Tinghae — and a tax reduction was granted for five years. As the long arm of the law was extended once more over the island, officers began to arrest the troublemakers who had been sheltering under Britannia's lax rule (they included, no doubt, many who had profited from the occupation and who were now 'squeezed', quite contrary to the Treaty of Nanking but without the British ever hearing of it). The Chinese authorities worked hard. By the middle of 1847 the refugee problem had been solved and there remained no homeless families to worry about.[4] In all, the year-long reconstruction had cost the provincial treasury 231,000,000 copper cash. One thing was certain — the emperor would not be sending a fleet to the Thames to demand compensation. Governor Liang visited the island for a final time in the spring of 1848 to find things back to normal:

> The farmers are tending their ancestral fields, the gentlemen are nourished by the moral benefaction of old, the merchants are prospering, everybody is settled back into their rightful occupation. Truly, all has taken on a most peaceful appearance.[5]

Once the disagreements over Chusan's return had been forgotten, the island continued to welcome Europeans escaping the heat of the treaty ports on the mainland. Each summer, with the permission of the magistrate,[6] the wharves became a home from home to missionaries and merchants. With a sickly feared in Ningbo, where the air sat suffocating and immobile over the city, Augustus Ward Loomis and Mary Ann arrived back on Chusan in 1849 to rally their health. On the waterfront beside Josshouse Hill they rented the house lately occupied by Mr Waterhouse the merchant.[7] It was rat-infested now, the roof needed mending,[8] and the high bamboo fence was a reminder of the danger of robbery,[9] but a fresh breeze was blowing in from a bay crowded with junks. As the mainland summer grew fiercer, more joined them: Miss Selmer, the young Swede who was assisting Mary Aldersey in her girls' school in Ningbo, Mr Lord with his wife and child, Mr Russell of the Church Mission Society, Mr Johnson up from the treaty port of Fuzhou (he and Miss Selmer would scandalise the missionaries by sharing an umbrella — 'and it's not more than three weeks since he first saw her!'),[10] Dr Ball the dentist, and an artist named Mr West who had travelled to China to capture its scenes for an American audience.[11] The botanist Robert Fortune, too, in Zhejiang once more to hunt down specimens of the tea bush for transplantation to the Himalayan foothills, arrived in the sweltering heat of 1850 with fond memories of his previous time on the island.

The passing of just four years had seen great changes.[12] The warehouses along the waterfront had burgeoned into a large town, and already it was difficult for Fortune to make out the houses where his friends had lived. The European hospital, still Chusan's only solid stone building, was yet standing, but it was being used as a customs house. An elderly mandarin, an opium addict, had taken up residence there and offered Fortune a bed. The next day he woke early to find the air still heavy with the smell of opium and the old man insensible. He dressed and walked out into the suburb. The contrast was profound. Asleep in that dim, fuggy room in the echoing building was a pitiable example of what China's scholar-officials had become, yet outside in the early morning sun the cool air was softly blowing in from the sea. 'The dew was sparkling on the grass,' Fortune remembered with delight, 'and the birds were just beginning their morning song of praise.'

Augustus Ward Loomis too was moved almost to poetry by the scenery around Tinghae:

> At the present time the fields are all clothed in the most beautiful green, and near sunset, when the tops of the hills are gilded by the sun's last rays, and other hills are sending their lengthened shadows along the plain, the shady groves and cottages of the people altogether afford a most charming landscape.[13]

In the city itself, the outward signs of British occupation had vanished so thoroughly that no-one who did not know its recent

271

history could ever have guessed it.[14] The temples and shrines had been repaired, the burned homes rebuilt. The English names chalked up at the street-corners had washed away. The tailors, the cobblers and all the rest who before the handover had considered an English shop-sign indispensable to trade had merged anonymously back into the Chinese street scene. Everything had returned to how it had been on July 4th, 1840.

Scarcely a decade was to pass after Chusan's handover before Britain and China were embroiled in a Second Opium War. The spark, as always, was the Canton trade — despite the Treaty of Nanking and the Davis Convention, foreign merchants were still not free to live and work within the city walls. As always, the fighting began in the south, on the Pearl River approaches to Canton. In the spring of 1858, sailing to the north to press his complaints home directly to the Qing government, Britain's plenipotentiary the Earl of Elgin stopped off at Chusan. Passing through Tinghae — a city that had by now a listless, abandoned air to it, utterly different from Ningbo and Shanghai across the water — the Earl of Elgin was approached by a French Catholic priest, the heir to Father Danicourt's mission. They walked together into the countryside, to the top of the highest mountain, from where they could look out over the valleys of Chusan and the archipelago spread out beyond. It was as beautiful a sight as ever. 'This is a most charming island,' wrote the Earl. 'How any people, in their senses, could have preferred Hong Kong to it, seems incredible.'[15]

In the north it was the same old story: an overwhelming show of force, a treaty agreed and signed at the barrel of a gun, and then, a year later, a refusal by an emboldened Manchu government to honour it. Only this time around, at the mouth of the Peiho River, it was the Royal Navy that was trapped and slaughtered by unexpectedly strong Chinese defences. Britain's pride and standing demanded a devastating response, and, once more, Chusan was to be seized. This time, though, Britain would be joined by the French — suspicions between those two ancient enemies ran deep, and the reasoning of both nations, it seemed, was that left to occupy Chusan on its own the other might not be above laying permanent claim to it.

A new generation of soldiers and diplomats, few of whom had seen action at the start of the 1840s, by now held positions of power in Hong Kong and the treaty ports. Just as the passing of time had lent a glow of nostalgia to Chusan, it had made some people forget those considerations of honour which in 1846 had outweighed all thoughts of gain. But what was there to gain now from placing honour on a pedestal, they argued, when the Chinese were as intractable as ever over their side of the bargain? One voice raised in favour of looking afresh at Chusan was that of Her Majesty's Consul in Canton, Sir Daniel Brooke Robertson.[16] Robertson was familiar with Chusan, having served as vice-consul in Shanghai during the last two years of British rule. Renewed war with China now presented Britain with a golden opportunity for finally getting hold of the island, he believed. In January of 1860, with another spate of fighting on the horizon, he formalised his ideas in a memo to the Foreign Office.[17]

In *The Expediency of Acquiring the Island of Chusan*, Robertson, like Robert Montgomery Martin fifteen years earlier, saw the potential for growing European crops in a rich soil and mild climate, for breeding sheep and cattle to supply a self-sufficient colony. Chusan, he reported, would be a sanatorium for men prostrated by the diseases of the tropical south. On that score, Britain's possession of Hong Kong would make Chusan all the more desirable — it was no longer a matter of abandoning one for the other. The wider situation on the China coast had changed, besides. Almost twenty years had passed since the Treaty of Nanking and Sir Henry Pottinger's decision to exchange Chusan for trading rights elsewhere. Shanghai in particular had matured, yet the Yangtze and the Huangpu that had to be navigated to reach it were far from easy. Large vessels, Robertson suggested, might prefer to unload in deep water at Tinghae. The vast increase in Shanghai's trade ought to have been foreseen, and it was a matter of regret that Chusan had not been annexed alongside it. 'It is useless now to look back,' he admitted, but when the unhealthiness of Hong Kong, the large amount of capital which has been sunk in making it habitable, and above all its utter unfitness for a military station from the fact of being dependent entirely on the mainland of China for daily provisions, is considered, it is impossible not to think that there was a mistake somewhere in the choice of it.[18]

It was also vital that, as British shipping grew in the Western Pacific, Britain had a naval base from which to put to sea at a moment's notice. If Chusan were British territory, Robertson predicted, echoing just what Karl Gützlaff had said many years before, naval stores and docks could be built, provisions, coal and materiel collected: 'It is not too much to say that Chusan might become in the China Seas what Malta is in the Mediterranean.' Technological advances underway in the wider world, too, were set to change the balance of the East China Sea. The US was rapidly expanding its steam commerce across the oceans, and with a transcontinental railroad in the offing a niche might open up for a coaling station on the Zhejiang coast: in 1860, the only options for refuelling were at Hong Kong far to the south or at Shanghai, 120 miles farther up the Yangtze and her winding tributary the Huangpu.

On April 14th, 1860, naval representatives of Britain and France met in Shanghai and decided to occupy Chusan straight away as a preliminary to a military expedition to the north.[19] Soon after daylight on the 21st, the British and French flagships and the P&O steamer *Grenada* dropped anchor in Tinghae harbour and a flag of truce was sent ashore to ask as politely as possible for the island's surrender.[20] The task fell to a man named Harry Parkes. Harry had been to Chusan before — he was the younger brother to Kate Parkes, wife of the medical missionary William Lockhart and cousin to Karl Gützlaff's wife Mary, and as a fourteen-year-old he had studied Chinese under Gützlaff in Tinghae. For a year he had remained there, toiling away at his studies in a little shed attached to the magistracy, familiarising himself with the dense language of courtly memoranda.[21] Now fluent in Mandarin,

Harry had been appointed as Her Majesty's consul in Shanghai, a diplomatic role in China second only to the consul in Canton.

At noon Harry landed with a delegation from the combined navies, but was perplexed to find that nobody had been sent out to meet them. Their unannounced arrival, surely, called for some feigned resistance at the very least? Instead a throng gathered about them to offer supplies and their services as factotums.[22] Chusan's general and civil magistrate were sent for and by mid-afternoon were sitting comfortably aboard the *Grenada* (as a P&O vessel, she was the closest the British and French could agree to a neutral venue) sipping maraschino and discussing their island's fate. The general (despite his liking for maraschino Yuan Junyou was in fact a Muslim, 'a tall, gentlemen-like fellow, with a quick, intelligent eye, and good countenance.')[23] and what was by all accounts a short, vulgar-looking magistrate[24] named Gan Bing took little persuading to hand over control of Chusan: on the adjoining mainland, the rebel armies of the Taiping Heavenly Kingdom were locked in a brutal struggle with the emperor's forces and this remote corner of the province was of little concern any more to Peking. There was clearly no point in dying for a vain cause.

And so, after becoming hopelessly lost for hours in the densest of sea-fogs, a landing party climbed to the top of Josshouse Hill and raised flags of conquest there, vying to see which could be set the higher, the Union Jack or the *Tricolore*. Early the next day, amidst refreshing spring showers, the allied commanders surveyed their new home.[25] The Vale of Tinghae was a mosaic of flooded paddy fields, where the emerald green of seedlings had begun to break the surface. Yellow swathes of mustard perfumed the wet morning air. Scattered grave-mounds rose from the flatness; temples nestled amongst stands of cedars. The few soldiers, now middle-aged men, who remembered the wharves before the handover of 1846 struggled to find the barracks they had laboured so hard to make comfortable. Once again the troops made their billets in the city temples, removing the gods from their plinths and putting them into storage. In the Chinese arsenals, weapons procured at great expense by Governor Liang had lain unused for fourteen years.[26] The Royal Engineers found piles of obsolete cannon that looked sure to explode if ever they were fired. The walls were lined with racks of swords, spears and pikes, all rusted beyond use. The same old muskets that had failed to hold back two invasions were piled alongside silk uniforms and padded trousers. Shields bore grotesque painted faces obscured by years of mildew. The Tinghae brigade was found to be at barely half strength. The strict requirement that it observe an annual muster and exercises had last been observed in 1852, once time had dimmed the memory of war. The shopkeepers reacted to the reoccupation as they always had; some, indeed, had only recently arrived, renting premises on the rumour that Chusan was once again to be occupied.[27] Signboards stashed away in 1846 were dusted down and proudly displayed once more.[28] Here was the familiar Stultz, No.1 London Tailor. Over there were E. Moses & Son, ostensibly an outfitter from Aldgate Pump, and Jim Crow, the fashionable tailor. In a barber's shop frequented by the allies, pictures cut from the *Illustrated London News* and the *Pictorial Times* soon hung on the walls. But again a large proportion of the wealthy population had fled the city with their possessions. The people who stayed behind were the same poor who had offered their services to Elliot and Pottinger. They were dressed in what looked like cast-offs from some other, richer town.[29] And there were so many beggars. They lay motionless by the roadside under rags, filthy and covered in sores.[30] It was tempting to consider how two decades under a social reformer like Karl Gützlaff might have left the city a better place.

The men had a quiet time of it while their officers organised hunting expeditions in the hills (one islander ran deer-shoots with a guarantee that 'no show deer, no catchee dollar').[31] General Yuan spent the evenings entertaining the allied officers, his dinner receptions famously consisting of twenty-seven courses, preceded by sherry and cheroots, accompanied by French champagne and rounded off with a pipe of Bengali opium. He tried to make his guests feel at home with roast geese and shoulders of mutton.[32] He sat to be photographed, a technology then in its infancy, and an image of him survives. He sits stock still in his robes and cap of office, staring into the lens. In the corner of his mouth he holds a pipe, as if to remind the viewer of the drug habit to which the arrival of Europeans ultimately condemned him and his countrymen.[33]

The vanguard of the allied forces spent just two uneventful months in Tinghae before the bulk of the expedition picked them up on their way to the Peiho River. In August the allies landed unopposed at Dagu and, just like in Chusan years before, took the forward-facing forts with ease by turning their flank. On the plains beyond, the great city of Tianjin surrendered rather than face destruction. An armistice was arranged to avoid an assault on Peking, but the British delegation was ambushed and kidnapped. A month later, Harry Parkes and the surviving hostages were finally freed in a terrible state, half their original number having died by design or neglect. China paid the price for this treachery: the Summer Palace, a vast and splendid collection of buildings and lakes, was looted and reduced to rubble while the allied command looked on with approbation. In Peking, under threat of annihilation, the emperor ratified the Treaty of Tianjin. With this, the Western powers forced China to grant them freedom to trade in a dozen more ports, the right to open legations in the capital and to travel freely in the interior, and to sail the Yangtze at will. Protestant missionaries, the successors to the men and women who had used Chusan as an ante-chamber to China, were from now on the absolute equals of Roman Catholics. In October, the last Western soldiers left Chusan for a third and final time, despite a brief but heartfelt insistence from the French commander Montauban that he would not simply hand back such a valuable possession.[34] Diplomatically, his political superiors overruled him: they had wrested everything they desired from the faltering Qing dynasty, and the Davis Convention with Victoria's sign-manual upon it remained sacrosanct. Chusan, so long as no other foreign power expressed an interest in it, was of more value to the British in Chinese hands than it was as an addition to their now extensive portfolio of rights and concessions in China. Just as had been the case in 1846, Britain's faith was still worth fifty Chusans. The desirability of a British Chusan had passed.

The year 1751 saw the printing of a book entitled *Illustrations of Tributaries to the Qing*. In one woodcut, the 'English Barbarian' is depicted in the knee-length breeches, frock coat and hat of an East India Company merchant.[35] A ringletted wig cascades down to his shoulders, and he holds a walking cane. In one hand he holds a china jar which he examines with an eye to buying. His wife has the look of a Nell Gwynn, with ample curly hair, a full skirt, and sleeves gathered below her elbows. The explanatory notes below read:

> England is a vassal state of Holland, and the dress and ornament of these barbarians is similar. The kingdom is quite rich. The men mostly wear woollen broadcloths and take pleasure in alcoholic drink. Their unmarried women bind their waists tightly, desiring to make themselves slender. Their hair falls down onto their shoulders. They wear short jackets but heavy skirts, and when they go out of doors they wear an extra coat on top. They always have snuff at hand.

A century later, in April of 1860, a party of Britons sailed one day for the holy island of Putuoshan to see about requisitioning a temple as a temporary hospital. In a shop in the island's one small settlement, they came across a book. On it, each of the world's races was depicted with a woodcut sketch and a pithy description. In one country, it was said, the people never died, but the country was thirty years' journey from Peking. Below this, the artist had encapsulated the people of Britain no longer as a merchant and his wife but as a pair of jovial soldiers carrying a large cannon. There was no mention of their achievements in the sciences, of their medicine, their steamships, their God…. The British were, the legend simply told the reader, 'famous for their construction of guns.'[36]

Epilogue

IN OCTOBER of 1911, seventy years almost to the day after Sir Henry Pottinger captured Chusan, an uprising broke out in the Yangtze port of Wuchang. By the end of the year, the Qing dynasty had collapsed. The two events were by no means unrelated. Britain's victories in the Opium Wars, and the relative ease with which she forced the Qing to cede trading rights and territory, had given the lie to the myth of an exalted Middle Kingdom surrounded by deferential barbarians. In the coming decades, the Qing would suffer one defeat after another, until its coastline and major rivers were pockmarked with foreign concessions and spheres of influence. The revolutionary ideology of men like Dr Sun Yat-sen — it is no coincidence that the founder of modern China was a Christian convert educated at a church school in Hawaii and baptised in Hong Kong — had arrived in China in the wake of the war, carried in Western writings on political and economic theory and in the minds of students who travelled widely for the first time beyond China's borders and who saw the reality of Western democracy. Marxism, a competing Western ideology, was later to enter China by similar means, and it was troops of the Communist Third Field Army who in May of 1950 finally dislodged Chiang Kai-shek's Nationalists — and the few Western missionaries still living and working there — from Chusan.[1]

In the *pinyin* romanisation adopted under Chairman Mao, Chusan is now known as Zhoushan, its capital Tinghae as Dinghai. More than one million people live on the 103 inhabited islands of the archipelago, which range in length from a few hundred yards to tens of miles. Dinghai has blossomed into a pleasant and wealthy city of tree-lined streets and tranquil parks. After four decades of disengagement from the outside world — and in this regard Mao's China was no less insular than the Qing — the waters of the archipelago were re-opened to foreign-registered shipping. In 2006, the ports of Ningbo and Zhoushan merged their interests to become one of the largest seaports on earth. This Ningbo-Zhoushan Port has plans to leapfrog into a global third place with the completion of five gargantuan container-ship berths on the same Kintang Island where Karl Gützlaff distributed his tracts and his mercurial ointment.

Where in the 1840s even a Western ship took days to sail from Dinghai harbour to the Shanghai bund, today it is possible to drive there non-stop in just four hours, first hopping from island to island by way of the five Zhoushan Cross-Sea Bridges before crossing Hangzhou Bay upon a 22-mile causeway that is second only in length to the Lake Pontchartrain Bridge in Louisiana. No longer a half-day's march but instead just a short drive away on Route 329, Shenjiamen (the fishing community of 'Sinkamoon' that Gützlaff had considered 'the very seat of iniquity')[2] has grown into China's most important centre for seafood processing — 10% of its seafood is landed here — with worldwide exports worth some US$50,000,000 each year. But the village of Sinkong on the west coast, with its long, sheltered harbour and deep anchorages, like a 'young Bosphorus', never developed into the great port that Lieutenant Ouchterlony of the Madras Engineers had envisaged. Now known as Cengang, it remains to this day home to just 16,000 souls, with a few machine-shops and boatyards strung out along a drab waterfront. Robert Montgomery Martin's grand dreams of a British city there never got beyond a barracks that housed two dozen men of the Royal Irish Regiment and their families, and a rented building that served as their hospital. The few issues of the *Singkong Gazette* that were printed on a simple press never grew to rival Hong Kong's *China Mail*.[3] Edward Cree's treatment of ophthalmia cases in exchange for poultry was the farthest that Western medicine penetrated. Today, run-down warehouses stare out over Sinkong Passage to the bare slopes of what the British knew as Poplar Island. It would require the same mastery of imagination to paint the neon skyline of a Hong Kong upon that blank canvas as it would to look out from today's Kowloon toward the skyscrapers of Victoria and see in their place the barren peak of 1840.

The navigation in this corner of the Pacific Ocean is still as treacherous as it was when the first East Indiamen arrived. In the shelter of Kintang Island the channel becomes a patchwork of spitting races and millpond calms as its depths are hurled to the surface by undersea contours. The wind gathers strength beyond Blackwall Island, then dies in the lee of Bell Island, where ships' wakes are smothered by a powerful riptide. The ferries' engines drop in pitch as they round Guardhouse Island, and the pattering of water on their hulls is echoed by the dozens of freighters that ride at anchor. Rather fittingly, the temple fort on Josshouse Hill, the first building in China to be forcibly occupied by a Western power, is now occupied by the People's Liberation Army. An observation tower overlooks the neatly laid out Harbour Square and the passenger wharves that line the waterfront. A little way off, Grave Island is untouched but for a navigation beacon. Too small to have attracted the attention of developers, it is quite possible that dozens of Royal Navy burials survive there.

But apart from the ghost of its old street-plan, not a trace remains ashore of the maritime suburb the East India Company knew, of the Red Hair Hall where Allen Catchpoole was held under house-arrest, of the handsome residence where Sir George Staunton was entertained, and where the ground had run with *samshoo* and warehouses had crackled as they burned. Even the stone-built Chusan Hospital for Europeans has vanished, where the plant-hunter Robert Fortune slept alongside an opium-addicted mandarin. The old British cemetery, which occupied a triangular half-acre at the foot of Josshouse Hill, has been entombed beneath homes and workshops. With the British occupation just a distant memory it had anyhow become 'a melancholy spectacle of neglect and disrepair',[4] with squatter families living amongst the dead and using their gravestones as tables and beds. A single memorial to the 431 men of the Westmoreland Regiment who died on Chusan has been rescued and moved a little way up the slope. It is the only British funerary monument to have survived the upheavals of the People's Republic.

On the vale below Josshouse Hill, Yuqian's earth rampart was carried away spadeful by spadeful in the 1950s leaving only the curve of Harbour Road to trace its line. The city walls too survived just a few years of Communist rule. Come Liberation in 1950 they had anyhow fallen derelict, and the tiled roofs and elegant carvings of the watchtowers had all gone. Then in 1955 their stone facing was removed, the tamped earth was carted away into the fields, and the solid wall became the broad expanse of Liberation Road. The paddy fields where the British pitched camp have disappeared under homes and shops as Dinghai has spilled out unbounded. The Cameronians' makeshift hospital at least has survived, that former pawnbroker's shop where hundreds of young Scotsmen were laid out on straw mattresses to die. It houses a government hostel, where guests slam down *mahjong* tiles and pound away at laundry. Beyond its courtyards, only patches remain of the Dinghai that the British would have known. Even though it was listed by the provincial government as a Famous Historic and Cultural City in 1991, before the decade was out swathes of the beautiful old town had been demolished, their centuries-old buildings sacrificed to property developers despite protests from the residents. On the site of the south gate, from where the Union Jack flew for six years, there now sits a branch of Kentucky Fried Chicken. But the very heart of Dinghai at least has been preserved, and the clock turned back to how it was under the Qing dynasty. It is being promoted as a living museum, a tiny corner of old China that is growing ever scarcer. There the great flagstones that pave Edward Cree's watercolours have survived, beside the shop fronts with their sliding wooden shutters and jutting balconies. The lofty fire-walls that divide one neighbourhood from the next have been replastered and painted in bright white. In the midst of those dog-leg alleyways, the great Zuyin Temple that once housed British soldiers has been splendidly restored.

Despite the best efforts of a few and the preferences of many, Chusan never became a Crown Colony. Still, for a few years, Victorian society had been on show here in all its complexity. There were its knights and aristocrats, artists and scientists, doctors and evangelists, and the wives and children of officers, privates, missionaries and merchants. Lieutenant-Colonel Colin Campbell, who handed Chusan back to the Qing, was laid to rest in Westminster Abbey as Baron Clyde after winning laurels in the

Crimea and commanding Britain's forces in India; Irish labourers and Bengali farmers who had signed up to escape poverty were buried in unmarked graves. Hundreds went to their deaths lamentably young in a country they never understood. Their relatives read months or years later, if at all, of their passing. Some of them no doubt arrived in Chusan with the intention of doing harm, but many more only wished the islanders well, and genuinely believed that by bringing Christ, medicine and English law to China they were helping to improve the lives of a quarter of humanity.

Captain Anstruther rose through the ranks of the Madras Artillery. His spell in gaol in Ningbo took nothing from his zeal for life, and by the time of the Chusan handover he was a major and a Companion of the Order of the Bath to boot. He reached the rank of major-general in India, the country where he spent most of his life, but toward the end returned to his ancestral homeland of Fife where in 1884 he died unmarried. As for Edward Cree, he bade farewell to his fellow Rattlesnakes in 1843, promoted to full naval surgeon aboard a modern steam sloop. He saw a young Singapore, waltzed all night at Mrs Wallace's ladies' finishing school in Penang, helped bring to book a piratical prince in Brunei, and watched as the final crates of the opium indemnity were hauled aboard his ship the *Vixen* in Victoria harbour. He thought Hong Kong's capital handsome, a great improvement on the fishermen's huts he had seen three years before, and it was there that he crossed paths again with Robert Fortune. In his first book, *Three Years' Wanderings*, Fortune had printed engravings of sketches which Cree had been so kind as to give to him when last they had met. Fortune, Cree noted, had not had the decency to acknowledge that contribution to his growing fame. Returning to Portsmouth, Cree fell in love with a girl named Eliza. By the time he left for the Baltic in 1854 she had borne him the first of eight children. As the war with Russia dragged on, Edward served on a steam frigate towing mortar-boats through the Dardanelles to lay siege to Sebastopol. As the Congress of Paris was being agreed, the chronic dysentery which had plagued him ever since drinking Chusan's contaminated water forced Cree to retire. In

1856 he arrived back at his home near Plymouth Hoe, from where in 1860 he no doubt followed accounts of the final occupation of Chusan. He did not begin the work of editing his sketches and journals until well into his seventies. As his writing deteriorated, his family bought him a typewriter. He died in 1901, aged 87, and was buried in Highgate. Robert Fortune meanwhile returned again to China as the Taiping rebels were violently carving out their heavenly kingdom in the Yangtze valley. He spent three years this time searching for plants, introducing to Britain the fragrant trumpets of *Rhododendron fortunei*. On behalf of the US government, who wished to establish a tea industry of its own, he went back once more in the late 1850s. He visited Japan, from where he introduced the variegated bamboo and the Japanese yew. His years of collecting in the east beautified Britain: he sent back peonies, wisteria, magnolia, dogwood, forsythia, viburnum, the Chusan palm and more. Without his passion there would be no *Weigela florida* in our urban gardens, no winter-flowering jasmine to brighten up the dark months.

William Lockhart left Chusan after burying his daughter Lizzie, and in 1843 he opened a mission hospital in Shanghai which proved to be exceedingly successful (in fact, it survives to this day as part of Jiaotong University Medical School). His wife Kate kissed him goodbye eight years later to be invalided back to England, and the two did not meet again until William returned home in 1858. Three years later he was back in China. He opened a hospital in Peking, travelled up the Yangtze to the new treaty port of Hankou, and even tested the waters in Japan. He died at his home in Lewisham in 1896. Kate herself outlived William by two decades, witnessing the fall of China's last imperial dynasty and passing away in Blackheath as the Great War drew to a close. Lizzie, if her tiny bones were not disturbed unnoticed in some building site, must still lie buried on Chusan.

The seemingly indefatigable Karl Gützlaff remained Chinese secretary in Hong Kong for only a few years. In 1844 he founded the Chinese Union to finance the dissemination of Protestant tracts in the interior, but five years later his wife and companion Mary died. She, like his late first wife, had lost a child soon after birth, and had left China taking with her some of their blind Chinese children. In the wake of this second bereavement Gützlaff spent time in Europe raising money for his Union, though as an undertaking it proved to be riddled with corrupt Chinese operators. During that time he married for the third time in twenty-one years. This last marriage proved to be even more fleeting: soon after returning to Hong Kong in 1851 Gützlaff sickened and died and was buried in Happy Valley.

Mary Ann Aldersey, so praised for her zeal and faith by the late magistrate of Dinghai, began to suffer in the heat of Ningbo where she had founded her girls' school. In 1852, well into her sixth decade, she sailed to Chusan to take the sea air. She retraced the old route to the Kin family home. The widow had died three years earlier, and her son, whom Mary remembered only as a useless opium addict, had given up the drug to administer the estate he had inherited. His sister, once such a bright spark, had retreated into herself and was uninterested by the reappearance of their old lodger. Mary sailed to Putuoshan, where for the benefit of the monks she spent her time holding impromptu Christian services in scarcely serviceable Ningbo dialect. In 1860, a by then frail Mary accepted an offer from a Presbyterian mission to take charge of her boarding school. She left for the colony of South Australia, where in McLaren Vale she settled down to retirement with some of the same nieces who three decades earlier had been her reason for staying in London. She died there in 1868, in a house she had named *Tsong Giaou* after a village in Zhejiang. Less than a year after she left her school it was overrun as the Taiping rebels swept through Ningbo. When the British relieved the city it was resurrected. It survived the fall of the Qing but not the Japanese occupation and Communist revolution.

The war orphan Afah travelled to England on the *Nemesis*, the steamer on which he had witnessed the Yangtze campaign of 1842, and was placed in the care of one Dr James Pope of Marylebone.[5] He learned to write English, a language he already spoke competently, and was baptised with the Christian names Lëang William. Captain Hall of the *Nemesis* arranged for him to be educated at a boarding school at Hanwell, where he was said to have become popular with the teachers and pupils. This little boy, rescued from Dinghai, was one day aboard the royal yacht introduced to Queen Victoria and Prince Albert, but then he slips from the historical record. The same is true of Anne Noble, who soon after her release from gaol in Ningbo sailed home taking with her a pair of blind girls from Mary Gützlaff's school. In late 1842 she seems to have been living in the Northumbrian village of Ovington, but then the trail goes cold. We cannot even be sure that the child she had been carrying during her imprisonment survived its birth, or say what became of the $8,000 subscription raised for her among the gentlemen of the British garrison.[6] As for HMS *Wellesley*, whose guns had opened the First Opium War, she saw out her days moored on the Thames as a training ship. She was sunk during the Blitz by a German bomb, the only wooden ship of the line to be destroyed from the air. Her enemy that day was as far in advance of her gunpowder broadside as General Zhang's gingals had lagged behind it. Eight years later, her mighty timbers of Indian teak were salvaged and reused in the post-war restoration of the Royal Courts of Justice on the Strand. Her figurehead now stands in the gateway to Chatham Dockyard.

But the stories of most of the people who lived upon Chusan during those years of British rule have been forgotten. Many of them were Indian, whether sepoys, lascars, or simply servants, and their names, if even they were written down, were long since prey to mould and bookworm. Then there were the women and children, all but invisible during their lifetimes, grudgingly acknowledged in regimental records if they were given nursing duties or laundry, or if they were an inconvenience to be accommodated in some outpost like Sinkamoon.[7] Mrs Bull, wife to the bosun of Edward Cree's *Rattlesnake*, lives on in his journals: she wanders the islands of Tinghae harbour with Chinese women clucking and fussing about her, examining her clothes, her large feet and her brown hair and asking if she is the Queen of England come to visit them. Just occasionally, in a personal diary or upon a list of the dead, army wives who had been lucky enough to draw lots to travel on the strength of a regiment have names. Elizabeth

Dunbar, a twenty-eight-year-old wife of the Royal Irish, died two days after bearing her husband's stillborn son. Jane Howes died aged just seven, two years before her four-month-old brother, Robert; a few weeks later their mother Ann followed them to the same plot. Elizabeth Meredith, a sergeant's wife, died at twenty-two. Eliza Wood was buried in the same grave as her young William, alongside another child who had not even been christened. Mary Peel gave birth to a child who did not live out the day; she herself passed away a fortnight later. Jane Maria Gregory, wife of a lieutenant colonel, was thirty-one when she died, just six months before Chusan was handed back. We will never know how many more there were.

In the tense years following the suppression of the demonstrations in Tian'anmen Square in 1989, the Chinese Communist Party made a decision to revisit the lessons of the Opium Wars.[8] It was an unexpected revival, for by that time the ardour with which first Chiang Kai-shek's Kuomintang and later the Communists themselves had placed the Opium Wars centre stage in China's modern history had rather faded.[9] But then in 1990 the 150th anniversary of the British capture of Chusan fortuitously coincided with a pressing need to find a way of repositioning the Communist Party as the saviour of China rather than its oppressor. In the years since then, China's rulers have extolled the patriotic and revolutionary credentials of the men and women who stood up to the British. They have been portrayed as proto-communists, the forerunners and antecedents of the People's Liberation Army who liberated China in 1949. They were, in truth, mostly opportunists whose kidnappings and murders were motivated by little more than the promise of silver dollars; but the truth, it has been said, should not get in the way of a good story. Just as the myth of the bereaved son who burned the British fleet in Tinghae was once preferred to the unpalatable truth of China's weakness, so the belief that the Chinese fought valiantly against their nineteenth-century invaders has found fertile ground with citizens who, understandably, long to see China respected as a strong nation.

By 1990, high-schools in China had stopped teaching the defeats of the 1840s.[10] Today, though, that has all changed, and sites associated with the war have been designated as Patriotic Education Bases (*Aiguozhuyi Jiaoyu Jidi*). Vast sums have been spent turning once-neglected battlefields into tourist sights, and 'red tourism' (*hongse lüyou*) has become a major part of China's domestic travel industry. One such Patriotic Education Base is on 49th Hill, the heights overlooking Dinghai harbour where the British routed Zheng Guohong's soldiers on October 1st, 1841. Just six years after Tian'anmen, as part of China's enforced resurgence in interest in the Opium War, the Opium War Relics Park was opened on the hill's eastern slopes. At its entrance there now stands a granite monument with a carved inscription:

> The Opium War erupted in 1840. On July 5th, the British bombarded Dinghai. The heroic defenders counterattacked, but General Zhang Chaofa was seriously wounded and soldiers and officials such as Magistrate Yao Huaixiang laid down their lives. On September 26th 1841, the British attacked again. Generals Ge Yunfei, Wang Xipeng and Zheng Guohong led 5,800 officers and men in a bloody battle lasting six days and nights, as one after another they died a brave and noble death for their country. This battle proved to be the most intense resistance to a British military invasion in China's modern history. To honour these martyrs, to make their deeds clear to future generations, and to propagate the spirit of patriotism, in 1995 the Zhoushan People's Government decided to found on that very battlefield a park to be both a memorial and a place to stroll.

A year later, the park was listed as a Patriotic Education Base for the schoolchildren of Zhejiang province. It is no coincidence that the inscription was dedicated in June 1997 — the very month that marked the end of British rule in Hong Kong and brought to a close a humiliating chapter that had begun with a single cannon-shot in Dinghai harbour. A stinging defeat on this otherwise obscure Zhejiang hillside has been reinterpreted as a rallying cry for Chinese nationalism.

Steps lead visitors to the Inscribed Tablets of the Hundred Officers, where a pathway meanders amongst tiers of polished black marble. On each of the tablets is carved an epigram, composed by a high-ranking officer of the People's Liberation Army and chased in gold. 'Do not forget this national humiliation,' reads one, 'but rouse yourself in pursuit of strength!' 'Wipe this national humiliation clean away and love this China of ours!' encourages another. 'May the noble spirit of these martyrs who defied the British never perish!' Others are more disquieting, and undeniably anti-British:

> Chusan was lit by the flames of war; but the people's determination to fight the British was resolute; together they spilled their blood in defence of their soil; yet vainly they suffered the injustice of Nanjing; a century of singular shame this morning has been washed away; their noble ambitions rewarded, our hearts are at peace; Hong Kong has returned to one rule; how can we ever again suffer those barbarian thieves to encroach on our borders?

The steps mount the saddle of the hill. Where the Westmoreland Regiment once clambered over naked rocks greasy from the morning drizzle, a woodland floor is now carpeted with moss, ferns and creeping ivy. Patches of flowers are beautifully spotlit, and there is the sound of birdsong. Scattered amongst the undergrowth are the hummocks of grave mounds, some lying in clutches, others alone. Headstones declare them to be the resting places of Chinese soldiers. They are still tended by the islanders: handfuls of joss-sticks bristle beside them. A little farther on, a stone tablet has been erected: 'Here fell General Zheng Guohong of the Chuzhou brigade, a national hero.' On the hill's ridge an essay has been carved in marble. It drips with symbolism:

> Today China has taken wing like the mythic *peng*, and Hong Kong has returned like a faithful magpie to its partner. The dragons are dancing in the Yangtze and rising from the Eastern Sea. And so we repair these shrines and temples, and continue a century of struggle. The parks and pavilions are extended, the

lofty and majestic peaks of these thousand islands are made strong.

Where the killing was at its worst that October morning, the Three Generals Memorial Square has been laid out. Its centre-piece is a colossal, rough-hewn megalith standing yards tall, from whose mass three faces stare defiantly in the direction of the British assault, as though the very rock of the island has been brought to life to defend Chusan. A trio of steel blades soars skyward like swords held aloft. A frieze depicts the fighting in a style that weaves surging socialist realism with the organic abstraction of an ancient bronze, anchoring the present, through the Opium War, to a distant cultural bedrock. A three-legged raven and a three-legged toad — ancient symbols of the sun and the moon — are testament to Yuqian's claim that the battle here lasted for six days and nights. His lie, that the Chinese stood firm and killed countless British soldiers, has attained the status of historic fact.

The path leads on to a museum built on the heights of the hill. A model of HMS *Wellesley* towers over the war junk cowering in her lee, and a Chinese gingal rusts away beside six feet of hefty British cannon. A statue of Captain Anstruther kneels patheti-cally, his hands tied behind his back, head bowed. Bao Zucai and his brother stand triumphantly behind their captive, their muscular arms gripping his neck and shoulders, bronze chests swollen with patriotic pride.

After the handover of Dinghai in 1846, a side-chapel in the temple of the god of war was devoted to the three generals who had died defending the city. Decades of neglect left what had been a miserable little temple to start with practically derelict. Its bronzes and stone tablets were missing, and every rainstorm would cause new leaks until its paintwork was black with damp. Then in 1884, with foreign ships again sniffing around Zhejiang, a brand new shrine was dedicated. When the next spring foreign ships threatened the Ningbo river, a rumour spread that ghostly lights had been seen along the coast. The people were calm, it was said, content that the souls of the generals were watching over them. Shortly before the Hong Kong handover in 1997, the shrine was moved to the crest of 49th Hill. In the cool of its great hall, life-sized models of the generals now sit swathed in silks and satins. Long necklaces of sandalwood mark them out as demigods. Above them, a plaque declares their faithfulness to be a worthy example. Inscribed pillars offer the schoolchildren who visit this place values to cherish: 'Maintain dignity with your heart, treat others with sincerity.' 'In performance of duty there is only loyalty, in times of crisis, courage.'

In 1994, a book entitled *The Complete Edited and Revised Annals of Zhoushan City* [11] was published in Zhejiang. Its editorial line was fully in tune with the Communist Party's new emphasis on the people's heroic resistance:

> During the Opium War, the British several times occupied Chusan, bringing terrible hardship to bear on the islanders. At a time of national crisis, the people of Chusan held high the flag of of patriotism, struggling indomitably with the British invaders, displaying a heroic spirit that moves one to song and to tears, and writing a glorious chapter in the annals of China's recent history.... You could say that the Opium War, started by the capitalist bourgeoisie-class government of Britain, forced China on to the humiliating developmental route of being a semi-colonial, semi-feudal society, and that the occupation of Chusan was the start of China's suffering in its recent history. [12]

The islanders' terrified, piecemeal reactions to the invasion have been portrayed as precisely the kind of guerrilla tactics which Mao used to defeat the Nationalists and the Japanese: everywhere the British went, they are said to have met with 'powerful attacks by the iron fists of popular justice.' Even their slogans were much the same, anachronistic proof of their revolutionary credentials: 'Ploughs, hoes, sticks and staffs, all can serve as weapons. Even women, girls and boys know to kill the rebels.' [13]

But in honouring Chusan's history, the Party is ignoring the reasons behind it: the autistic inability of the Qing to comprehend a changed world; the xenophobia of a culture that considered itself superior and all others barbarian; the concentration of power in the hands of men who could not be held to account by the people they ruled. The sanctioned version of the Opium War does not stop to question how a few thousand men, women and children could sail halfway around the globe to demand terms from a nation of 400 million. Visitors to the Opium War Memorial Hall are not told that the British steadfastly refused for the most honourable of reasons to renege on their promise to hand back Chusan, nor are they told that Chinese soldiers died because the ignorance and embezzlement of their commanders had left them woefully ill-equipped. For it was Chinese corruption, as Karl Gützlaff saw all too clearly, that resulted in 'the miserable fortifications that were thrown up, the half-starved soldiers, the wretched match-locks, the useless powder, the honeycombed guns, the miserable display of the whole Imperial army.'[14] Perhaps visitors are not told this because they would be canny enough to draw obvious and unwelcome parallels with the present day. The Communist Party wants to cast itself as the saviour of China, but if an impresario were tasked with casting the Party in the most fitting of the roles demanded by the First Opium War, it would not be as the relatively few brave individuals who opposed the British out of a sense of patriotism and loyalty; instead he would cast it as the venal mandarins whose fabricated memorials misrepresented the truth and condemned China to defeat after defeat.

On the plaque explaining the kidnap of Captain Anstruther there is no mention of his knees being clubbed until he could no longer walk, or of how his elderly servant was beaten to death with rocks. And there is certainly no mention of the dozens of men, some of them just teenagers and many of them guilty only of serving as camp followers, who were abducted, tortured and beheaded in exchange for silver dollars. As the humane and thoughtful Edward Cree noted in his journal, the war cost the lives of many thousands of human beings, and great destruction of property and misery and sorrow to many. But a great many of those lives were British and Indian, and not all of the misery and sorrow was borne by the Chinese. Life for the barbarian invaders was brutal and short, whether men, women or children:

of the 591 men of the Westmoreland Regiment who left England for foreign service in 1821, just nine were still alive when the regiment returned home in 1844;[15] four out of every five were to die serving in China. It is terribly sad that China and Britain cannot join together in mourning the violence done on both sides while being thankful that it started them out on paths that are converging in peace. For without the horror of that war, Hong Kong would likely be just one more island in the Gulf of Canton, Shanghai a town of no great consequence, and China would be poorer for their absence. Chusan ought to celebrate itself not as a symbol of victimhood but as a place where China and Britain began to explore one another. Perhaps, once the Communist Party has made way for a democratic government which feels no pressing need to trumpet its patriotic credentials, this will become possible. My own hope — a lot to wish for so long as the Communist Party insists on seeing China forever portrayed as the only victim of war — is for a joint Anglo-Chinese excavation of the British burials on Grave Island in Dinghai harbour, and for a memorial to the men interred there, with an inscription mutually agreed upon by the Chinese and British governments. It would be a step toward healing.

Hong Kong's prosperity can with hindsight seem preordained, and Palmerston's disparagement of it as 'a barren rock' quaintly amusing. The handover of Chusan in 1846 might then be seen as a reasoned gambit, as though the path we look back on proves wrong anybody who had argued for a different policy. But Hong Kong started out as a blank canvas, and in retrospect there were no insurmountable impediments to making a successful colony of it. Just two thousand souls had been living at Chekchu at the raising of the Union Jack, and anybody who chose to live in Victoria was placing himself voluntarily under British rule. Governor Pottinger and his successors had no entrenched gentry to contend with as did Stephens and Schoedde on Chusan. Both Hong Kong and Chusan were occupied by the Japanese during World War II — Japan's treatment of the Chusanese proved to be incomparably more brutal than Britain's — and come August of

1945 Hong Kong might easily have returned to the rule of Chiang Kai-shek's Republic of China as so many of the foreign concessions already had; President Roosevelt had suggested as much. In the end the Japanese surrender was formally accepted by the first allied force to arrive, a British fleet under Rear-admiral Harcourt. Post-war reconstruction was carried on under the Union Jack, with Hong Kong absorbing hundreds of thousands of Chinese fleeing the civil war raging over the border. A once-British Chusan might also have returned to British rule in 1945, or it might equally have been reclaimed by Chiang Kai-shek's Republic only to be invaded by the Red Army a few years later. We can only speculate. Either way, just four years passed before Mao shut China's door to wipe away at a stroke both the economic disadvantages Chusan had faced from her unwelcome proximity to Shanghai and the advantages Hong Kong had drawn from nearby Canton. For thirty years the New Territories might as well have bordered France, yet the Chinese flair for business thrived under the impartial stability of British law; the same would have been true of a British-administered Chusan. During the turbulence of the Cultural Revolution, it seemed for a few months as though political agitation might fatally undermine British rule in Hong Kong; in the face of such a threat, insular Chusan, had it remained a British possession and military base, would have been more resilient.

The twentieth century saw China split into four most uneven jurisdictions. The largest, the People's Republic, still regularly rattles its sabre across the Taiwan Strait at the second-largest of them, for Taiwan is a snub to the Communist Party's avowed aim of national unity. There was never any need to chivvy along the return of Portuguese Macao, that tiny spit of land which made its fortune from the Chinese addiction to gambling. And once it had decided that 'to get rich is glorious' and that to recover capitalist Hong Kong would be no bad thing, Beijing had only to watch and wait for 1997 to arrive; once the expiry of the lease on the New Territories brought the People's Republic flush with Kowloon, the remainder of the colony would have been unviable. Sir Daniel Brooke Robertson's advice to the Foreign Office in

1860 was proved accurate: Hong Kong, entirely dependent on the mainland, ultimately proved unfit as a permanent possession. Better that London negotiate an amicable return than see it wither. But the much larger and self-sustaining Chusan might have been — if London could keep its nerve in the face of inevitable pressure from an ever more self-confident People's Republic — impervious to anything but an overwhelming invasion. Just as Beijing and Taipei have reached a pragmatic impasse over the Taiwanese island of Kinmen, only three miles from the Communist mainland, so Beijing and London might have learned to live with a quirk of history whose usefulness to China's economic growth — like Hong Kong — outweighed its anachronism. More likely, though, the British Crown Colony of Chusan would have become a festering point of disagreement — a barbarian arrow eternally pointed at China's heart.

A scene unchanged since the 1840s: Buddhist monks processing into the Zuyin Temple, Dinghai (© L. D'Arcy-Brown)

Sources & Bibliography

A. Contemporary sources in Western languages.
(i) Printed books.

Alexander, W. *The Costume of China*. 1805; *Picturesque Representations... of the Chinese*. 1814.

Anderson, A. *Narrative of the British Embassy to China*. 1796.

Baker, C.W. *An Artillery Officer in China, 1840-42* (in *Blackwood's Magazine*, July-Dec., 1964).

Barrow, J. *Travels in China*. 1806.

Bernard, W.D. *A Narrative of the Voyages & Services of the Nemesis*. 1844; *The Nemesis in China*. 1847.

Bingham, J.E., RN. *Narrative of the Expedition to China*. 1843.

Burrows, M. *Memoir of Admiral Sir Henry Ducie Chads, GCB*. 1869.

Cantor, Dr T. *General Features of Chusan* (in *Annals & Magazine of Natural History*, ix. 1842).

Cranmer-Byng, J.L., ed. *An Embassy to China, being the journal kept by Lord Macartney*. 1962.

Cunningham, Dr J. *Observations and Remarks made during his residence on the island of Chusan* (in Harris' *Navigantium*. 1748).

Cunynghame, Cpt. A. *An Aide-de-Camp's Recollections of Service in China*. 1853.

Davis, Sir J.F. *China, During the War and Since the Peace*. 1852; *Chinese Miscellanies*. 1865.

Denham, Cpt. *Journals Kept by Mr Gully & Captain Denham During a Captivity in China*. 1844.

Dunne, J.H. *From Calcutta to Peking; being notes taken from the journal of an officer between those places*. 1861.

Ellis, Lady (ed). *Memoirs & Services of the Late Lt-Gen. Sir SB Ellis, KCB, Royal Marines, from his own Memoranda*. 1866.

'A Field Officer.' *The Last Year in China, to the Peace of Nanking*. 1843.

Forbes, Lt. F.E., RN. *Five Years in China*. 1848.

Fortune, R. *Three Years' Wanderings in China*. 1847; *A Journey to the Tea Countries of China*. 1852.

Grant, A. *A Diary of Chinese Husbandry, from Observations made in 1843-44*.

Gützlaff, K. *Missionary Travels to China to Distribute Bibles*. 1839.

Gützlaff, K. *Gaïhan's Chinesische Berichte*. 1850.

Halloran, A.L. *Wae Yang Jin*. 1856.

Harris, Cpt. R. *Remarks on Heaving Down a 72-Gun Ship*. 1850.

Hüttner, J.C. *Voyage à la Chine*. 1799.

Jocelyn, Lord R. *Six Months with the Chinese Expedition; or Leaves from a Soldier's Notebook*. 1841.

Knollys, H. *The China War of 1860*. 1875.

Lindsay, H.H. *Is the War with China a Just One?* 1840.

Little, A. *Gleanings from Fifty Years in China*. 1910.

Lockhart, W. *The Medical Missionary in China*. 1861.

MacKenzie, K.S. *Narrative of the Second Campaign in China*. 1842.

MacPherson, D. *Two Years in China, a Narrative of the Chinese Expedition*. 1843.

Martin, R.M. *Report on the Island of Chusan*. 1844 (published by order of the House of Commons, 1857); *China Political, Cultural & Commercial*. 1847.

Masefield, P., ed. *The Land of Green Tea. Letters & Adventures of Colonel Baker of the Madras Artillery*. 1995.

Matheson, J. *The Present Position & Prospects of the British Trade with China*. 1836.

Milne, W.C. *Life in China*. 1858.

Mountain, A. *Memoirs & Letters of the Late Col. Mountain*. 1858.

Murray, Lt. A. *Doings in China*. 1843.

Noble, A. *Narrative of the Shipwreck of the 'Kite'*. 1841.

Ouchterlony, J. *A Statistical Sketch of the Island of Chusan*. 1841; *The Chinese War*. 1844.

Power, W.T. *Recollections of Three Years' Residence in China*. 1853.

Scott, J.L. *Narrative of a Recent Imprisonment in China, after the Wreck of the Kite*. 1841.

Smith, G. *A Narrative of an Exploratory Visit to each of the Consular Cities of China and to the Islands of Hong Kong and Chusan*. 1847.

Staunton, Sir G. *An Authentic Account of an Embassy from the King of Great Britain to the Emperor of China*. 1798.

Swinhoe, R. *Narrative of the North China Campaign of 1860*. 1861.

Urmston, Sir J.B. *Chusan & Hong Kong*. 1847.

Vickers, T.H. *The Events of the War in China in 1841*. 1881.

Walrond, T. *Letters & Journals of James, Eighth Earl of Elgin*. 1872.

White, W., ed. *'John' of the Highflyer. A Sailor-Boy's Log-book from Portsmouth to the Peiho*. 1862.

Wilson, Dr. J. *Medical Notes on China*. 1846.

Wolseley, G.J. *Narrative of the War with China in 1860*. 1862.

In addition, HM Government's *British Parliamentary Papers* series (BPP), under *Accounts & Papers*, contains the text of treaties and official proclamations.

(ii) Periodicals and newspapers.

Les Annales de la Propagation de la Foi (*APF*)
The Chinese Repository (*CR*)
The Englishman & Military Chronicle, Calcutta (*EMC*)
The India Journal of Medical & Physical Science (*IJMPS*)
The Journal of the Horticultural Society of London (*JHS*)
The Missionary Register (*MR*)
The Nautical Magazine (*NM*)
The Times, London (*Times*)
The United Service Journal and Naval & Military Magazine (*USJ*)

(iii) Manuscripts.

(a) British Library (©The British Library, cited and quoted with kind permission) (BL):

'Materials for a History of a series of attempts first by the English and afterwards by the United East India Company to acquire and establish a trade at the port of Chusan in China, from the year 1699 to 1759' India Office Records (BL IOR G/12/14).

'Portion of a Diary kept in the attempt to form a settlement at Chusan for the New Company, 1701-02' India Office Records (BL IOR G/12/16).

'Journal of John Tarver, chief mate of the Stringer galley' (BL IOR L/MAR/B/688A).

'Journal of Cpt Henry Duffield of the Trumball' (BL IOR L/MAR/A/CXXXVIII).

'China Materials' (BL IOR G/12/6) contains letters and a diary with details on the provision of accommodation for the East India Company from 1700.

William Alexander's *'Journal'* (BL Mss Add 35174) (BL Alexander) and Sir Erasmus Gower's *'Log of the Lion, 1792-94'* (BL Mss Add 21106) (BL Gower) have details of the visits to Chusan by the ships of the 1793 embassy.

'*Up the Gulph - the letters of Hugh Henry Monk, assistant surgeon, RN, 1840-1843, during the first opium war*' (BL Mss Eur C575/3) (BL Monk) has first-hand accounts of the 1840/41 invasions and life on the island.

'*Journals of Two Expeditions to China, 1840-41*' by Major Thomas T. Pears (BL Mss Eur B368) (BL Pears) provides a wealth of detail on the invasions and subsequent occupations of Chusan.

'*Travels of Thomas Machell to China, the South Seas, India, Arabia and Egypt, from 1840-1848*' (BL IOR Mss Eur B369/1) (BL Machell) has eyewitness accounts by a young midshipman on the *Worcester*.

'*Letter from Chusan*' written by Lt. Lawrence Shadwell of the 98th Regiment to the Rev. Stuart A. Pears of Corpus Christi College, Oxford (BL Mss Eur C644) (BL Shadwell) contains opinions on missionary work and of Sir Henry Pottinger.

'*Letters of Lt. Wm Edward Prescott Cotton... to his wife*' (BL Mss Eur Photo Eur 207) (BL Cotton) contain observations of life upon Chusan from June to September 1842 from this soldier of the 41st Madras Native Infantry.

Official letters in BL Mss Eur D643 (BL Nicolls) to and from Sir J. Nicolls, c-in-c of HM forces in India, cover the occupation in 1840.

The correspondence of Robert Peel, Lord Aberdeen, William Gladstone, Sir James Graham and others holds the discussions which took place in the last years of British rule on Chusan, and which led ultimately to the decision to hand the island back: *Aberdeen Papers* (BL Aberdeen); *Peel Correspondence* and *Peel Papers* (BL Peel). *The Correspondence of Sir Robert Peel, 3rd Series, B. General Correspondence*, Add. MS 40554 (BL Peel-RMM) holds the letters which passed between Peel and Robert Montgomery Martin in 1845.

(b) The National Archives, Kew (TNA):

TNA file FO17 holds the Foreign Office records on China. '*Diary of a Residence on board the ship Scotland in Chusan harbour*' is at FO17/49(182). FO682 contains original copies of Chinese-language diplomatic correspondence between the British in Zhejiang and

their Chinese counterparts. FO931 has translations of Chinese documents received by the British. T1 holds the files of the Commissariat.
The logs and muster books of the warships involved are to be found
by name in the Admiralty files (ADM), while the pay and muster
books of the British Army regiments, containing detailed records
of regimental life, are in the War Office records by regiment (WO).
WO28 holds a wealth of military documents on the China Expeditions from 1840-44, including WO28/300, which contains the very
detailed *General Orders* for the British army, where all manner of
transient facts are recorded. The 1860 occupation is reported in
ADM1/5735. The *Army and Navy Lists* are useful sources on names,
ranks and regiments. A revealing map of Tinghae's British cemetery
dating from 1890 is at MFQ1/1243/1, and a painstaking 1840s survey
of the whole island by Lt. Havilland of the 55th and Lt. Sargent of the
18th is at MR1/151/3.

(c) Other holdings:

The School of Oriental and African Studies archives of the Council
for World Mission (CWM) (© Council for World Mission, by kind
permission) hold the correspondence of the London Missionary
Society in South China. Their *List of Missionaries* is extensive and
detailed. Of great help are Alan Hughes' *'Lockhart Correspondence'*
(MS380645/1) and *'Biography of Dr William Lockhart'* (MS380645/2)
(both ©Alan P. Hughes), and the LMS microfiched correspondence,
*'Missionary Archives. South China, including letters, 1832/33-1857,
CWM 2'* (LMSMA).

The Hong Kong Public Record Office holds letters between Robert
Montgomery Martin and Sir James Urmston in *'Papers referring to
the failure to annex Chusan Island by the British, at the time of the
Treaty of Nanking'* (HK PRO Papers) (©Hong Kong Public Record
Office).

Cornell University's Rare & Manuscript Collection in the Carl A.
Kroch Library holds the *Augustus Ward Loomis Papers* (CUL Loomis), which include a number of letters describing life on Chusan in
1849 (©Cornell University).

The Museum of the Staffordshire Regiment in Lichfield (MSR) holds
'An Account of the voyage of HM 98th Regiment aboard the Belleisle,

CHUSAN

1842-42' by Captain Edie of the 98th.

Birmingham University Library holds the Karl Gützlaff Collection (BUL KGC) and Church Missionary Society Archives (BUL CMSA). The latter contains details of the Church of England's first mission to China at C.CH.L1 and C.CH.M1.

The National Army Museum in London holds many works which are difficult to track down elsewhere, including a fascinating collection of early photographs of Chusan from the Second Opium War. The museum's unpublished manuscripts from the period include a letter from Color Serjeant J. Henderson to his father, 19/10/1840, Acc. no. 9006-219-2-1 (NAM Henderson) (©National Army Museum, by kind permission).

The Museum of the Border Regiment in Carlisle Castle, besides housing a number of fascinating artefacts brought home from Tinghae, is the inheritor of the records of the 55th Westmoreland Regiment (Carlisle MBR), including regimental songs, general orders and despatches, and translations of Chinese documents which have not survived elsewhere. (©Museum of the Border & King's Own Royal Border Regiments, by kind permission).

The excellent Jardine Matheson Archives (JMA) in Cambridge University Library contain a mass of private letters to and from the company in Macao and Hong Kong and correspondents on Chusan. *'Jardine Matheson: In-correspondence: unbound letters: Private, Chusan, 1837-1843'* are on microfilm reel 580 (JMA reel 580); *'Jardine Matheson: in-correspondence, unbound letters: Chusan, 1840-1860'* are on microfilm reel 528 (JMA reel 528); *'Alexander Matheson Private Letter Book, December 1844 to January 1846'* is at C6/4 (JMA C6/4) (©Matheson & Co. Ltd, by kind permission).

Last, but far from least, the Caird Library in the National Maritime Museum, Greenwich, is now home to the invaluable *Cree Journals* (Cree). All material by kind permission of the owner and copyright holder, Henrietta Heawood. *The Cree Journals* (Exeter: Webb & Bower, 1981) are the source of the images on pages 62, 91 and 146, with kind permission of Richard Webb.

B. Secondary sources in Western languages.

Aldersey White, E. *A Woman Pioneer in China: The Life of Mary Ann Aldersey*. 1932.

Algernon, S. *The Iniquities of the Opium Trade with China*. 1838.

Allom, T. & Wright, G.N. *The Chinese Empire Illustrated*. 1988.

Bamfield, V. *On The Strength: The Story of the British Army Wife*. 1974

Baynham, H. *From the Lower Deck: The Old Navy 1780-1840*. 1969.

Bretschneider, E. *History of European Botanical Discoveries in China*. 1898.

Carnac Temple, Sir R. *The Diaries of Streynsham Master, 1675-1680*. 1911.

Carter, T. *A Historical Record of the Twenty-Sixth, Cameronian Regiment*. 1867.

Coates, P.D. *The China Consuls*. 1988.

Cook, H. *The North Staffordshire Regiment*. 1970.

Costin, W.C. *Great Britain & China, 1833-1860*. 1937.

Cox, E.H.M. *Plant-Hunting in China*. 1945.

Danicourt, E-J. *Vie de Mgr. Danicourt de la Congregation de la Mission*. 1889.

Eames, J.B. *The English in China*. 1909.

Elleman, B.A. *Modern Chinese Warfare, 1795-1989*. 2001.

Fay, P.W. *The Opium War, 1840-42*. 1975; 'The Protestant Mission and the Opium War' in *Pacific Historical Review*, 40:1971; 'The French Catholic Mission in China' in *Modern Asian Stud.*, 4:1970.

Featherstone, D. *Weapons & Equipment of the Victorian Soldier*. 1978.

Frontier & Overseas Expeditions from India, vol.6. 1911.

Gardner, B. *The East India Company: A History*. 1971.

Graham, G. *The China Station: War & Diplomacy, 1830-1860*. 1978.

Gretton, Lt-Col. G. le M. *Campaigns & History of the Royal Irish Regiment*. 1911.

Harfield, A. *British & Indian Armies on the China Coast, 1785-1985*. 1990.

Headrick, D. *The Tools of Empire: Technology & European Imperialism in the Nineteenth Century*. 1981.

Hibbert, C. *The Dragon Wakes*. 1970.

Hucker, C. *A Dictionary of Official Titles in Imperial China*. 1985.

Hummel. *Eminent Chinese of the Ch'ing Period.* 1943.

Johnston, S.H.F. *The History of the Cameronians (Scottish Rifles) vol.1, 1689-1910.* 1957.

Kendrick, Col. N.C.E. *The Story of the Wiltshire Regiment.* 1963.

King, F.H.H. *Survey Our Empire!* 1979.

Knollys, Col. H. *The Life of General Sir Hope Grant, vol.2.* 1894.

Kuo, P.C. *A Critical Study of the First Anglo-Chinese War.* 1935.

Lambert, A. *The Last Sailing Battlefleet.* 1991.

Lane-Poole, S. *The Life of Sir Harry Parkes.* 1894.

Leland, C.G. *Pidgin-English Sing-Song.* 1876.

Levien, M., ed. *The Cree Journals.* 1981.

Lloyd & Coulter. *Medicine & The Navy, 1200-1900, vol.4.* 1963.

Lloyd, C. *The British Seaman.* 1968.

Lovell, J. *The Opium War.* 2011.

Lovett, R. *History of the London Missionary Society, 1795-1895.* 1899.

Markham, G. *Guns of the Empire.* 1990.

McIlwain, J. *HMS Trincomalee.* 1994.

Moidrey, Père J. de. *La Hierarchie Catholique en Chine... 1307-1914.* 1914

Morrison, E.A. *Memoirs of the Life and Labours of Robert Morrison.* 1839.

Morse, H.B. *Chronicle of the East India Co. Trading to China.* 1926.

Moule, A.E. *The Story of the Cheh-Kiang Mission of the Church Missionary Society.* 1878.

Munn, C. 'The Chusan Episode: Britain's Occupation of a Chinese Island, 1840-46' in *Journal of Imperial and Commonwealth History*, vol.25, no.1, Jan. 1997.

Musgrave, T. *The Plant Hunters.* 1998.

Noakes, G. *A Historical Account of the Services of the 34th & 55th Regiments.* 1875.

Patterson, Mjr. J. *Camp & Quarters: Scenes and Impressions of Military Life.* 1840.

Petre, F.L. *The Royal Berkshire Regiment, vol.1.* 1925.

Peyrefitte, A. *The Collision of Two Civilisations.* 1993.

Phillimore, A. *The Life of Sir William Parker, vol.2.* 1879.

Proudfoot, W.J. *Biographical Memoir of James Dinwiddie, LLD.* 1868.

Rait, R.S. *The Life & Campaigns of Hugh, 1st Viscount Gough, vol.1.* 1903.

Reason, J. *The Witch of Ningbo*. 1940.

Rennie, D.F. *The British Arms in North China & Japan*. 1864.

Schlyter, H. *Karl Gützlaff als Missionär in China*. 1946.

Shadwell, Lt-Gen. *Life of Colin Campbell, Lord Clyde*. 1881.

Singer, A. *The Lion & the Dragon*. 1992.

Smith, G. *Physician & Friend: Alexander Grant FRCS*. 1902.

Society for Promoting Female Education in the East. *Female Agency Among the Heathen*. 1850.

Strachan, H. *Wellington's Legacy: the reform of the British army, 1830-54*. 1984; *From Waterloo to Balaclava*. 1985.

Trustram, M. *Women of the Regiment*. 1984.

Wakeman, F. *Strangers at the Gate*. 1966.

Waley, A. *The Opium War through Chinese Eyes*. 1958.

Walsh, F. *A History of Hong Kong*. 1997.

Wei Tsing-sing, L. *La Politique Missionaire de la France en Chine, 1842-1856*. 1957.

Werner, E.T.C. *A Dictionary of Chinese Mythology*. 1961.

Winton, J. *Hurrah for the Life of a Sailor*. 1977.

Worcester, G.R.G. 'The Chinese War-Junk' in *The Mariner's Mirror*, 34. 1948.

C. Sources in Chinese.

Yapian Zhanzheng Dang'an Shiliao. Zhongguo Diyi Lishi Dang'anguan. Tianjin, 1992 (*YPZZDASL*).

Yapian Zhanzheng zai Zhoushan Shiliao Xuanbian. Zhejiang Renmin Chubanshe. 1992 (*YPZZZZS*).

Zhejiangsheng Dituce. Zhonghua Ditu Xueshe. 1999.

Huangqing Zhigong Tu. Qianlong 16 [1751], reprinted Peking, 1986.

Chouban Yiwu Shimo, Daoguang. Published 1856, reprinted in *Jindai Zhongguo Lishi Congkan*. Taibei, 1970 (*CBYWSM*).

Zhoushan Shizhi. Zhejiang Renmin Chubanshe. Hangzhou, 1992.

Zhoushan Haiyu Daojiao Zhi. Zhou Xike ed. Zhoushan, 1991.

'Zhoushan Shizhi' Bianxiu Shimo. Zhang Xinya ed. Zhejiang Renmin Chubanshe. Hangzhou,1994.

Zhoushanzhi. Ming Tianqi 6 [1626], reprinted by Chengwen Chubanshe. Taibei, 1983.

Guangxu Dinghai Tingzhi. Qing Guangxu 3 [1877], and *Dinghai Xianzhi*. Qing Guangxu 11 [1885], both reprinted as part of

Zhongguo Difangzhi Jicheng. Shanghai Shudian, 1993. Besides containing the contemporary annals of Dinghai County, the reprint of the 1877 work contains an immensely useful 1920s map of Dinghai and its wharf district, by which landmarks from the 1840s can be pinpointed.

Qingji Zhiguanbiao. Wei Xiumei. Taibei, 1977.

Acknowledgements

My sincere thanks to Richard Morel, curator of the East India Company records at the British Library, for commenting on a draft of Chapter 1, and my apologies for not using his insights into the rivalries between the New and Old Companies which coincided with the Company's early trade at Chusan, simply because of the complexity of sculpting them into a narrative focusing upon the 1840s rather than the 1700s. Any inaccuracies in my depiction of the East India Company on Chusan are wholly my own; to Henrietta Heawood, for permission to use the invaluable *Cree Journals*, and Mike Spathaky for his help in tracing both them and Henrietta; to Richard Webb, of Webb & Bower, for permission to reproduce images from the published edition of *The Cree Journals*; to Malcolm Cherry for reading and commenting on a draft; to the British Library and the National Archives for permission to cite the materials forming the backbone of this work; to the Cadbury Research Library at Birmingham University; to the Council for World Mission; to Matheson & Co. Ltd for permission to use and cite the Jardine Matheson Archives; to the Hong Kong PRO for copies of the *Urmston Correspondence*; to Cornell's Carl A. Kroch Library for providing copies of the *Augustus Ward Loomis Papers* before the author had even sent payment; to the Museum of the Border Regiment, Carlisle; to the National Army Museum, London; to the Royal United Services Institute for allowing access to their library; to Gary Kronk for information on the Great March Comet. Cheers to Jonathan Foster-Smith of Shine Design for his support and patience. Especial thanks to David Rees for sacrificing two perfectly good weekends (including a bank holiday that turned out to be rather less rainy than expected) to cast his discerning eye over the final typescript; and last but not least to my wife, Professor Becky, for her help, understanding and encouragement in the writing of this book.

Author's Note

This book is the result of some twelve years of research and three trips to Chusan, and was put on hold and restarted time and again as other writing projects demanded my attention. It has gone through several radically different incarnations to reach its final form, and one dark episode in which a computer glitch erased all formatting and garbled many of my notes. From a scholarly point of view, there are as a result points in the text for which I have given only partial references, and occasionally no reference at all. Readers who would like to follow up on textual points for which I have not made a source clear are welcome to contact me through the publisher; I shall do my utmost to locate an exact reference from within my voluminous papers.

Note on Romanisation and Names

As will be apparent to readers with a knowledge of Chinese, the text uses an admixture of Romanisations for places and personal names — mostly *pinyin* for its near-global currency today and its fair approximation of Chinese sounds, but also Wade-Giles and the idiosyncratic spellings of contemporary sources, besides common Western usages such as Canton (for Guangzhou). There is, intentionally, little consistency in my choices, which were made depending upon their ubiquity in any given period, their familiarity to non-experts, and their orthographic elegance (or otherwise). I have used Tinghae and Chusan throughout the substantive chapters, since to use the *pinyin* would have led to ugly anachronisms. Alternative spellings which readers might encounter in other studies of the Opium War period have been included in the *Index*, making it easier for non-Chinese speakers to recognise that, for example, the man whom I call Yuqian is the same man referred to by Fay as Yukien and by others as Yu-ch'ien.

Before the standardised *pinyin* of the 1950s, the name which is now written Dinghai was rendered in a variety of spellings by English speakers — Tinghai, Tinghaï, Ding-hae, Ting Hie, Ting-hae-heën (i.e. district), etc — of which Tinghae seems to have been the most commonly used. However spelt, it is pronounced like the English words 'ding high'. The name dates back to 1687, and means 'the seas calmed'. Chusan is now officially spelled Zhoushan. Its English spelling similarly varied widely — Cheuxan, Tcheou-shan, Cheuchan, Tchusan... — but by the nineteenth century Chusan was by far the most common. Chusan means 'the island of boats', probably a reference to its fishing fleet, though the name is also taken as a reference to its silhouette, said to resemble a junk (it would take a brave crew to sail a junk so unseaworthy looking). The island first appears in the centuries before Christ as Yongdong (i.e. 'east of [Ningbo's] Yong river'), was known as Wengshan ('the sage's island') in the eight century, and from 1073 to 1386 was renamed Changguo ('making the nation prosperous'). Its present name seems to have been first recorded in 1169 (in *Qiandao Siming Tujing*).

Endnotes

Prologue

1 See *Note on Romanisation and Names*, p.307.
2 BL Peel 40451 18/10/1845.

Chapter 1

1 *Zhoushan Shizhi* p.377 notes that there are records of the Portuguese establishing themselves in the Chusan archipelago: Zheng Shungong's *A Mirror of Japan* (1565) records that in 1526 a criminal named Deng Liao 'enticed the barbarians to engage in illicit trade at Shuangyugang'. By 1540 there are said to have been some 3,000 people there, trading in summer and returning to Macao to overwinter and with firearms enough to keep the Ming army at bay (Pan Jixing, *Scientific Exchanges between China and the World* p.162).
2 A 'factory' was the name used at the time for a trading settlement which housed the Company's 'factors', or agents: it was not a factory in the modern sense.
3 *Zhoushan Shizhi* p.201.
4 BL IOR G/12/14, 23/11/1699; Morse's *Chronicle* and the observations of the physician James Cunningham in *Observations and Remarks* provide background to this section.
5 BL IOR G/12/6.
6 BL L/MAR/B/137B.
7 BL IOR G/12/14, *Diary of Henry Rouse.*
8 BL IOR G/12/16, 22/10/1701.
9 *Ibid.*
10 *Diaries of Streynsham Master, 1675-1680*, p.320.
11 BL IOR G/12/14, 21/12/1700.
12 *Ibid.*
13 BL IOR G/12/14, 3/1/1701.
14 *Ibid.*
15 BL IOR G/12/14, 21/12/1700.
16 BL IOR G/12/14.
17 *Ibid., Diary of Henry Rouse* notes that the Chinese complained about how drunk the sailors were.
18 *Ibid.*, 21/12/1700.
19 *Ibid.*
20 BL IOR G/12/14, *Diary of Henry Rouse.*
21 *Ibid.*, 13/1/1701.
22 BL IOR G/12/14, 6/7/1701.
23 *Ibid.*, 1/2/1702.
24 BL IOR G/12/14 sets out the expulsion of the King's consul-general in detail.
25 *Ibid.*, p.62.
26 BL IOR G/12/14, 4/9/1702.
27 *Ibid.*
28 Letter of 10/2/1703, in Morse, *Chronicle* p.120.
29 BL IOR G/12/14, 22/11/1703.
30 *Ibid.*, 21/12/1700.

Chapter 2

1 BL IOR G/12/14, 17/1/1758.
2 The description of the China trade in these pages draws on Fay, *The Opium War.*
3 The failed diplomacy and worsening relations between China and Britain from the 1790s to the outbreak of war have been written on extensively elsewhere and are simply sketched out here. This summary of the salient reasons for the war also draws on Peyrefitte's *The Collision of Two Civilisations* and Fay's *The Opium War.*

4 Lord Palmerston's instructions on the eve of war reasserted his view that the Chinese were free to ban any article they pleased (FO17/40(130)).

5 The following section, besides citing primary accounts by men involved in the embassy, draws its background from Singer, *The Lion and the Dragon* and Peyrefitte, *Collision*.

6 BL Gower, p.70.

7 Staunton's *Authentic Account* provides this and many of the observations informing this narrative; Barrow too provides a scientific eye on the proceedings.

8 BL Alexander, p.16.

9 Staunton, p.32.

10 See also Barrow, *Travels* p.35, for an account of the visit.

11 Mary Aldersey (*Female Agency* p.251) would later observe that Chusan's women spent an hour each morning arranging their hair.

12 BL Alexander, p.16.

13 Barrow.

14 Cranmer-Byng, *Embassy* p.65.

15 Hüttner, *Voyage* p.3.

16 BL Alexander, p.34; BL Gower.

17 See Wilson, *Medical Notes*, 22/9/1842.

18 BL Gower.

19 BL Alexander, 30/11/1793.

Chapter 3

1 Fay, *The Opium War* p.43.

2 BPP, *Correspondence Relating to China*, 1840, 36 (223) 5.

3 FO17/9 (126) *The Present State of our Relations with China*.

4 Lane-Poole, *Life of Sir Harry Parkes.*

5 BL Pears, p.221 has a good description of Gützlaff.

6 Lane-Poole.

7 *Journal of a Voyage*, *CR*, vol.2 June 1833, p.49 contains the detail of Gützlaff's visits.

8 FO17/36(66) Palmerston to the Admiralty, 4/11/1839.

9 *Oxford DNB*; Lovell, *The Opium War* p.62.

10 *Oxford DNB*.

11 FO17/40(130), amongst other FO documents containing Palmerston's orders.

12 *USJ* 1840 vol.1 p.117.

13 *USJ* 1840 vol.3 p.109.

Chapter 4

1 BL Pears, pp.61/75 records the composition of the squadron.

2 BL Nicholls, 8.

3 Cree, vol.4 3/6/1840.

4 BL Pears, p.213; Ouchterlony, *Statistical Sketch*.

5 There were reportedly so many opium vessels in Chusan in 1839 that a few balls of the drug amounted to nothing: JMA reel 580 28/3/1839.

6 *EMC*, 5/10/1840 has a description of the day's events.

7 Jocelyn, *Six Months*.

8 BL Pears, p.216 provides details of what the British saw.

9 Ouchterlony, *Statistical Sketch* 3/7/1840.

10 Levien, p.55.

11 *Ibid.*

12 Ouchterlony, *Statistical Sketch* 4/7/1840.

13 Levien, p.55.

14 *USJ* 1841, vol.1 p.125 has Sir Gordon Bremer's account

of the meeting; Jocelyn,
Six Months gives another
eyewitness account.

15 Reproduced in *USJ*
1841, vol.1 p.128.

16 *CR*, vol.9 p.230.

17 Jocelyn, *Six Months*
p.53; Levien, p.56.

18 Urgungga's memo-
rial of DG20/6/13,
YPZZDASL vol.2 p.161.

19 Lin Zexu, in *YPZZZZS*
p.55, DG20/7/10.

20 *YPZZZZS* p.28, DG20/6/13.

21 Davis, *China* p.4, citing the
original Chinese memorial.

22 Mountain, *Memoirs
& Letters* p.161.

23 The attack can be pieced
together very well from
eyewitness accounts: *EMC*,
9/10/1840 and *Times*, 8/12/1840
have Burrell's report; *EMC*,
12/10/1840 has an account by
'Paddy Fields'; *EMC*, 13/10/1840
has an account by 'an intelligent
sailor'; *USJ* 1841, vol.1 p.122 and
Times, 8/12/1840 carry Burrell's
detailed reports to his superiors;
USJ 1841, vol.1 p.125 carries
intelligence from Sir Gordon
Bremer to the Admiralty; Levien
and Cree, vol.4 have Edward's
thoughtful observations; BL
Pears and Ouchterlony have
good incidental detail.

24 Lambert, *The Last
Sailing Battlefleet.*

25 Ouchterlony, *Statistical
Sketch* 5/7/1840.

26 *NM*, 1841.

27 BL Pears, p.224. It was Captain
Pears who handed him the flag

and asked him to hoist it.

28 BL Monk, p.2.

29 *USJ* 1841, vol.1 p.113. The
brass 6½-lber had been
cast in Moorfields by the
gun-founder Richard Phillips
at a cost of £22/14s 6d. It
would eventually make its
way to a museum in India.

30 *Times*, 9/12/1840.

31 Ouchterlony, *Statistical
Sketch* 5/7/1840.

32 Cree, vol.4 10/8/1840 describes
an armoury in Tinghae.

33 *Times*, 8/12/1840.

34 Levien, p.61.

35 Masefield, *Land of
Green Tea* p.66.

36 Ouchterlony, *Statistical
Sketch* 5/7/1840.

37 BL Pears, p.224.

38 Baker, *Artillery Officer*,
letter of 11/7/1840.

39 *CR*, vol.9 p.230.

40 Ouchterlony, *Statistical Sketch*
5/7/1840; a correspondent
to *NM*, 1841 reported that
men had to wade through
spilled samshoo.

41 *CR*, vol.10 p.515.

42 *Ibid.*

43 *EMC*, 19/10/1840.

44 *Times*, 8/12/1840.

45 Ellis, *Memoirs* p.115.

46 FO17/40(142), 20/7/1840.

Chapter 5

1 E.g. *YPZZZZS* p.22, DG20/6/8.

2 *YPZZZZS* p.23, DG20/6/10.

3 *YPZZZZS* p.24, DG20/6/10.

4 Lord Macartney himself
had noted this point in
1793: Singer, p.131.

5 Davis, *China* p.17.

6 BL Pears, p.224; Cree (Levien p.58) notes that some of the islanders were already looting the warehouses on the wharves.
7 BL Pears, p.224.
8 Jocelyn, *Six Months.*
9 *USJ* 1841, vol.2 p.307 (Lt-Col. Wilkie).
10 *YPZZZZS*, p.78 DG/20/9/2.
11 BL Pears, p.234; Cree, vol.4 23/9/1840.
12 Wakeman, *Strangers at the Gate* p.22.
13 Details of the British scheme are in *EMC*, 19/10/1840.
14 BL Nicolls, 17/7/1840.
15 BL Nicolls, 8/8/1840.
16 CWM MS380645/1, letter from Chusan, Jan 1841.
17 *EMC*, 19/10/1840.
18 *Times*, 9/12/1840.
19 BL Pears.
20 *EMC*, 12/10/1840.
21 *CR*, vol.10.
22 Bingham, *Narrative.*
23 FO17/49(182), *Diary of a Residence*, 12/9/1840.
24 Bingham, p.337.
25 *CR*, vol.9 p.231. The *Repository*, published monthly in Canton by the American missionary Elijah Coleman Bridgman, was (and remains) a treasure-trove of informed articles on every aspect of life in China.
26 *CR*, vol.10.
27 Recounted in *CR*, vol.9 p.231.
28 *CR*, vol.10.
29 Ellis, *Memoirs* p.116.
30 *EMC*, 31/12/1840.
31 Levien, p.9. Levien also provides a biography.
32 Levien, p.59.
33 Published in *EMC*, 19/10/1840.
34 Bingham, *Narrative* p.325.
35 BL Pears.
36 *CR*, vol.10 p.328.
37 See e.g. the accounts in *EMC*, 12/10/1840 and 13/10/1840.
38 *CR*, vol.10 p.328.
39 *IJMPS*, 1845 p.217.
40 *CR*, vol.10; BL Pears, p.234 and Cree, vol.4 4/8/1840.
41 Cree, vol.4 23/9/1840.
42 *CR*, vol.10.
43 Bingham, p.340.
44 *CR*, vol.10.
45 Ouchterlony, *The Chinese War* p.77.
46 Cree, vol.4 17/7/1840.
47 BL Pears, 22/8/1840.
48 Cree, vol.4 22/9/1840.

Chapter 6
1 BL Pears, p.212 notes that the British were using East India Company charts on which the Red Hair Hall was marked.
2 *EMC*, 12/10/1840.
3 Levien, p.60. *CR*, vol.10 has an invaluable sketch-map which, when compared to the 1920s map in *Guangxu Dinghai Tingzhi*, allows us to determine which buildings were put to which purpose.
4 *CR*, vol.10.
5 FO17/49(182), *Diary of a Residence*. Letters in JMA reel 580 make it clear that opium went on being sold from ships, and at a 'capital' price.
6 Coates, *The China Consuls.*
7 See e.g. the Catholic missionary's reaction in *APF*, 13/10/1844.
8 Cree, vol.4 14/7/1840.
9 BL Pears, p.224.

10 BL Pears, 19/7/1840.
11 The hill appears in popular engravings as 'Irgao-shan' (Mount Irgao), possibly a dialect form of Zhen'ao shan, its name since the twelfth century.
12 WO28/300/MS4, 1/9/1840.
13 YPZZZZS p.78, DG20/9/2. See also YPZZZZS p.171, DG20/12/19.
14 YPZZZZS p.93, DG20/9/10.
15 EMC, 12/10/1840.
16 EMC, 19/10/1840; a different, anonymous account was published in EMC on 14/11/1840.
17 CR, vol.9 p.232.
18 Jocelyn, *Six Months.*
19 *Ibid.*
20 *Ibid.*
21 EMC, 1/12/1840.
22 Mountain, p.165.
23 Levien, p.61.
24 YPZZZZS p.55, DG20/7/10.
25 Cree, vol.4 21/8/1840.
26 *Times*, 15/3/1841.
27 WO28/300/MS4, *General Orders, HQ, Tinghae.*
28 CR, vol.10.
29 BL Pears, p.254.
30 *Ibid.*, 19/7/1840.
31 Cree, vol.4 13/8/1840.
32 *Ibid.*, 3/8/1840.
33 *Ibid.*, vol.4 5/8/1840.
34 Levien, p.62.
35 EMC, 1/12/1840.
36 BL Pears, 24/9/1840.
37 EMC, 30/12/1840. JMA reel 580 12/11/1840 recounts how four villagers were shot dead and two more injured by sepoys out foraging. Gützlaff found it impossible, given that both sides seemed to be lying

about the incident, to discover who had been to blame.
38 EMC, 1/12/1840, the event taking place on 19/8/1840.
39 Bingham, p.282 has the best account; also BL Monk, MacPherson, p.56.
40 The accounts disagree as to which boy shot whom.
41 BL Pears, 22/8/1840.
42 Masefield, p.69.
43 YPZZZZS, p.232 DG21/r3/27.
44 JMA reel 580 25/8/1840.
45 EMC, 1/12/1840.
46 CR, Sep 1840 p.326.
47 EMC, 17/12/1840.
48 *Ibid.*
49 BL Pears, 19/7/1840.

Chapter 7
1 *Ibid.*
2 *Ibid.*
3 BL Pears has an account of the progress of the proclamation around Chusan.
4 YPZZZZS, p.142 (Chinese original).
5 BL Pears, 28/8/1840.
6 CR, vol.10 p.498.
7 BL Pears, 30/8/1840.
8 *Ibid.*, 31/8/1840.
9 *Ibid.*, 1/9/1840.
10 *Ibid.*, 2/9/1840.
11 FO17/49(182), *Diary of a Residence*, 17/9/1840.
12 A fierce debate was conducted in the *Englishman*, the *Friend of India* and the *Eastern Star* over whether the premature award of the Bengal regiments' victualling contract to one supplier had frozen a better quality but more expensive competitor out of the running.

13 WO28/300/MS4, 1/11/1840.
14 *Ibid.*, 1/9/1840.
15 Cree, vol.4 has various entries telling how Edward befriended the locals, often being invited aboard junks in the harbour.
16 Cree, vol.4 27/9/1840.
17 *Ibid.* 18/9/1840.
18 *Ibid.*
19 MacPherson, *Two Years in China* p.27.
20 *EMC*, 22/2/1841 has Anstruther's account of his kidnap; MacPherson, p.49 has the letter he wrote from Ningbo, detailing his capture and imprisonment.
21 FO17/49(182), *Diary of a Residence*, 17/9/1840.
22 Phillimore, *Historical Records of the Survey of India* vol.4 pt.1 (quotation from the unpublished diary of a schoolfriend of Anstruther).
23 BL Pears, 13/10/1840.
24 *Ibid.*, 17/9/1840.
25 FO17/49(182), *Diary of a Residence*, 17/9/1840.
26 BL Pears, 17/9/1840 has a description of the subsequent events.
27 Lahoo was possibly a valley to the northeast of Sinkong.
28 JMA reel 580 25/8/1840.
29 FO17/49(182), *Diary of a Residence*, 19/9/1840; BL Pears, 19/9/1840.
30 Brigade Orders, 21/9/1840, reprinted in *EMC*, 1/12/1840.
31 JMA reel 580 25/8/1840 recounts the events.
32 See e.g. the list in *YPZZZZS* p.86, DG20/9/3.
33 The story of the *Kite* and of Anne Noble and the others can be pieced together from sources including Anstruther's letters, but the most important are Anne's own *Narrative of the Shipwreck of the 'Kite'* and John Lee Scott's first-hand *Narrative of a Recent Imprisonment in China*.
34 Levien, p.67.
35 Noble, p.2.
36 CWM MS380645/1 letter from Chusan, Jan 1841.
37 Levien, p.72.
38 *NM*, 1842 p.632.
39 *EMC*, 25/5/1841.
40 *EMC*, 9/2/1841, letter written from Ningbo prison, 17/12/1840.
41 *EMC*, 9/2/1841.
42 *Ibid.*
43 *EMC*, 22/2/1841.
44 Ellis, p.279.
45 Attachment to memorial of DG20/9/3 in *YPZZZZS* p.82.

Chapter 8

1 BL Monk, p.4.
2 *Ibid.*
3 Cree, vol.4 25/9/1840.
4 *EMC*, 31/12/1840, letter of 7/11/1840.
5 *EMC*, 30/11/1840.
6 It is worth noting that the exact diagnoses are unclear: contemporary records call the most devastating sicknesses 'agues and fluxes', and the symptoms described are imprecise. Contaminated water, we can be certain, was behind much of the illness. The term 'malaria' was used to describe intermittent fevers, but the disease we now know to be transmitted by

mosquitoes was not necessarily differentiated from other fevers.

7 Ellis, p.136 vividly describes the hospital.

8 BL Monk, p.16 lists various treatments tried by the fleet's surgeons.

9 *CR*, vol.10 p.498; *IJMPS*, 1845, the course of the disease described by Alexander Grant.

10 Wilson, *Medical Notes on China* p.46.

11 NAM Henderson.

12 BL Nicolls, 18/10/1840.

13 Ouchterlony, *The Chinese War* p.53.

14 MacPherson, p.12.

15 *EMC*, 31/12/1840, letter of 7/11/1840.

16 *EMC*, 1/12/1840, report of 25/9/1840.

17 *IJMPS*, 1845 p.145.

18 Levien, p.66 and Cree, vol.4 10/10/1840.

19 ADM101/105/2 (notes of HMS *Iris*' surgeon); In JMA reel 580 24/11/1840, Gützlaff notes that the islanders too were suffering dreadfully from the 'devouring epidemic'.

20 *NM*, 1841 p.696; *Times*, 13/7/1841; Wilson, *Medical Notes* p.17.

21 BL Pears, 24/10/40.

22 Mountain, August 1840.

23 BL Nicolls, 20/9/1840 and 1/10/1840 (where Burrell explains his reasons for not moving the men into quarters earlier: with the weather warm and the Elliots in the north, it had seemed inexpedient to go about a full-scale movement of troops).

24 *EMC*, 30/11/1840.

25 *Times*, 7/1/1841; Masefield, p.75.

26 *EMC*, 1/12/1840.

27 JMA reel 580 7/11/1840.

28 MacPherson, p.55.

29 The Cameronians' muster book is now in the National Archives, Kew.

Chapter 9

1 Hummel, *Eminent Chinese* has biographies of Qishan and Yilibu.

2 FO17/49(182), *Diary of a Residence*, 26/9/1840.

3 Cree, vol.4 20/10/1840 has a comical watercolour.

4 FO17/50(39).

5 FO17/49(182), *Diary of a Residence*, 27/10/1840.

6 See e.g. the report from the governor-general of Fujian-Zhejiang in *YPZZZZS* p.48, DG20/7/6.

7 *YPZZZZS* p.62, DG20/7/19.

8 Wakeman, *Strangers at the Gate*.

9 *YPZZZZS* DG20/10/6, p.105; English translation in *EMC*, 31/12/1840.

10 *EMC*, 1/12/1840; JMA reel 580 6/10/1840. The number of junks varies with the source, from just two to more than one hundred. They were clearly numerous enough to have been a feature of some note in Tinghae harbour.

11 *EMC*, 30/12/1840; Bingham, p.353.

12 JMA reel 580 19/10/1840. Gützlaff wrote to Matheson so frequently that his letters often opened with a joke about his being James' 'indefatigable correspondent'. Gützlaff had, of

course, visited Chusan aboard opium vessels before the war, and Matheson was a major figure in the trade. Matheson, too, was a proponent of Britain's acquiring Chusan: in 1836 he had penned *The Present Position & Prospects of the British Trade with China*, arguing that if Britain were to bypass the Canton trade by annexing territory, that territory ought to be Chusan.

13 Ouchterlony, *Statistical Sketch*. In *NM*, 1841, the surveyor, Collinson, gives the position as 30° 0' 10" N, 122° 14' E by chronometer, making his latitude almost perfect and his longitude just 9' out.

14 *EMC*, 17/2/1841.

15 *EMC*, 1/12/1840.

16 FO17/14(142), letter of 20/7/1840.

17 JMA reel 580 14/12/1840.

18 *Ibid.*, 25/1/1840.

19 WO28/300/MS4, *General Orders, HQ, Tinghae*.

20 *CR*, vol.10 p.500; the *Cree Journals* have a watercolour of such a flogging.

21 Masefield, p.75.

22 WO28/300/MS4, *General Orders, HQ, Tinghae*.

23 *CR*, vol.10; Bingham, p.337.

24 Ellis, p.290.

25 FO17/49(182), *Diary of a Residence*, 26/10/1840.

26 *Times*, 15/3/1841; Cree, vol.4 26/10/1840.

27 *CR*, vol.9 p.641.

28 Cree, vol.4 8/12/1840.

29 WO28/300/MS4, *General Orders, HQ, Tinghae*.

30 Cree, vol.4 30/11/1840.

31 Masefield, p.75.

32 WO28/300/MS4, 1/11/1840.

33 *Ibid.*

34 *CR*, vol.10 p.500.

35 Cree, vol.4 8/12/1840.

36 *CR*, vol.9 p.641.

37 JMA reel 580 24/11/1840.

38 *Ibid.*, 26/9/1840. Gützlaff repeated the same point a fortnight later, and it became a frequent refrain in his letters to Matheson.

Chapter 10

1 *EMC*, 9/2/1841.

2 Davis, *China* p.184.

3 FO17/100(72).

4 JMA reel 580 24/12/1840.

5 Hummel, *Eminent Chinese* has a biography.

6 Cited in Davis, *China* p.8.

7 *YPZZZZS* p.161, DG20/12/13.

8 *Ibid.* p.164, DG20/12/17.

9 *EMC*, 20/3/1841.

10 Bingham, p.372.

11 Cree.

12 JMA reel 580 24/1/1840.

13 Noted in WO28/300/MS4, *General Orders, HQ, Tinghae*.

14 Levien, p.70.

15 The following section on the impasse at Canton draws on Fay, *The Opium War*.

16 FO17/40(136), 4/11/1839.

17 FO17/38(152) Elliot to Palmerston, 16/2/1840.

18 FO17/38(158) Elliot to Maitland, 21/2/1840.

19 FO17/40(142).

20 FO17/61(93-105) contains Elliot's justification for his actions.

21 See e.g. the edict of DG20/12/18 in *YPZZZZS* p.167.

22 *YPZZZZS* p.173, DG20/12/25.

23 *Ibid.* p.193, DG21/2/4.
24 WO28/300/MS4, *General Orders, HQ, Tinghae.*
25 Levien, p.72.
26 *EMC,* 16/4/1841.
27 This was adjacent to Tinghae's main gate.
28 *CR,* vol.10 p.504; Bingham, p.378.
29 CWM LMSMA, the digest of Lockhart's journal has an account.
30 *EMC,* 17/4/1841.
31 Scott, *Narrative.*
32 CWM LMSMA, letter from aboard *Blundell* 27/2/1841; in MS380645/1 Lockhart notes in passing that Anne was six months pregnant in mid-January.
33 Ouchterlony, *The Chinese War* p.127.

Chapter 11
1 Memorial of DG21/3/20, *YPZZZZS* p.221.
2 Cited in Davis, *China* p.179.
3 See e.g. *YPZZZZS* p.200, DG21/2/21.
4 *YPZZZZS* p.202, DG21/2/12.
5 *Ibid.* p.207, DG21/2/19 (cited in Davis, *China* p.178).
6 *YPZZZZS* p.216, DG21/3/6.
7 *Ibid.*
8 *YPZZZZS* p.217, DG21/3/15.
9 Cited in Davis, *China* p.172.
10 *YPZZZZS* p.217, DG21/3/15.
11 *Guangxu Dinghai Tingzhi,* p.277.
12 *YPZZZZS* p.216, DG21/3/6.
13 *YPZZZZS* has biographies and memorial inscriptions, from which salient facts can be extracted from amongst the formulaic eulogies.

14 *YPZZZZS* p.217, DG21/3/15.
15 *Ibid.* p.232, DG21/r3/27 gives an exhaustive account of Yuqian's fortification of Chusan.
16 *Ibid.* p.220, DG21/3/20.

Chapter 12
1 FO17/45(36), Palmerston to Elliot, 21/4/1841.
2 Walsh, *A History of Hong Kong* p.114.
3 FO17/53(41ff), Palmerston to Pottinger, 31/5/1841.
4 FO17/52(20), Auckland to Hobhouse, 11/8/1841.
5 *EMC,* 19/12/1840.
6 BL Machell, p.85.
7 Noakes, p.73.
8 *Ibid.; EMC,* 8/5/1841.
9 4/9/1841, quoted in Harfield.
10 *YPZZZZS* p.270, DG21/7/9.
11 *Ibid.* p.278, DG21/8/6.
12 The iron steamship *Nemesis* was the British trump card. She belonged to the East India Company, a flat-bottomed gunboat (she drew a mere six feet) manoeuvrable enough to carry arms into shallow river deltas. *Nemesis* was equipped with 120hp engines to drive her paddlewheels, and sails to economise on coal. Bulkheads divided her into watertight compartments, making her all but unsinkable. She was formidably armed, with a 32-lber at either end and a platform for firing Congrève rockets. The Chinese had seen nothing like her before: though small by the standards of Britain's wooden wall, she was still twice the size of their largest war junks. The

Nautical Magazine published
a description of her from a
Chinese memorial: 'On each
side is a wheel, which by the use
of coal fire is made to revolve
as fast as a running horse....
At the vessel's head is a marine
god, and at the head, stern
and sides are cannon, which
give it a terrifying appearance.
Steam vessels are a wonderful
invention of foreigners, and are
calculated to afford delight to
many' (1843, p.346). When they
saw the destruction she could
bring, the Chinese reassessed
their coy appraisal, attempting
to copy the steam-driven
paddlewheels but succeeding
only in making the British scoff
incredulously at the result — a
junk with a pair of hand-
powered wheels and a funnel
which blew smoke from a fire
unrelated to its propulsion (Bernard, *The Nemesis in China*).

13 BL Pears, p.367ff has an account
of the skirmishes leading up
to the second invasion.
14 *USJ* 1842, vol.1 p.412, Parker's
report to Auckland.
15 Bernard, *Narrative* p.193.
16 WO28/300/MS4, 29/9/1841.
17 Recorded in Carlisle MBR,
*General Orders for the
Expeditionary Force*, 29/9/1841.
18 Murray, 30/9/1841. Murray, a
lieutenant of the Royal Irish
aboard the *Sophia*, provides
interesting details which others
fail to record, such as how his
men could see the Chinese
muzzle flashes in sufficient time

to watch 'with great delight' for
the balls as they approached.
19 There are accounts by eyewit-
nesses to the day's fighting in
EMC, 20/12/1841; *USJ* 1842, vol.1
p.412 contains Parker's naval
report; p.419 contains Gough's
army report; p.487 has an
account of the skirmishing; BL
Pears, 1/10/1841 has a detailed
account from this observant and
knowledgeable officer; Cree,
vol.5 has extra insights; also
Ouchterlony, *The Chinese War*
p.177ff and MacPherson, p.212ff.
20 Vickers, *Events of the
War in China*.
21 Murray.
22 *Ibid.*
23 BL Machell, 1/10/1841
has another account of
this gruesome event.
24 Carlisle, MBR, *Record of
the Services of the 55th*.
25 FO17/54(225). Pottinger's
note on Ge's death directly
contradicts his Chinese eulogies,
which insist that he died fighting. Pottinger's account is on
the whole the more believable.
26 Murray.
27 Power, p.218; Murray.
28 Murray.
29 *USJ* 1842, vol.1 p.487.
30 Edward Cree (vol.5) had
watched Ge being buried
on the beach in his hand-
some, green silk dress.
31 FO17/54(102), Pottinger to
Palmerston, 19/10/1841.
32 One memorial partially translated in Davis, *China* p.194; *YP-
ZZZZS* p.284-92, DG21/8/15-24.

33 *CR*, vol.11 p.60.
34 *NM*, 1842 p.190, circular from Pottinger.

Chapter 13
1 FO17/54(92), Pottinger to Palmerston, 2/10/1841.
2 FO17/54(200), 16/11/1841.
3 Cree, vol.5 3/10/1841.
4 Murray.
5 Cree, vol.5 3/10/1841.
6 Smith, *Physician & Friend*.
7 Ellis, p.246.
8 Smith.
9 *Times*, 26/10/1842.
10 Bernard, *Narrative* p.203.
11 *Ibid*. p.xi.
12 See e.g. BL Machell.
13 *CR*, Nov 1841 p.625; Cree, vol.5 18/10/1841.
14 Ellis, p.246.
15 *Ibid.*, p.283.
16 Bernard, *Narrative* p.203.
17 *USJ* 1842, vol.1 p.419, in Gough's report to Auckland.
18 *IJMPS*, 1845.
19 *USJ* 1842, vol.1 p.419.
20 *IJMPS*, 1845.
21 FO17/54(108), text of Pottinger's *Proclamation*, given 6/10/1841.
22 WO28/300/MS4, *General Orders, HQ, Tinghae*.
23 BL Machell. The latitude too was unfamiliar to the Indians: this far north it grew light at 4am, and they were forever asking their officers the correct time (BL Pears, 21/6/1840).
24 BL Machell.
25 Levien, p.95.
26 Cree, vol.5 5/12/1841.
27 FO17/49(182), *Diary of a Residence*, 24/9/1840; Levien, p.95.
28 Ellis, p.284.

29 *Ibid.*
30 *Ibid.*, p.298.
31 *Ibid.*, p.284.
32 *Ibid.*, p.288.
33 BL Machell.
34 Levien, p.95.
35 Masefield, p.105.
36 BL Machell.
37 Both incidents are recounted in *EMC*, 19/5/1842, repeating reports in the *Canton Press* of 15/3/1842.
38 *EMC*, 19/5/1842.
39 Hummel, *Eminent Chinese* has a biography.
40 FO17/56(38).
41 Ouchterlony, *The Chinese War* p.226.
42 *Ibid.*
43 *IJMPS*, 1845 p.537.
44 Ouchterlony, *The Chinese War* p.226.
45 *NM*, 1842 p.561.
46 *EMC*, 13/7/1842 and 22/8/1842 have many examples.
47 Murray, p.125.
48 Smith, *Physician & Friend* 28/4/1842.
49 Baker, letter of 1/6/1842.
50 Mountain, p.190.
51 *Ibid.*
52 *EMC*, 13/7/1842.
53 *Ibid.*, 25/6/1842.
54 In FO17/112(140), Gützlaff's *Extracts from Chinese State Papers*.
55 *EMC*, 25/6/1842.
56 Levien, p.69.
57 Milne, p.124.
58 *CR*, vol.11 p.614.
59 The original manifesto is reproduced in *YPZZZZS* p.535 and in translation in *CR*, Dec 1841 p.646.

60 Reported in *EMC*, 14/7/1842.

61 See e.g. Davis, *China* vol.2 p.19.

62 *EMC*, 15/8/1842, 23/8/1842 and 25/8/1842 have accounts of how the British all but lost control of Tinghae during this time.

63 *EMC*, 6/10/1842.

64 BL Cotton, letter of 24/7/1842.

65 Carlisle MBR, *Translation of a Paper found under Joss House Hill by Serjeant Campbell, 49th Regiment.*

Chapter 14

1 FO17/56 contains *Precis of Intelligence from Chinese spies.*

2 In classical Chinese, *yin* means 'to reverence', though this meaning has now been lost. It is a different character from the *yin* which forms one half of the *yin/yang* duality.

3 WO28/300/MS4, 20/3/1842.

4 In, for example, the *Precis of Intelligence* in FO17/56(113).

5 Bernard, *Narrative* p.271ff and *Nemesis* p.284 recount the events on Daishan; also *EMC*, 10/5/1842; *USJ* 1842, vol.3 p.292 has a letter from Gough to Auckland; Ouchterlony, *The Chinese War* p.250 has more.

6 *A Translation of a Letter Picked up in the Streets of Ting Hai on the 1st April 1842* (Carlisle MBR) notes that the guards at the city gates had been halved and suggests that a date be set for an attack and pay be distributed to braves on Chusan.

7 A translation of the abridged version of the memorial in *CBYWSM*, vol.46 p.175, reproduced in Bao Jiangyan's 'An Investigation into Zheng Dingchen's Fire-Attack on Dinghai' (*Zheng Dingchen Huogong Dinghai Kao*).

8 Details of the attack are found in ADM 51/3589, ADM 53/750; Parker's report is reproduced in *USJ* 1842, vol.3 p.306; BL Machell provides an eyewitness account from the deck of the *Worcester*.

9 Cpt Dennis appears elsewhere to have been military magistrate of Sinkong (Bingham, vol.2 p.313).

10 Bingham, vol.2 p.313.

11 The intrigues can be followed in *YPZZZZS* p.333ff and are examined in Bao Jiangyan (n.7, above).

12 *YPZZZZS* p.340, DG22/4/4.

13 *YPZZDASL* vol.5 p.289, DG22/4/12.

14 Bernard, *Narrative* p.xiii.

15 Hummel, *Eminent Chinese* has a biography.

16 Levien has Edward Cree's shocked account and watercolours of the day's aftermath.

17 *NM*, 1844 p.463.

Chapter 15

1 Cree, vol.6 2/10/1842.

2 Wilson, *Medical Notes* recounts the story of the *Minden*.

3 MSR, *An Account of the voyage of the Belleisle*.

4 Shadwell, *Life of Colin Campbell* records the sufferings of the 98th in the Yangtze and the relative salubrity of Chusan. Cook, *The North Staffs*, records that by 1851 the 98th would have been serving abroad for nine years, during which time they had lost 1,164 men, not one of them in battle.

5   BL Nicolls has detailed records of sickness among the 98th: by the end of September 1841, 163 men had died, not one of them from enemy action.
6   Wilson, *Medical Notes*, p.84.
7   *Ibid.*
8   *Ibid.*, p.112.
9   *CR*, vol.11 p.614.
10 FO17/82(11).
11 *EMC*, 16/12/1842.
12 Cunynghame.
13 FO17/54(263), 1/12/1841.
14 *CR*, vol.11 p.119.
15 FO17/54(280), Pottinger's *Proclamation*, 14/12/1841.
16 Ellis, p.288.
17 Cunynghame.
18 Cree, vol.6 23/1/1842.
19 FO17/66(282), 25/3/1843.
20 Cree, vol.6 4/10/1842.
21 Cunynghame, ch.7.
22 Cree, vol.6 11/10/1842.
23 FO17/67(43, 73, 84 and 94).
24 Cree, vol.6 17/6/1842.
25 *Ibid.* 26/12/1842.

Chapter 16
1   Smith, *Narrative* p.261.
2   *CR*, vol.10.
3   BL Monk, p.24.
4   BL Pears, 19/7/1840.
5   MacPherson, p.4.
6   Davis, *Chinese Miscellanies*.
7   *CR*, vol.9 p.422.
8   *EMC*, 12/10/1840.
9   BL Monk, 16/7/1841.
10 BL Cotton, letter of 29/6/1842.
11 Cunynghame.
12 *Ibid.*
13 *Times*, 26/10/1842.
14 *Ibid.*, 1/5/1844.
15 *EMC*, 31/1/43.
16 Musgrave, *The Plant Hunters* has a biography. Fortune's experiences in Chusan are recounted in his two books, *Three Years' Wanderings* and *A Journey to the Tea Countries of China*.
17 Cox, p.75.
18 Fortune, *Three Years' Wanderings*, p.179.
19 *Ibid.*, p.61.
20 *Ibid.*
21 *Ibid.*
22 *Ibid.*, p.69.
23 *IJMPS*, 1845.
24 Davis, *Chinese Miscellanies*.
25 Fortune tasted 'excellent buns and short cakes' in Chusan: *Wanderings*, p.46.
26 Cunynghame.
27 Fortune, *Wanderings*, p.70.
28 *Ibid.*, p.71.
29 Davis, *China* vol.2.
30 Fortune, *Wanderings*, p.71.
31 Repeated in *CR*, vol.10 p.500.
32 Smith, *Physician & Friend* is an edited biography of Grant.
33 Fortune, *Wanderings*, p.325.
34 Thomas Allom's *China Illustrated* p.90.
35 His observations are recorded in his *Diary of Chinese Husbandry*.
36 Davis, *Chinese Miscellanies*.
37 Edward Cree (vol.6 14/1/1842) describes and sketches one.
38 *IJMPS*, 1845.
39 *Ibid.* p.217.
40 Gützlaff, *Gaïhan's Chinesische Berichte*, p.20.
41 BL Pears, 24/10/1840.
42 *Ibid.*
43 *APF*, p.251.
44 *Ibid.*
45 Davis, *Chinese Miscellanies*.
46 Grant, Feb 14th.

47 Morrison, *Memoirs*.
48 The local customs are set out in *Zhoushanzhi* (1626), *Guangxu Dinghai Tingzhi* (1877) and *Dinghai Xianzhi* (1885).
49 Davis, *Chinese Miscellanies*.
50 *Ibid.*
51 *Ibid.*

Chapter 17
1 Ellis, 9/1/1842.
2 *Times*, 1/5/1844.
3 The everyday details of garrison life survive in countless incidental mentions in diaries and contemporary published accounts, from the bills of lading of ships supplying Chusan, from requests in letters to relatives back home, and so on.
4 *EMC*, 13/6/1843; Cree, vol.7 17/3/1843 has a delightful description.
5 This, and a regimental hospital in Sinkong, were rented from local landowners. The same went for the posts in Sinkamoon: WO28/272.
6 Power, *Recollections* p.255.
7 *IJMPS*, 1845 p.217.
8 Power, *Recollections* p.260.
9 Shadwell, *Life of Colin Campbell* p.215.
10 Power, *Recollections* p.255.
11 Game was even sent by ship as a luxury to Hong Kong and Macao: JMA reel 528 19/1/1844.
12 Power, *Recollections* p.255.
13 Cree, vol.5 12/1841, vol.6 1/1842, and vol.7 1-2/1843.
14 Power, *Recollections*.
15 *Ibid.*
16 *Ibid.*
17 Davis, *China* vol.2.

18 *Ibid.* p.53.
19 FO17/58(276), 12/11/1842.
20 Allom, p.103.
21 FO17/89(3-19).
22 FO682/1975/139.
23 FO682/1975/140.
24 FO682/1975/148.
25 FO17/58(272), Pottinger's *Proclamation* of 11/11/1842.
26 Smith, *Narrative* p.272.
27 *Ibid.* p.274.
28 Davis, *China* vol.2 p.56.
29 The misunderstandings over the annual fishing fleet are in FO17/78(102ff).
30 Power puts Chusan's seasonal fishing population at some 175,000.
31 Gützlaff, *Journal of a Voyage*, in *CR*, vol.2 June 1833.

Chapter 18
1 The observations on Protestantism and Catholicism in this section draw on Fay, *The Opium War*, 'The Protestant Mission and the Opium War' and 'The French Catholic Mission in China'.
2 This dichotomy can still be seen in the People's Republic of China, where even in the twenty-first century Protestantism and Catholicism are treated as distinct religions.
3 *MR*, March 1840, p.131.
4 CWM LMSMA, letter from Milne 15/7/1840.
5 CWM LMSMA, *Proceedings with Reference to a Mission on the Island of Chusan*, in a letter from Macao 8/1840.
6 *Ibid.*
7 CWM, *List of Missionaries*

(384) and MS380645/2 together provide a detailed biography.

8   CWM LMSMA, *Proceedings with Reference to a Mission.*

9   CWM, *List of Missionaries* and letter from Tinghae 25/10/1840.

10 CWM, MS380645/2.

11 CWM LMSMA, digest of Lockhart's journal, 22/9/1840.

12 CWM, MS380645/1(Jan 1841) and /2.

13 CWM LMSMA, letter from Tinghae 25/10/1840; JMA reel 580 14/8/1840.

14 CWM LMSMA, letter from Tinghae 25/10/1840.

15 *Ibid.*

16 *Ibid.*

17 *Ibid.*

18 *Ibid.*

19 *CR*, vol.10 p.453.

20 *Ibid.*

21 *Ibid.*

22 Lockhart records his observations in *The Medical Missionary in China.*

23 *CR*, vol.10 p.453. Quinine had first been isolated in 1820 and was soon being mass-produced.

24 *CR*, vol.10 p.459.

25 ADM101/105/2 (notes of HMS *Iris*' surgeon).

26 CWM MS380645/1, letter from Macao 18/8/1841.

27 *CR*, vol.10 p.453-9.

28 *IJMPS*, 1841 p.612.

29 Wilson, *Medical Notes*, p.21.

30 *MR*, Oct 1841, p.465.

31 *MR*, Mar 1842, p.139.

32 *MR*, Mar 1843, p.142.

33 CWM, *List of Missionaries* (384) and MS380645/2.

34 CWM MS380645/1, insert

from Kate herself in a letter from Dinghae 29/6/1843.

35 CWM LMSMA, letter from Morrison in Macao 22/3/1841 (quoting *Isaiah* 35:1).

36 Gützlaff, *Gaïhan*, letter of 12/6/1843.

37 *Female Agency among the Heathen.*

38 *Ibid.*

39 The Rev. David Abeel, *An Appeal Addressed to Christian Ladies.*

40 Gützlaff, *Voyages* p.384.

41 The story of Mary's life is in Reason, *The Witch of Ningbo.*

42 Mary's work in the East Indies is in *Female Agency*, p.242ff.

43 *Ibid.*, p.251.

44 *Ibid.*

45 *Female Agency* has a colour facsimile.

46 Gützlaff sets out an account (often suspiciously subjective) of his work on Chusan in *Gaïhan*. Schlyter provides a good analysis in *Karl Gützlaff als Missionär in China.*

47 Gützlaff, *Gaïhan*, letter of 12/6/1843.

48 *Ibid.*, letter of 17/10/1842.

49 For official Chinese complaints over Gützlaff's social policies and the behaviour of British troops towards the islanders, see e.g. FO17/65(28), FO17/66(201ff) and FO17/66(369ff).

50 The original Chinese documents are in *YPZZZZS* pp.548-52. There are translations of some of them in FO17/66(209), FO17/67(116) and FO17/69(36, 92).

51 Gützlaff, *Gaïhan*, letter

of 12/6/1843.

52 Davis, *Chinese Miscellanies*. Tinghae's population was to swell to 35,000 by the end of British rule.

53 The foundling hospital was well built and roomy and in July 1840 had contained fifty children (CWM LMSMA, Lockhart's journal, 3/2/1841).

54 Davis, *Chinese Miscellanies*.

55 Gützlaff, *Gaïhan*, letter of 16/3/1843.

56 CWM MS380645/1, Lockhart writing from Dinghae 29/6/1843.

57 See e.g. Schlyter's account of Gützlaff's mission.

58 Gützlaff, *Gaïhan*, letter of 16/3/1843.

59 *Ibid*. This was the Great March Comet of 1843, which was visible for two months around the globe.

60 *Ibid*.

61 BUL KGC DA19/3/1/1/1-4(2).

62 Gützlaff, *Gaïhan*, letter of 16/3/1843.

63 *Ibid*., letter of 10/7/1843.

64 *Ibid*., letter of 16/3/1843.

65 *Ibid*., letter of 12/6/1843.

66 *Ibid*; *EMC*, 9/8/1843.

67 Gützlaff, *Gaïhan*, letter of 10/7/1843.

68 *Ibid*.

69 *Ibid*., letter of 28/8/1843.

70 *Ibid*.

71 The details of Danicourt's life and work on Chusan, though partisan, are in Danicourt, *Vie de Mgr Danicourt*.

72 Gützlaff, though he thought him a clever man, had rather barbed views on Danicourt's

hailing 'seemingly from the lower classes': *Gaïhan*, letter of 17/10/1842.

73 Fay, 'The French Catholic Mission in China', p.118.

74 BL IOR G/12/14.

75 Danicourt, *Vie*.

76 *APF*, 2/1/1843.

77 *APF*, 13/10/1844.

78 *APF*, 2/1/1843.

79 *APF*, 13/10/1844.

80 Danicourt, *Vie*.

81 *APF*, 2/5/1854.

82 Danicourt, *Vie*.

83 *Ibid*.

Chapter 19

1 BUL CMSA C.CH.L1 p.38ff and C.CH.M1 p.11ff contain the CMS's account of the mission and, along with Smith's *Narrative*, are the source for this section.

2 The background to the mission is in Moule, *The Story of the Cheh-Kiang Mission*.

3 The voyage alone demanded substantial funds: when the missionary G.T. Lay travelled from London to Chusan via Suez his passage cost £270, a five-figure sum today (FO17/71(126)).

4 Smith, *Narrative* p.255.

5 *Ibid*. p.271.

6 *EMC*, 19/12/1842.

7 Phillimore, p.532.

8 Smith, *Narrative* p.272.

9 *Ibid*. p.276.

10 *Missionary Register*, Mar 1848 p.122.

11 BUL CMSA C.CH.M1.

12 FO17/100(1), Davis to Aberdeen, 2/6/1845.

13 Smith, *Narrative* p.317.

14 BL Pears, 3/9/1840.
15 E.g. FO17/49(342), George Elliot to the Admiralty, 21/10/1840.
16 FO17/90(96).
17 JMA reel 580 2/10/1840.
18 Masefield, p.105.
19 Mountain, p.190.
20 BL Shadwell, letter from Chusan 11/7/1845.
21 *IJMPS*, 1845.
22 FO17/89(3), 21/10/1844.
23 Power, p.239.
24 *Ibid.*
25 Fortune, *Wanderings*, p.314.
26 *China Mail*, 27/11/1845.
27 *CR*, vol.14 p.550.
28 *Ibid.* p.552.
29 *Ibid.* p.545ff; FO17/96(201) covers the advice to Davis over Canton.
30 *Ibid.*, conveniently laying out the various newspapers' positions.
31 *Friend of India*, 18/9/1845.
32 *China Mail*, 27/11/1845.
33 King, *Survey Our Empire!* is the source for the biographical detail on Martin and of much of the secondary material on his views regarding Hong Kong and Chusan (pp.220-75) which informs this section.
34 Forbes, p.365ff has tables of goods passing through Chusan and Shanghai in 1845: at less than £50,000 in total, Chusan's trade was a tiny fraction of Shanghai's £2.3 million.
35 *Ibid.*
36 *Ibid.*
37 Smith, *Narrative* p.275.
38 BL Peel-RMM, (11).
39 Published by order of the Commons in 1857. Noting that many of Martin's points were similar to Gützlaff's, it was suspected that Gützlaff might have been behind Martin's *Report*. The *Report*, though, is far less balanced than Gützlaff's letter to the FO, and Martin was quite willing to advocate the retention of Chusan contrary to the Treaty of Nanking, a move which Gützlaff did not countenance.
40 A copy is in FO17/91(172-177).
41 In FO17/100(63), Davis makes this and other points concerning Martin's disparagement of Hong Kong.
42 FO17/90(100).
43 BL Peel-RMM, (17) 8/2/1845.
44 *Ibid.*
45 BL Peel-RMM, (20) 9/2/1845.
46 FO17/54(200), 16/11/1841.
47 BL Peel-RMM, (20) 9/2/1845.
48 *Ibid.*, (24) 10/2/1845.
49 Preserved in BL Peel, 10/3/1845.
50 After his appointment as provincial governor in 1844, Liang Baochang gathered intelligence from sources in Tinghae and forwarded updates on troop movements, shipping, etc: *YPZZZZS* p.417ff.
51 BL Peel, letter of 14/8/1844.
52 Power, *Recollections.*
53 Davis, *China* vol.2 p.126.
54 *Times*, 4/11/1845.
55 FO17/100(228).
56 BL Peel, Graham to Peel, 18/10/1845.
57 BL Aberdeen, f.61.
58 *Ibid.*, f.67.
59 *Ibid.*
60 FO17/96(78).
61 The French seem to have

been sanguine over Chusan's worth, and understanding of Britain's decision: Ambassador Lagrené had already reported to Guizot, the French foreign minister, that 'From a political and military point of view, we might doubt that Hong Kong has any reason to envy Chusan, so much so that doubtless in a few years public opinion in England will be completely in line with the farsighted and profound thinking which fixed the limits and the conditions of British territorial power in these waters' (Wei Tsing-sing, p.413).

62 BL Aberdeen, f.83.

63 *Ibid.*, f.87.

64 The FO's correspondence with Davis over the question of a foreign power occupying Chusan, of its possible retention, and of the latitude given to Davis in negotiating its retention is to be found in FO17/96.

65 FO17/96(78).

Chapter 20

1 The documents detailing the mutual suspicion over Canton and the talks which led to the Davis Convention are in FO17/88(e.g.135), FO17/102, FO17/109(11-69), FO17/111(e.g. 6), FO17/112. The Chinese documents which passed between Davis and Qiying are found in FO682/1978/56-65 and FO682/1979/1-57a.

2 ADM 101/105/2.

3 FO17/109(20).

4 FO17/96(251), FO to Davis, 24/10/1845.

5 Davis had suggested this to Aberdeen in a letter of 27/6/1845, FO17/100(90).

6 FO682/1978/66.

7 Davis had proposed the idea of a secret treaty to Aberdeen in September: FO17/101(128).

8 FO17/111(6).

9 FO682/1979/19.

10 FO682/1979/24.

11 *Ibid.*

12 FO682/1979/39.

13 FO17/112(57)

14 FO17/113(100).

15 FO93/23/3.

16 Accounts by Davis and Campbell of the handover are in FO17/113.

17 *YPZZZZS*, p.441 DG26/5/29.

18 A translation of Xian Ling's address is recorded in Shadwell, p.138.

19 *YPZZZZS*, p.448 DG26/7/6.

20 FO17/113(93, 97); Shadwell, *Life of Colin Campbell*, p.136.

21 In FO17/112(140), Gützlaff's *Extracts from Chinese State Papers*.

22 FO17/89(28), Davis to Aberdeen, 23/10/1844; FO17/96(27), FO to Davis, 22/2/1845. FO17/100(5) has Davis' proclamation to the islanders assuring them of British protection.

23 Davis, *China* vol.2 p.144.

24 FO17/113(100).

25 Forbes, p.365.

26 The details of the departure are in FO17/113(93).

27 Davis, *Miscellanies* notes that a British-built trading suburb to replace the one burned in 1840 had grown up at Dong-gangpu, the furthest navigable

point on the river which
crossed the Vale of Tinghae.

28 Gützlaff, *Gaïhan*, letter of
4/8/1846, written on his
return to Hong Kong.
29 *Ibid.*
30 Forbes, p.169.
31 *Dinghai Xianzhi*, DG26/6/13.
32 *CR*, vol.15 p.376.

Chapter 21
1 Memorial of DG26/8/4,
YPZZZZS, p.450
2 *APF*, 13/10/1844.
3 *NM*, 1843 p.820.
4 YPZZZZS, p.462 DG28/2/12.
5 *Ibid.*
6 CUL Loomis, letter of 2/8/1849.
7 *Ibid.*, letter of 4/7/1849.
8 *Ibid.*
9 *Ibid.*, letter of 2/8/1849.
10 *Ibid.*
11 *Ibid.*
12 Fortune, *Journey* p.340ff.
13 CUL Loomis, letter of 4/7/1849.
14 Fortune, *Journey* p.344.
15 Walrond, *Letters &
Journals* p.233.
16 Coates, *The China Consuls*
has a brief biography.
17 *The Expediency of Acquiring the
Island of Chusan* is in FO17/343.
18 Robertson would be proved
right when in the 1980s the
time came to discuss the end
of Britain's lease on the New
Territories: a factor that weighed
heavily in the decision to hand
back Hong Kong island and
Kowloon, both of which had
been acquired in perpetuity, was
their utter reliance on the territory north of Boundary Street.
19 The accounts of the brief 1860

occupation which inform
this section are found in
Swinhoe, p.6ff; Kendrick, p.83ff;
Knollys, p.55ff; Rennie, p.9ff;
Wolseley, p.17ff; Lane-Poole,
vol.2 p.333 and Dunne.
20 Wolseley.
21 Lane-Poole.
22 Rennie, p.9.
23 Wolseley.
24 *Ibid.*
25 *Ibid.*
26 *Ibid.*
27 FO17/337(293)
28 Dunne; Rennie, p.9.
29 Wolseley.
30 *Ibid.*
31 Dunne, 18/5/1860.
32 *Ibid.*, 2/6/1860.
33 *Ibid.*, 3/6/1860. The image is in
the National Army Museum.
34 PRO30/22/49(213), Lord Elgin in
Peking to Lord John, 31/10/1860.
35 *Huangqing Zhigong Tu*,
vol.1 p.46.
36 Wolseley, 23/4/1860.

Epilogue
1 Lockhart, Gützlaff, Danicourt
and the rest would be delighted
to discover that Christianity did
in the end take root on Zhoushan, with Catholic and Protestant
congregations to be found
right across the island today.
2 Gützlaff, *Journal of a Voyage*,
in *CR*, vol.2 June 1833.
3 Cree, vol.7 13/3/1843.
4 Isabella Bird, *The Yangtze
Valley and Beyond*.
5 Bernard, *Narrative* p.xiii.
6 CWM MS380645/1, letter
from Macao, 19/4/1841.
7 E.g. WO28/272, 12/9/1843,

records the employment of Chinese coolies to clean the quarters occupied by soldiers' families. *General Orders* of 4/10/1844 mention that both women and children were stationed with the men, and that a nurse was employed to tend to the soldiers' wives.

8 Lovell, ch.19.

9 *Ibid.*, ch.18.

10 *Ibid.*, p.344.

11 *Zhoushanshizhi Bianxiu Shimo* (Zhejiang Renmin Chubanshe).

12 *Ibid.*, p.200.

13 *Ibid.*, p.211.

14 FO17/100(80).

15 Noakes, *Historical Account*, p.93.

Index

Aberdeen, Lord *170, 214, 240, 248, 253-4, 258*

Afah (orphan) *149, 170, 185-6*

Agriculture on C. *194-8, 241-2, 249, 270, 273*

Aldersey, Mary Ann *222-5, 228, 232-3, 270, 285*

Amherst, Lord *42, 49, 184, 209*

Amoy *136, 138, 173, 181, 183, 209, 237, 243, 248, 257*

Anstruther, Philip *13, 51, 97-100, 102-4, 113, 127-30, 137, 142-3, 148-9, 155, 177, 217, 283, 290, 292*

Auckland, Lord *61*

Baker, Charles W. *59, 242*

'Blondel de Westa' *103-4, 121*

Bourchier, Sir Thomas *250*

Bremer, Gordon *61*

Bu Dingbang *82-3, 86-7, 100, 102, 127, 130, 147, 177*

Burrell, George *66-7, 72, 74, 77-9, 85-7, 93-6, 99-100, 106-9, 115-6, 119, 121, 124, 126, 130, 134, 137, 139, 149-51, 218, 252*

Caine, Wm *66, 78, 85, 93, 225*

Cameronian Hill *79, 106, 108, 148*

Campbell, Colin *207, 263-4, 282*

Canton
early trade *17-20, 24-6*; trade confined to *31-2, 43*; 19th-century trade *33-5, 44, 48-50, 209, 244-6*; conditions at *67, 72, 187, 190, 192, 246, 254*; talks at *111-4, 117, 119, 122-4, 126, 138, 242, 257*; as treaty port *173-4, 245, 257-62, 272, 275*; missionary work at *216, 220, 237*

Catchpoole, Allen *21-9, 35*

Cemeteries
British *25, 105, 109, 148, 264, 267, 281, 293, 301*; Chinese *74-5, 131, 194, 227, 235, 264*

Ch'i-shan *see* Qishan

Chinese views of the British *205-7, 239-40*

Ch'i-ying *see* Qiying

Chusan
location and climate *14, 20, 65, 114, 190-1, 219, 246, 250*; invasions of (1840) *51,* (1841) *138,* (1860) *274*; desirability *15, 20, 117, 123-6, 136-7, 174, 190-1, 210, 236, 238, 241-54, 258, 272-4*; rationale for occupying *45, 49-50, 124, 136, 226, 240, 258, 273-4*; problems of occupying *83, 126, 147, 162, 203-4, 227-9, 245, 250-2*; surveys of *72, 97-8, 114, 241, 301*; French interest in *252-4, 262, 266, 272-3, 277*; US interest in *254, 262*; return to Chinese rule *257-69*

Confucius Temple, Tinghae *68, 127*

Cree, Edward *53, 70, 84, 86-7, 96-8, 107-8, 122, 148, 152-3, 158, 174, 178, 180-1, 185, 192, 199, 201, 206-8, 225, 280, 282-3, 286, 292*

Cunningham, James *21-2*

Customs, local *122, 190-2, 194-204, 219, 267*

Danicourt, Father *232-6, 266, 272*

Daoguang *43, 64, 170, 244, 261-2*

Davis Convention *261-3, 272, 277*

Davis, John *186, 209-10, 213, 215, 240, 245-7, 249, 253-4, 257-66, 269*

Dennis, John *151, 159, 168, 320*

Dinghai *see* Tinghae

Duell, Richard *141*

Dutch, the *17-8, 28*

Earth wall, Tinghae harbour *132, 138-40, 142-3, 148, 152*

East India Company *93, 98, 174, 209*; early trade *18-32, 37, 59, 123, 278*; opium trade *34*

Elepoo *see* Yilibu

Elgin, Earl of *272*

Elliot, Charles *49-50, 61, 64, 78, 83,*

85, 99, 111-5, 117, 119, 122-6, 135-6, 151, 171, 175, 177, 223, 242, 276

Elliot, George 49, 64, 85, 99, 113-4, 117, 137

Fenghua 155

Food 38, 192, 195-8

Fire, risk of 77, 116

Fishing industry 36, 52, 59, 95, 134, 150, 153, 192, 213, 242, 308

Fortune, Robert 189-94, 244, 271, 283-4

49th Hill 79, 91, 114, 139-43, 152, 159, 268 (ill.), 288, 291

Fuzhou (Foochow) 173, 183, 209, 231, 237-8, 248, 271

Gan Bing 275

Gaoting village 165

George III, King 14, 35, 40-1

Ge Yunfei 133, 142-4, 149-50, 288

Gough, Hugh 137, 139-41, 149-50, 155, 158, 160, 164-5, 170, 211

Graham, James 15, 250-1, 253-4

Grand Canal of China 44, 133, 171, 174

Grant, Alexander 148-9, 188, 194-200, 230, 243

Great March Comet 229

Green Standards 53, 55-6, 63, 102, 112, 141, 172

Guangzhou see Canton

Gützlaff, Karl
character 46; urges action against China 44-5, 48, 83; missionary and social reformer 46-8, 90, 130-1, 225-32, 266-7, 284; works for British 48, 53, 93-6; civil magistrate 66-9, 71, 74, 77, 80, 85, 109, 178, 211, 213-4; views of Chinese 114, 120, 198, 222, 292; argues for C.'s retention 117, 240, 242, 249, 274; spies 130, 163, 165, 265; death 285

Gützlaff, Mary 225, 274, 284, 286

Hangzhou (Hangchow) 20, 44, 66, 80, 131, 155, 158, 170-1, 207

Harbour, Tinghae 52-4, 79, 114, 132, 137-93, 154, 178, 280; islands 41, 70, 84, 96, 105, 154, 175, 241; trade at 26, 47, 84, 111, 152, 179, 248; desirability of 14, 20, 242; fire-attack on 112, 121, 165-70

Herbert, Sir Thomas 250

Hong Kong
compared to C. 15, 124, 131, 135-6, 174, 176, 178-9, 190, 240, 242-4, 246, 248, 251, 253, 258, 272, 274; location 124, 254, 274; possession of 126, 135-6, 173, 250-1, 273; reputation of 183, 190, 240, 247, 250-1, 274, 283

Hospitals 41, 90, 105, 110, 116, 127, 175-6, 217-8, 220-1, 227-8, 234-5, 266, 271, 278, 280-2, 284

Iching see Yijing

Ilipu see Yilibu

Islands of the C. archipelago
Bell (Xi Xiezhi) 175, 281; Daishan 165-6; Grave 105, 148, 281, 293; Kintang (Jintang) 47, 280; Lowang (Liuheng) 36, 39; Macclesfield (Xiao Wukuishan) 168; Putuoshan 47, 95, 114, 233, 238, 267, 278, 285; Tea (Panzhi) 168, 242; Trumball (Da Wukuishan) 70, 140-3, 168, 180, 240; Tygoosan (Daxieshan) 211, 214

Japan 19-20, 120, 242, 284-5, 293-4

Jardine, Matheson & Co. 77, 82, 115, 251

Jesuits 20, 184, 189, 215, 232

Josshouse Hill 52, 54, 56-8, 60, 74, 76 (ill.), 77-8, 91, 98, 105, 114, 116, 131-2, 138, 141-2, 148, 153, 167, 238, 248, 264, 266, 270, 275, 281

Kangxi 27, 35, 132

Kanlon village (Ganlan) 151, 211

Keying *see* Qiying

Kidnappings
   of British *84, 89, 98-9, 130, 155-160, 176-7, 188, 210, 217, 269, 277;* of Chinese *82, 147, 153, 157-8*

Kintang Sound *65, 67, 79, 113, 119-20, 139, 147, 210, 257*

Kishen *see* Qishan

Lahoo valley *99-100*

Lan Li *22-7, 34-5, 53*

Liang Baochang *269-70, 275*

Liu Yunke *138, 144, 169*

Lockhart, Wm and Kate *217-222, 225, 237, 274, 284*

London Missionary Society *158, 216-7, 222, 224*

Macao *17, 19, 36, 124, 216-7, 232-4*

Macartney, George *35-7, 40-1, 184*

Manufactures, English *15, 18, 21, 25, 27, 29, 31, 35, 47, 125, 152, 248*

Martin, Robert M. *246-54, 258, 273, 280*

Matheson, James *114, 117, 124, 241-2*

Medical Missionary Society *217, 221*

Melbourne, Lord *135, 170*

Milne, Wm *158-9, 216, 224*

Ming dynasty *19, 21, 120, 202*

Missionaries *14, 20, 47, 183-4, 189, 215, 245, 266, 270-1, 279*
   Protestant *44, 46-8, 186, 199, 215-38, 266, 277, 284;* Catholic *215, 231-6, 272;* C of E *237-9*

Morrison, John *77, 216, 218*

Morrison, Robert *199, 223*

Mowah village (Ma'ao) *151*

Mu Sui *23-4, 27-8*

Nanking (Nanjing) *171-3*

Nanking, Treaty of *173-7, 183, 188, 209-10, 213, 221, 226, 237, 240, 242, 245, 249-2, 254, 257, 264-6, 270, 272-3*

Newspapers and periodicals
   China Mail 244, 246, 253, 259, 280; Chinese Repository 68, 186, 245, 267; Englishman 90, 106-7, 158, 186, 189; Friend of China 245-6; Friend of India 246, 253; Missionary Register 216; United Service Journal 50;

Ningbo (Ningpo) *13, 19, 24, 65, 67, 97, 214, 225, 238, 240, 279;* trade at *20;* Chinese refugees *79;* kidnapped British *82, 98-99, 102-3, 157;* Chinese authorities *111-3, 119, 127, 207, 210-1, 213, 252, 263;* kidnapped Chinese *129-10, 158;* captured by British *147, 155, 158;* attacked by Chinese *163-4;* treaty port *173, 183, 209, 237, 248-9, 265, 272;* girls' school *224, 271, 285;* missionaries *237, 239, 266, 270*

Noble, Anne *13-4, 51, 100-4, 113, 127, 147-8, 286*

Oglander, Lt-Col. *66*

Opium *106, 147;* British trade in *33-4, 43, 49, 51, 111, 180, 248;* ban on *33-4, 161;* destruction of *48, 50, 111, 123-4, 135;* use and sale on C. *38, 47, 51, 54, 66, 77, 132, 161, 179, 189, 219-20, 224, 248, 266, 271, 276*

Ouchterlony, John *241, 280*

Palmerston, Lord *43-5, 48-50, 61, 66, 83, 85, 111, 123-6, 135-6, 147, 170, 173, 179, 246, 250, 254, 262-3, 293*

Parker, Wm *137, 139, 147, 165-6, 168, 170, 250*

Parkes, Harry *274, 277*

Pearl River *17-9, 32, 119, 123, 272*

Peel, Sir Robert *170, 214, 249-53*

Peiho River (Bai He) *36, 39-41, 44, 49, 85, 111, 172, 272, 277*

Piracy *18, 22, 55, 72, 133, 213-4, 238*

Pishoon village (Beichan) *151*

Portuguese, the *17-20, 124*

Pottinger, Henry *136-8, 147-8, 150-1, 153, 155, 162, 170-1, 173-4, 177-9, 186, 188, 195, 197, 211, 214-5, 227-8, 232, 240, 246, 248, 250, 270, 273, 276, 279, 293*

Qing dynasty *14, 19, 42, 55, 112, 120, 169, 171, 263, 272, 277, 279*

Qingling village *130*

Qishan *111, 120, 122-3, 138*

Qiying *171, 173, 213, 257-65*

'Red Hair Hall' *22-3, 26-8, 37, 39, 41, 57, 77, 132, 281*

Refugees, after C.'s invasion *79-80, 89, 113, 132, 269-70*

Regiments, British *13, 51, 58*; 18th Royal Irish *57-8, 66, 78, 85, 89, 96, 98, 116, 119, 127, 137-8, 141-2, 150, 181, 206, 280, 287*; 26th Cameronians *58, 66, 79, 81, 90, 96, 98, 105-6, 108, 110, 137, 148, 282*; 49th Hertfordshires *58, 60, 66, 79, 96, 98, 108, 110, 116, 137, 151, 157*; Bengal Volunteers *58, 79, 96, 108, 119*; Madras Artillery *59, 96-8, 115, 119, 137, 142, 148, 242, 263, 283*; Madras Engineers *58, 74-5, 91, 96, 98, 114, 132, 137-8, 241, 280*; Madras Native Infantry *137, 141, 161, 243*; Royal Engineers *276*; Royal Marines *153*

Resistance to British rule *87-91, 96, 98-9, 112, 120-1, 129, 140, 143-5, 154, 158-69*

Robertson, Sir Daniel Brooke *273-4, 294, 327*

Royal Marine Square *152, 206, 266*

Rule of law, British *65-8, 115-6, 151, 178-9, 205, 210-4, 226-9, 238-41, 243-4*

Saltoun, Lord *214, 250*

Samshoo *25, 59-60, 108, 115-6, 139, 151, 156-7, 161, 163, 196, 239*

Schools *224-5, 228, 233, 240, 266,*
271

Shadwell, Lawrence *177-8, 242*

Shi Shipiao *27-8, 34-5, 53*

Schoedde, James *178, 190, 213-4, 229, 293*

Shanghai *170, 173, 183, 207, 209, 221, 237, 240, 272, 274*; compared to C. *248, 252, 273*

Shaoxing (Shaohsing) *133, 155, 163*

Ships

East India Co: *Eaton, Macclesfield, Trumball 21*; *Hindostan 35-6, 42*; *Nemesis 138-40, 143, 149, 155, 165-6, 168, 170, 263, 285, 317*; *Onslow, Chesterfield 31*; naval vessels: *Alligator 59*; *Atalanta 52-3, 93-6, 114*; *Belleisle 175-6*; *Blenheim 51, 88-9, 99*; *Blonde 128, 148*; *Columbine 124, 127*; *Jupiter 168*; *Lion 35-6*; *Melville 51*; *Minden 175-6*; *Pluto 261*; *Rattlesnake 53, 70, 86, 97, 121, 127, 153, 180-1, 208, 283, 286*; *Vulture 261*; *Wellesley 51, 53-6, 58, 64-5, 111, 137, 286, 290*; *Wolf, 267*; privately owned: *Clarence 36-7, 39*; *Grenada 274-5*; *Kite 13-4, 51, 100-2*; *Lapwing 267*; *Lyra 129, 138, 147*; *Rustomjee Cowasjee 51*; *Sylph 47*; *Worcester 153*

Shu Gongshou *130*

Sickness and disease *109, 126, 176, 218-21, 314*; dysentery *42, 66, 82, 85, 90, 98, 101-2, 105, 108, 175-6, 283*; malaria/fever *42, 82, 85, 96, 107-8, 117, 160, 176, 195, 219, 243, 246, 249*; scurvy *105*; typhus *105*; cholera *105, 175*

Silk

Trade in *14, 18-20, 25-32, 248, 252*; native to C. *224, 242*

Silver, as currency *18, 21, 25-34, 117, 127, 164, 248, 252*

Sinkamoon (Shenjiamen) *48, 95, 150-1, 213-4, 266, 280, 286*

Sinkong (Cengang) *87, 99, 120, 150, 168, 206, 208, 241, 266, 280*

Smith, George *183, 237-40*

Society for Promoting Female Education in the East *222*

Spying, by the Chinese *74, 80, 87, 89, 94, 112, 169, 252*

Sport and pastimes *205-9*

Staunton, Sir George *36-8, 78, 185, 281*

Stead, Cpt., murder of *129, 138, 147*

Stephens, Thomas *66, 78, 151, 159, 293*

Taiping Heavenly Kingdom *275*

Taiwan *17-8, 20-1, 294-5*

Taxes, tariffs and duties
Chinese *19, 31, 183, 213, 270;* levied on British *25, 28, 34, 183;* levied by British on C. *125, 161, 178, 238-9, 244, 248, 252;* levied by British gov. *34, 43, 48*

Tea
trade in *18-9, 24, 26-7, 32, 34, 226, 248, 252;* grown on C. *53, 71, 107, 200, 242*

Theatre Royal Chusan *207, 266*

Thom, Robert *77, 81, 214*

Tianjin (T'ientsin) *27, 277*

Tinghae (Dinghai)
situation and descriptions *14, 21-2, 37-8, 51, 65, 72-4, 77-8, 80, 82, 85, 104, 115, 117, 131, 152, 179, 184-5, 187, 192-3, 198, 203, 205, 210, 269-72, 275, 279-81;* defence of *55-60, 63, 137-8;* Chinese administration *65-66, 130;* refugees *79-80;* arsenals *58, 127, 134, 275-6;* captured (1840) *60,* (1841) *142;* free port *178;* census *227;* citizens anticipate retention *240;* trade slow *248, 252, 265;*

British leave *265*

'Traitors', Chinese *129-30, 264-5*

United Service Club, Tinghae *117, 121, 127, 266*

Urgungga *63-4, 80, 104*

Violence, toward Chinese *87-9, 100, 138, 154, 157-61, 165, 228, 239*

Wang Xipeng *133-4, 143, 288*

Ward Loomis, Augustus and Mary Ann *238, 266, 270-1*

Waterhouse, Benjamin *115, 251-2, 266, 270*

Wellesley, George *177, 188, 230, 242*

Western views of the Chinese *185-92, 194-5, 198, 220, 222, 234-5*

William III, King *21-2, 24, 28*

Wu'ergonga *see* Urgungga

Xian Ling *263-4, 267*

Yangtze River *14, 20, 180, 279, 284;* trade *17, 125, 273-4;* military importance *44, 170-1, 173, 177, 188, 215, 226, 232, 248, 250;* survey *101*

Yao Huaixiang *53, 66, 288*

Yijing *155, 160, 163-7, 169, 171*

Yilibu *111-4, 119-21, 126, 128-30, 155, 171, 173-4, 178, 213*

Yuan Junyou *275-6*

Yu Buyun *147*

Yu-ch'ien *see* Yuqian

Yukien *see* Yuqian

Yuqian *120, 126, 129-34, 137-9, 142-4, 147-8, 150, 152, 155, 290*

Yuyao *147, 155, 211*

Zhang Chaofa *53-8, 63-5, 133, 288*

Zheng Dingchen *164-9*

Zheng Guohong *127, 133, 143, 164*

Zhenhai (Chenhai) *119, 129, 139, 147, 155, 163-4*

Zhenjiang (Chenkiang, Chinkiang) *171-2, 176, 215*

Zhou Shifa *169-70*

Zuyin Temple, Tinghae *62 (ill.), 78, 149, 282, 296 (ill.)*

Lightning Source UK Ltd.
Milton Keynes UK
UKOW03f1219200814

237246UK00001B/6/P